A Legacy
of Caring

A Legacy of Caring

THE FIRST HUNDRED YEARS OF THE
CROSSNORE SCHOOL

HOWARD E. COVINGTON JR.

THE CROSSNORE SCHOOL
Crossnore, North Carolina

Designed and typeset by Kachergis Book Design
in Filosofia

The paper in this book meets the guidelines for
permanence and durability of the Committee on
Production Guidelines for Book Longevity of the
Council on Library Resources.

Publisher's Cataloging-in-Publication
(Provided by Quality Books, Inc.)
Covington, Howard E., Jr.
A legacy of caring of the first hundred years of the
Crossnore School / Howard E. Covington, Jr.
p. cm.
Includes index.
ISBN 978-0-615-62620-8
1. Sloop, Mary T. Martin, 1873–1962.   2. Crossnore
School—History.   3. Orphanages—North Carolina—
Avery County—History. 4. Schools—North Carolina—
Avery County—History.   5. Avery County (N.C.)—
History, Local.   I. Title.
HV995.A942C76 2012   362.73´2´09756862
QBI12-600084

cloth   08 07 06 05 04 5 4 3 2 1

paper   08 07 06 05 04 5 4 3 2 1

Contents

Foreword

It is amazing to stand on this mountaintop and behold The Crossnore School's legacy of caring. As you read Howard Covington's account of this amazing place, you will find that from our most humble beginnings, when Dr. Mary Martin Sloop housed a small group of boys in a barn so that they had access to the one-room schoolhouse in town, to the lovely village of homes and well-equipped classrooms that we have on campus for children today, our constant passion has been helping the thousands of students who have come our way to "rise above their circumstances" by providing them access, in Dr. Sloop's words, "to a fine education."

Poverty has always been a common denominator of the children we have served. Family crises have been equally present, whether caused by the alcoholic father of yesteryear constantly hiding from the law while making moonshine on mountain creek banks or the drug-addicted parents of today hiding from law enforcement and cooking methamphetamine in their kitchens. I have often said that as Dr. Sloop and I bookmark a century of caring for children in need, the only thing that has really changed is the drug of choice.

For an entire century, Crossnore has been a shelter from life's storms for countless abused and abandoned children, for children who were adopted and then un-adopted when challenges arose, for the big brother who got in trouble for stealing food to feed his younger siblings, for children and teens whose parents were incarcerated, for the preteen whose mother was dying and unable to care for him, for the child who had a learning difference and needed more individualized instruction or the neglected and malnourished sibling group of five little sisters who needed the safety of Crossnore. Students in need have found a sanctuary here in these mountains, a lifeline of hope.

In the midst of this vast array of student needs, we see *all* children as children of promise. In the powerful words of one of our students, Michael Jones, now a senior at New York University, "Crossnore allowed me to live outside of a difficult situation, to reevaluate that situation from a distance and to plan for a future beyond my past. The result is an explanation of my present that has more to do with what went right than what went wrong."

The key to helping our students plan a future beyond their past, as illustrated throughout our colorful history, has been the combined efforts of dedicated houseparents (resident counselors), devoted teachers, caring coaches, and support staff who have been committed to the school's mission. The transformation we witness in the lives of our students, the change in trajectory of their lives, has always happened through relationships—relationships with an adult on campus or a family in the community that reached out and truly made a difference in the life of a child.

None of the miracles of this past century would have been possible without the generous support of our DAR friends, summer volunteers, caring donors, and foundations that truly have a heart for children in need. Crossnore's legacy of caring is *your legacy of caring!*

One of our precious summer friends, Harrison "Toto" Williamson, said it best: "Crossnore is an example of what happens when God and good people get together."

My earnest prayer is that God and good people will continue to get together and shape a new century of providing both home and school for children in need, children of promise.

May Christ's promise in Matthew 25:40 bless all who have helped us nurture the children in need for this first century of caring, as well as those who will share their love with tomorrow's hurting children.

I believe in miracles!

PHYLLIS H. CRAIN
Executive Director
Spring 2012

A Legacy
of Caring

1
An Epiphany of Shame

ONE EVENING in the summer of 1999, Phyllis Crain was walking along a path on the campus of The Crossnore School, a unique mountain home for children suffering from the neglect of their mothers, fathers, and even the state of North Carolina. As the school's executive director for only a few months, Crain was the sixth successor to Mary Martin Sloop, the job having passed through five men since the legendary founder's death in 1962. One by one, Crain walked past tired and worn buildings. The scene reminded her of a run-down summer camp. One relic that was still in use and standing atop a nearby hill dated to the Sloop era. It was, quite literally, a safety hazard.

As Crain took her mental inventory, she was struck by a stunning reality: the school's newest and finest structures—among them an administration building and a comfortable home provided for the person who held her job—had little to do with restoring hope, opportunity, confidence, or even just a smile to the children Crossnore claimed to serve.

Crain said she experienced an "epiphany of shame," and she resolved to flip the priorities and make them more consistent with God's word—"the last shall be first." Out of this conviction would come the overhaul of an institution adrift in the shifting trends of child welfare and literally dependent upon the timely death of a generous benefactor to balance the books at the end of every year. Over the next few years, Crain would lead her board of trustees and Crossnore's long-time friends around the country, the National Society of the Daughters of the American Revolution, through an audacious effort to raise millions of dollars. In this way, she would renew Crossnore's mission, enabling the school to live up to its history and become, after ninety years, a bona fide educational institution.

The big-ticket items were new cottages to meet the needs of youngsters, most of whom had never experienced anything like a normal home life. Even more expensive was a classroom building for the recently organized charter school that had been created to serve Crossnore children. There was more to it than that, of course. Crain wanted to plant fiber optic cables to connect campus buildings as new water and sewer lines were laid to provide safe drinking water. Improvements in staff housing, a clinical psychologist, renovations, and recreation facilities were part of the plan. Eventually, Crain would shape the odd lot of buildings on the hillside into a pleasing and attractive "neighborhood" with sidewalks, a playground, and even puppies. Finishing touches included donations of bronze sculptures of children at play and landscaping that would make a master gardener proud.

Crossnore has long traded on a single word: "miracle." The term became forever attached to the school after founder Mary Martin Sloop's lively memoir, *Miracle in the Hills*, was published in 1953. But as The Crossnore School approached its centennial, Crain would embody a new miracle in the face of challenges that were as daunting as those that confronted Sloop in the early years of the twentieth century—if not more so. She would transform Crossnore in the face of public policy that had all but repudiated the value of residential care for disadvantaged children. And she would accomplish these goals while undergoing treatment for Stage IV cancer.

Sloop liked to say she took in children from "six years to six feet" who would show up at her doorstep seeking help. Some had no homes, while others had lost one parent or even two. Many were strangers to basic necessities: warm clothes, regular meals, hope. She provided a safe and loving place where life was Spartan but at least there was a bed, hot food, caring people, and the opportunity to attend an extraordinary public school. This school's curriculum was enhanced by extra teachers whose salaries were paid with money raised through Sloop's begging and bartering in the days before foundation grants and government aid.

"God, gumption, and grit" built Crossnore, she once told a correspondent. She devoted a lifetime to the place, influenced the lives of thousands of children, and was honored in 1951 as "Mother of the Year." Her habits were simple, and her mission was clear: educate a child, and you raise the circumstances not of one life but of the lives of the generations to come.

The Crossnore School occupies much of the tiny town of the same name that sits just off US 221 near the edge of the Blue Ridge escarpment in North Carolina's Avery County. When Crain arrived there in 1999, she found an institution struggling to survive within a rigid child welfare system that seemed to prefer bureaucratic tidiness, simplistic slogans, and mindless economy to dealing with a twelve-year-old whose drug-addicted mother chose her boyfriend over her own daughter. Mary Martin Sloop had often said that moonshine created the misery she had to deal with. Crain's modern-day equivalent is meth labs.

"We are a trauma-informed community," Crain said late one afternoon in her office on the Crossnore campus. She is an administrator with a $6-million annual budget who can speak with the love and compassion of a grandmother and the precision of a Ph.D. She is both. Her emotions overflow with frustration when it comes to the well-meaning theoreticians she believes complicate children's lives: "This will give you some idea. After thorough assessment of every child in care at Crossnore, 80 percent have post-traumatic stress disorder. We are a trauma-informed community. Children and teens in care today have suffered multiple traumas, such as being moved around in the dysfunctional foster care system through multiple placements. Most are dealing with abandonment, as well as the abuse and neglect that are too common today. Children today are really carrying heavy loads. A part of me longs for the world of yesteryear, when poverty alone was the common denominator. What a simple thing that would be."

The Crossnore campus begins, literally, at the roadside, at the

Miracle Grounds Coffee Shop, a self-help business created and run by Crossnore students. It continues up the steep hill behind, past the Blair Fraley Sales Store and on to a quaint stone building called Homespun House, a working museum and tribute to a heritage of mountain weaving. Residential cottages with broad porches are above, set in the wooded hillside. They provide as much of a homelike setting as possible for about eighty students. The Crossnore Academy, a charter school, is on the hilltop near a gymnasium with a fully equipped fitness center. Nearby is the latest addition, the Mariam Cannon Hayes Fine Arts Building, a performance hall and campus auditorium. On the back side of the campus, just down from the gymnasium and playing fields, is a house where academy graduates can live while they continue their education at nearby colleges in a program called Stepping Stones. Crain also follows the studies of some thirty former campus residents annually who are on scholarships at colleges and universities. On the flat below are a horse barn, paddock, and pasture, all part of the school's equestrian therapy program.

Crain explained: "For all practical purposes, this is a lovely prep-school setting with most of the services and all the opportunities, except it is for the most polar-opposite population, for the most disadvantaged children in the state, rather than the most privileged. It is everything we can provide to allow a child to rise above his or her circumstances. It is not a minimalist view. We are not into warehousing of children. We are not just bathing kids and sending them to school tomorrow."

The transformation of Crossnore didn't come easily or without serious personal challenges. Crain was in the midst of Crossnore's first real capital campaign when she was diagnosed with cancer that had begun in her breast and spread to her spine, ribs, left clavicle, and the femur neck of her right hipbone. Her prognosis was so bleak that the trustees—who, like her doctors, didn't expect her to survive beyond eighteen months—went ahead and named a new cottage in her honor. Yet nine years on, as Crain prepared for Crossnore's centennial, she was convinced that the Lord had put her at Crossnore for a darned good reason. She had prayed over her decision to resign as superintendent of the Avery County school system to join the Cross-

nore staff. She was ready to leave a job that had exhausted her, especially through "adult trivial-pursuit games and small-minded, visionless decision-making around children's education." But what was her next step? She sought something more meaningful.

"I prayed for serving children in a place where there was purity of purpose, where everybody is involved for all the right reasons," she said, recounting that transition and the changes that had come to the campus—and to her—since those early days. Her hair is no longer shoulder length and deep brown, but gray and cropped short, a result of cancer treatments. Yet radiation, chemotherapy, and years of uncertainty and pain have not diminished her ready, broad smile, dulled her lively eyes, or silenced a shrieking, girlish laugh that can penetrate walls. Her emotions are closer to the surface now, especially as she talks about the children whose lives touch hers. Hanging on her office door is a cheery sign that reads, "Free Hugs / One Size Fits All." At the same time, she is a woman who has never shied from candor and frank assessment.

Is Phyllis Crain Crossnore's second Mary Martin Sloop? It is easy to compare the two. They share similarities on many levels. Of education: Sloop was a medical doctor who assisted her physician husband in his practice; Crain earned her doctorate in education from the University of South Carolina. Of Christian faith: Prayer is central to Crain's life; Sloop believed in work and prayer. Both saw that every child was in a church pew on Sunday morning. Of determination: Sloop busted up stills and challenged the sheriff to do his job. Crain succeeded in getting special legislation approved by the North Carolina General Assembly. The two women also share a common purpose: "I believe, and Dr. Sloop really believed, that the best way to help kids rise above circumstances is to provide them access to a fine education."

Sloop never considered herself an educator. In fact, for its first eighty years, the campus did not have a school of its own. The children living in the Sloop-run dormitories attended Avery County public schools, which were built on land donated by the nonprofit organization that Sloop, her husband, and a handful of farmers organized in 1917. She did care deeply about education at all levels and was instrumental in getting a two-room public school building opened in 1913, and she labored year after year to expand academic offerings that served the entire community, children as well as adults. Students were taught their ABCs, while young mothers learned about the care of infants. Farmers studied horticulture to learn better farming methods and to form co-ops to boost their income. Beginning during the Depression, high school graduates could continue their education in a limited version of a junior college that taught stenography, bookkeeping, and the basics of business. Perhaps Sloop's best-known creation was the Crossnore weaving department. She modeled this and many of the other campus activities on what she learned from the self-help educational program of Berea College in Kentucky.

Sloop struggled constantly to raise enough money to pay the cost of housing and feeding as many as two hundred children for nine months each year. Her most successful venture was the sale of used clothing, which by the late 1920s and early 1930s arrived in boxes and barrels at the railway freight station seventeen miles down the mountain. Her network of correspondents numbered in the thousands. At one time, she had nearly forty thousand readers of a quarterly bulletin that she filled with stories about the needs of the campus, the special talents of the children, and a passionate plea for anything second-hand, from clothing to kitchen appliances to office supplies. Crain later produced an outdoor drama that vividly portrayed the work of the Sloops and brought to life Aunt Pop and Uncle Gilmer, the couple who ran the Sales Store for forty years.

Behind Sloop's every effort was a desire to improve the quality of life for the students, as well as the families that lived in the surrounding hills. For

The arches at the base of the campus bell tower open to seat for a quiet rest. The tower, built in the 1950s and later covered with native stone, is a familiar landmark for students and alumni.

example, she bartered with local farmers to obtain produce for the campus kitchen after sending an agricultural extension agent around to help growers increase the yields of their gardens. It boosted their income—she paid in credits they could use for clothing at the Sales Store—and improved the table fare of the boarding students at the same time.

The Sloop era ended in the 1960s, and the freestanding campus adjusted to a new model of operation, edging ever closer to a dependent relationship with government social service agencies. The campus got a few new buildings and hired its first social worker. A series of directors maintained Crossnore's close connection with the DAR and depended on the story of Sloop and her mission to court benefactors, whose legacies continued to benefit the campus decades after her death. The proceeds of a trust established by a DAR benefactor fifty years earlier paid for the new administration building and director's residence that Crain found when she arrived.

If The Crossnore School had a future when Crain signed on, it was not apparent. What had worked for Sloop was not sustainable. Clearly, the place needed a new miracle if it was to survive. As Crain was considering an offer to join the staff, a close friend and a Crossnore board member warned her against taking the leap. The challenges looked too great. Most of Crossnore's children still came from the mountains, but they were "society's orphans," whose flight from tragic situations made their care even more urgent than that of the children who had found their way to Crossnore looking for help a half-century earlier.

The pendulum swings to and fro. In the early years of Sloop's boarding program, the state cared little about what happened to children in distress. Nongovernmental institutions like orphanages—most of them church related—were the only option. Later, along came social welfare programs and government money (first administered through Aid to Families with Dependent Children), as well as state-financed placement of children. For a variety of reasons, foster care became the answer to "congregate care," which was found wanting and fell from favor. By the 1990s, the emphasis was on restoring the family as rapidly as possible, leaving little sympathy for institutions like Crossnore that had once provided a safe haven for children.

"It sounds so good," Crain said. "Let's do the rehabilitation of the entire family within the family. It sounds so good. Every child deserves a loving home. It sounds so good. It is best if that is the child's biological home. It sounds so good until it plays out in the life of a child who needs to be kept safe." In short, Crain's files are filled with story after story of multiple placements in foster homes and examples of families that just *shouldn't* be reunited. The disruption of children's lives is the cost, leaving students two to three years behind their classmates at school. In some cases, stability is only a word that looks good on paper. "What children in North Carolina's foster care system are grieving for and long for is a healthy childhood," she said. "And not one has ever told me that they dream of another foster-home placement."

Crain struggles against the system, keeping a light in the window for children whom it has failed. When she took the job, she knew something of Mary Martin Sloop, another tough, resilient, and deeply caring woman. Sloop was someone who had overcome daunting challenges and made a difference for an entire section of the high country of the southern Appalachians. She had transformed the lives of thousands of youngsters who faced a world that circumstances had stacked against them. As Crain would later say, even as cancer dogged her daily life, "That is what life is about—doing what you can to make a difference. And in the end, there is peace."

2
The Sloops

"I CANNOT YET DECIDE," a magazine writer observed in the mid-1920s, "whether Dr. Mary Martin Sloop is the reason for Crossnore, North Carolina, or whether Crossnore is the reason for Dr. Mary Martin Sloop."

"Miz Sloop," as her neighbors called her—reserving the title of "Doctor" for her husband, who also was a physician—would be remembered most for helping transform a dilapidated one-room school into a center of learning for a remote, neglected, and impoverished corner of the North Carolina mountains. But first and foremost, in those early years, she was a town builder. And a most unassuming one at that. She had come to Crossnore in 1911 with her husband and a daughter who was not quite three years old to raise her family, to aid her husband in his surgery, to care for the sick and injured, and, "incidentally, to help our fellow man."

Crossnore was little more than a crossroads when the family arrived and moved into a small cabin where they made a home and Doctor saw his patients. In the flat beside a small creek that drained a quiet mountain valley about a quarter-mile from their home, they found a combination post office and general store that served as the center of a scattered community of roughly two dozen residents. There seemed to be little that was really "settled" about this settlement. Even the man who had given his name to the place, George Crossnore, just up and left one day, never to be heard from again.

However, by 1917, when the Sloop's second child—a son born the year after they arrived in Crossnore—was about ready to begin his education, the community had two churches, one for the Baptists and another for the Presbyterians, with active Sunday schools and preachers in the pulpit. There was a community club and a good citizens' league, a cooperative cheese factory, a garage, a community worker, a trained nurse visiting in the homes, and an electric power plant. The one-room school had been replaced by a building with five rooms that operated for nine months each year, not the minimum of four and a half months required by the state, and it was staffed with qualified teachers. Mary Sloop hadn't swung the hammer, but she had been the catalyst for the ambitions of the community. "She doesn't make people do things," the magazine writer noted. "She merely makes them realize that they can."

Mary Martin Sloop

Sloop came from a family of scholars and doers. Her father was teaching at the University of North Carolina when the Civil War began and a company of students and faculty members elected him to lead them into the service of the Confederacy. After the war, he returned to the classroom and settled at Davidson College, a small Presbyterian institution north of Charlotte, where he taught chemistry and geology. His daughter, Mary, one of ten children, was born there on March 9, 1873. In addition to his teaching duties, William J. Martin served as an interim president of the college and helped the school right itself during those difficult years in the South. From its classrooms came the men who would be part of the industrial and com-

Eustace Sloop

mercial awakening of the region. They would build the textile mills, fill the pulpits, and doctor the sick. One would even lead the nation. Among Martin's students was "Tommy" Wilson, the son of a Presbyterian minister. The nation would know him as Woodrow Wilson when he was elected president of the United States in 1912.

Martin saw to the education of his entire family and sent his daughter to school at the nearby Statesville Female College for Women. She finished in 1891, intent on fulfilling a childhood dream to earn a medical degree and enter missionary service with the Presbyterian Church. Instead, she was called on to look after her ailing mother, a duty that consumed the next twelve years of her life. Her older brother William Jr. had a medical degree and a doctorate in chemistry. He, too, remained in Davidson, where he succeeded their father as chairman of the chemistry department upon the elder Martin's death in 1896. In 1912, a year after the Sloops moved to Crossnore, William Jr. became president of the college.

Mary refused to be idle during her decade as a caregiver. She audited courses at the college in preparation for entering the North Carolina Medical College, which occupied a two-and-a-half-story brick building with tall windows and turrets in the Queen Anne style. It stood just off the college grounds, not far from the Martin home. She began her formal medical studies in 1902 after the death of her mother, who would not have approved of her choice to pursue a professional career. Mary was the only woman among sixty-one students. One of her classmates was Eustace H. Sloop, whom she had met in 1893 when he came to Davidson as an undergraduate. He excelled as an athlete and as a student. Tall, with broad shoulders and a gentle countenance, Eustace was the "handsomest man in the medical school," according to the class record of the medical school. "Miss Martin" was one of two chosen as "best man morally."

They were separated during the balance of their medical education. Mary finished at Woman's Medical College of Pennsylvania, as it wasn't considered proper for women to attend anatomy classes with men. Meanwhile, "Doctor," as she called Sloop even then, completed his studies in North Carolina and went on to earn a postgraduate degree at Jefferson Medical School in Philadelphia. In the winter of

1907, when Mary was the first resident physician at Agnes Scott College, a Presbyterian school in Georgia, the two made plans to marry the following summer.

By the early years of the twentieth century, the North Carolina high country had been attracting summer visitors for some time. Mary's father was one of the first to build a house near the town of Blowing Rock. A few years later, a seasonal resort hotel sat perched at the very edge of the Blue Ridge escarpment. Martin went to the mountains to engage in the scientific study of rock formations. In time, he and other early scientific explorers from Davidson became part of a full Presbyterian summer colony, and they organized a church in 1886. In 1905, Mary's brother William helped draw the plans for a church building to be built of native stone. It was still unfinished in the summer of 1908 when Mary and Eustace Sloop were married there in the early morning amid decorations of mountain flowers and evergreens. After a mid-morning wedding breakfast at her brother's house, they set out on horseback for a honeymoon stay at the Eseeola Lodge at Linville, about twenty miles away. They planned to make their home in the North Carolina mountains and serve as medical missionaries.

Mary was a teenager when she first expressed her desire to do missionary service to the Reverend Dr. Jethro Rumple, a prominent Presbyterian pastor, Davidson College trustee, and friend of the family. (The Blowing Rock church was named in his honor.) When she finally was old enough to choose her missionary career, the church twice refused her services. She wanted to go to Africa, but she was told the Presbyterians were not sending white women for duty there. She then asked to be sent to China, only to be told she was too old—she was thirty-three at the time—to learn the language. Eustace, too, had a calling. He had worked during the summers with the Reverend Edgar Tufts, a Presbyterian who opened a school for girls in the far reaches of the North Carolina mountains northwest of Blowing Rock near the Tennessee state line. If the world beyond the United States would not have them, the Sloops decided, they would serve closer to home.

After their honeymoon in Linville, the Sloops rode on to the town of Plumtree and a school for boys that was operated by Tufts's brother-in-law, the Reverend Joseph P. Hall. The boys' school was not far from Tufts's school for girls in Banner Elk. Sloop coached the boys in athletics—he had been an outstanding player on the Davidson football team—when he wasn't seeing patients. In their first year, the couple lived in an apartment in the school dormitory before they found a small house of their own. They also rehabilitated a broken-down two-room house for their medical office. Three years later, just two weeks before Christmas, the Sloops left Plumtree for Crossnore, which was about twenty miles of rough road to the southwest.

Mary Sloop later wrote that friends had urged them to resettle and bring medical care to the Linville River valley, but there may have been more to their exit from Plumtree than that. There was already a doctor in Plumtree, and one small village couldn't sustain both him and the Sloops. In addition, the couple may have had a disagreement with the Reverend Hall. A year after their move, the presbytery overseeing Hall's work in Plumtree ordered him to repay money that the Sloops had invested in the school. The official body never censured Hall, but he was recalled from the churches he served and was listed as an "evangelist" without a "charge" assigned by the Presbyterian Church.

Plumtree was small, but it did have a few stores, and it was the center for the mica mines in the area. There was far less at Crossnore. Even the hills had been stripped of their riches by timber companies that had clear-cut the mountainsides of vast tracts of chestnuts and oaks by the time the Sloops arrived in 1911. That was the same year that the North Carolina General Assembly created Avery County, lending an air of excitement and anticipation for the future. Crossnore certainly had nowhere to go but up, with its one small store and a rough one-room community building of plank-covered logs that served as the schoolhouse, community center, and meeting place for Sunday religious services.

This old building served none of its purposes very well. The interior was dark and gloomy, and sheets of paper had replaced broken windowpanes. The ceiling boards were loose, the walls blackened by smoke that had escaped the leaky stovepipes. Handmade desks were scarred with the carvings of distracted youths. But it was the only space available, and the community had learned to accept even this modest bounty. At least, Mary Sloop observed, those at the services

The school building that opened in 1913 to replace a dilapidated long structure was soon enlarged as enrollment grew.

they attended on their first Sunday were attentive and appeared eager to learn about the Lord, especially after she showed some of them her Oxford teaching Bible, which included a concordance and other annotations. It wasn't long before she had young people eager to own one just like it. She provided copies at her own expense to reward those who could recite two hundred Bible passages to her satisfaction.

Sloop's generosity and eagerness to teach the Bible probably helped overcome some of the suspicion the local people held of outsiders. The Reverend Monte Johnson was a boy when he got one of Mary Sloop's Bibles. Years later, he said he had watched the Sloops ride in and eyed them coolly. "For hundreds of years the mountain people had known the lumbermen who had robbed us of forests, and the cattlemen who drove sharp bargains," he said. "It was difficult to understand why a 'furriner' should have other motives. It took time for some of us to understand that they were there to help us."

Universal public education was becoming a serious ambition for the state of North Carolina by the second decade of the twentieth century. Yet it was slow to be realized in communities like Crossnore. One-room schoolhouses predominated in Avery County, where nearly fifty of them were scattered about the valleys and hollows. Teachers hired by the county barely qualified for the title. They were unable to carry students much beyond the equivalent of the fourth grade. The Sloops had to be concerned about the future for their daughter, Emma, who would be of school age soon, and their son, William, who was born in November 1912. The sorry condition of the schoolhouse was a worry for others in the community, as well, including Alexander A. Johnson, who was one of those who had urged the Sloops to relocate to Crossnore. By the time they arrived, Johnson had already sent the oldest of his ten children out of Avery County across the mountains to Berea College in Kentucky, where an academy educated youngsters from Appalachia who had more promise for learning than could be satisfied back home.

With support from Johnson and others, Mary Sloop badgered officials of the new county to pay for an additional teacher, and then she began pushing for money to pay for a new school building of two rooms. It opened in 1913. Meanwhile, she remained distressed over the prospects of teenage girls like those who attended the sewing classes she had begun holding in her home. Some of them wanted more education, but the prevailing mountain culture required them to forsake those dreams and submit to marriage at an early age. She learned that one of her students, Hepsy, was destined to marry at the age of thirteen unless she intervened. Finally, she convinced Hepsy's father to allow her to enroll at Lees-McRae Institute (later Lees-McRae College), Edgar Tufts's school for girls in Banner Elk. Sloop found a benefactor in Davidson to pay Hepsy's expenses.

Tufts's school was on the far side of Avery County, about twenty miles away, but it may as well have been in another country because of the poor condition of the roads. As Sloop prepared Hepsy for her extended stay at the school, she discovered that the teenager had nothing suitable to wear. This time, Sloop wrote to her cousins down the mountain and asked for dresses and other apparel that would outfit

Alex A. Johnson encouraged Mary and Eustace Sloop to settle in Crossnore. In this family picture taken by Eustace Sloop, the patriarch is standing by the post, surrounded by his talented children, who became ministers, teachers, and nurses. He saw his children educated at Berea College and was one of the first trustees of Crossnore School Incorporated.

Hepsy for school. When the donations arrived, Sloop discovered that the clothing was the right size and the quality excellent, but the dresses were more suited for a funeral than a classroom. Everything was black. Sloop was in despair when a neighbor who was aware of the predicament told her, "I wish them dresses was big enough for me. I'd shore buy one of them, and that would help a bit."

"Then the idea came," Sloop wrote later in her memoir. "I took out armloads of those black dresses and hung them on the front porch of her home. The neighbors saw them, and the word went around. And they came and bought, and bought, and bought."

The proceeds from the sale of that first shipment of clothes set in motion a unique philanthropy that would sustain Mary Sloop and her plans for Crossnore—and would remain strong a century later. Sloop wrote more letters with appeals for used clothing. Friends and family responded, and soon her front porch was full of items to sell. Customers eager to buy arrived at her house before she had finished the breakfast dishes. Soon, she had money to buy fabric, ribbons, and undergarments for Hepsy and others in need. Sloop kept writing, asking her correspondents to send whatever they could. She wasn't particular; she would take clothing for men as well as for women. Boxes and barrels of clothing began arriving at the rail station in Spruce Pine, about ten miles away.

When Hepsy set out for her second year, there were more girls who wanted to go with her, and Sloop had raised enough money to pay their expenses, too. The response to her appeals had been such that she was no longer able handle it all herself while looking after two young children, one of them a toddler. She enlisted the aid of her neighbors, Gilmer Johnson and his wife, Poppie Jane, who were known as Uncle Gilmer and Aunt Pop. Gilmer sported a long handlebar mustache that reached nearly all the way to his ears. His wife was small and wiry, as "energetic as a cricket," Mary Sloop recalled.

Working together, Sloop and the Johnsons set Saturday as the regular sales day and laid out the clothes on tables on a patch of ground Uncle Gilmer enclosed with chicken wire. The gate opened at 10 a.m., so that people who lived the farthest from Crossnore would not be disadvantaged in the rush for the most popular items—which seemed to be just about everything. In time, the outdoor sales were moved into a rough building put up to house what came to be called the Sales Store.

Sloop kept writing her letters. "Do not leave out anything that is given you to send," she told one friend in 1914. "Trust me to find a use for it. If it is too handsome for schoolgirls, we will sell it; if it is

Donations of clothing and other items for the Sales Store arrived in crates and barrels at a train depot more than ten miles away and were hauled by wagon to Crossnore. Mary Sloop is on the wagon, leaning across the top of one large delivery.

Mary Sloop conducted the early sales of used clothing outdoors, hanging goods for sale from clotheslines. Sloop is bundled in a coat and standing to the right of the tree. Photo courtesy of North Carolina Collection, University of North Carolina at Chapel Hill.

Aunt Pop and Uncle Gilmer Johnson ran the Sales Store for nearly forty years.

too old, we will sell it; if it is too large, we will cut it down; if it is too small, we will let it out. You send it and we will use it. Clothes of every kind, grade, age, and size and anything else—house furnishings, books (especially Bibles), pictures, anything." She even wanted loose bits of fabric. "I told one dressmaker friend that I could educate a girl with what she swept up off her floor."

Nothing was given away. Sloop believed that mountain folks were proud people who didn't take to charity. They were hardworking, independent, and proud of their Anglo-Saxon ancestors who had migrated south in the early years of the nation. "Our best people have never felt poor, and we don't want them to acquire that feeling," she later said. "That is why we encourage them to earn money with which to buy." Accordingly, items were priced and sold for what people could afford. A good pair of shoes might sell for fifteen cents.

She kept a record of all those who responded to her letters, and she replied to each donor. These became the first names on a list that grew as each shipment arrived at the Sales Store. It was not long before her list was so long that she could not send out individually written letters with her appeals. Instead, she substituted a printed broadside that was packed with details of what the money realized from the sales had wrought. At the end of these newsletters was a call for more donations.

Mary Sloop's education and love of literature came through in the longer printed pieces. She used vivid descriptions and strong verbs to bring a far-flung audience right into a mountain community and way of life that few would ever experience themselves. Recipients could see the boy who was proudly wearing a pair of old kid gloves, castoffs that had come with an apology for so modest a donation. They learned of a young woman who walked five miles to buy

Customers lined up early when word spread that a new shipment of goods had arrived at the Sales Store. Mary Sloop is standing beside the open trunk in this photo, which was probably staged for the benefit of visiting photographer Bayard Wooten. Photo courtesy of North Carolina Collection, University of North Carolina at Chapel Hill.

books. "Somebody said, 'What use can you make of men's cuffs?'" she wrote. "It is true that they will not sell. A mountaineer sometimes wears a collar but never a cuff. But we treasure them, and cut them into squares, take a nail and drive a hole thru them, and we have a good tag, and it takes five hundred to a thousand for all the items offered for sale, so we have saved a great deal of money."

"It is certainly true," she wrote, "that there is nothing that has been seen by the human race since the world began, that I cannot sell, from a tin bucket to a candle shade."

Sloop drew a straight line for her readers from the money raised in the sale of cast-off clothes to the nails and lumber purchased to build a school barn or pay the salary of a trained nurse, a community worker, or a teacher. "If I could have the scraps discarded by the Dressmakers (and often the home-dressmakers,) in one season, I could install the water plant."

The early newsletters came from a woman who was deeply sensitive to the needs of people and aware of the pride of heritage and family. She was confident and bold in her requests, just as she was in her own life. Sloop had been raised as a gentlewoman, but she could also handle a horse, had tramped to the top of Mount Mitchell, and knew the kin of the region's great bear hunter, Big Tom Wilson. She was gracious, literate, and well-bred, but she also carried a pistol on occasion. Many were surprised at the audacity and courage of a woman who stood barely five and a half feet tall but who could command notice with a beatific countenance and sparkling eyes.

The receipts from the Sales Store grew steadily, and Mary Sloop used the money with care. After Hepsy's first year, sixteen more girls just like her were ready the next year. In Sloop's third year, she had twenty-six asking for help, with that many more waiting for their chance. Most were attending Lees-McRae, but she was also paying the expenses of students extending their education at Berea College, whose registrar, Ethel Todd, paid a visit to Mary Sloop. In a 1915 report to Berea's president, Dr. William G. Frost, Todd wrote, "She finds out everything she can about the person, gives all the advice she thinks necessary, and perhaps puts them on trial for a year to make good in some particular line of character about which she is doubtful before sending them away and investing in them."

Within just a few years, that distressing shipment of black dresses had become a generous revenue stream that was making a difference in the lives of people and helping to underwrite a growing number of projects on Mary Sloop's list of community improvements.

3

We Hope to Rise

As a young woman living in Davidson, Mary Sloop had often found herself surrounded by intelligent and serious young men for whom a college degree was but the first step to success in later life. One of them, Eustace Sloop, finished at the top of his class, and he became her husband. Another promising classmate in the early 1890s was Walter L. Lingle. By the time the Sloops moved to Crossnore, Lingle had left one of the most prestigious pulpits in the South to create the Assembly Training School at the Presbyterians' Union Seminary in Richmond, Virginia. Lingle's name was on Mary's mailing list, not as a source of clothes for the Sales Store but for assistance in improving the physical, educational, and spiritual life of her neighbors in the North Carolina mountains.

Lingle and Sloop shared a common belief that the Gospel was best expressed by doing, not preaching, and that society's sins of poverty and neglect deserved the attention of the church as much as did the fate of a unbeliever's soul. It was not a theology universally shared by Presbyterians, who focused efforts at salvation on the individual, not society at large. Nonetheless, in 1911, just before the Sloops arrived in Crossnore, Lingle left the First Presbyterian Church in Atlanta for the seminary, where he taught Christian sociology and began training prospective clergy and laymen for Christian service. He once wrote that it was better for a young theologian "to know something about the housing conditions of Richmondites than to be intimately acquainted with the family life of Hittites that have been a long time dead."

During the second decade of the new century, Lingle's school commissioned men and women to staff many of the social gospel agencies of the denomination, including its settlement houses, institutional churches, and mountain schools that combined spiritual and religious training with the elements of reading, writing, and arithmetic. Mary Sloop appealed to Lingle for the names of people who might aid in her work at Crossnore, and she enrolled these individuals in her movement to raise the standard of living in her community. Some came as what another generation would call social workers. Others were college-trained teachers. A desire to "save" the young women of Appalachia was a common theme among the missioners and those who sent them on their way.

The Presbyterians were trying to keep pace with other denominations that had their own mission efforts under way in the southern Appalachians. In the mid-1890s, the Episcopalians had created the Missionary District of Asheville and installed a bishop who was opening churches and establishing boarding schools for mountain children. Two of them were within a day's ride of Crossnore. The Episcopalians' Right Reverend Junius Horner sounded a lot like Mary Sloop when he reported to the church in 1913, "We must reach the people where they are, with schools and churches and give them instruction in house sanitation and care of health."

After gaining support from the county school board for a new school, Sloop pressed the members each year to expand it. In order to justify the new classrooms, she had to show there were a sufficient number of children to be served. Armed with the authority of a new truancy law that required children under seventeen to attend at least four and a half months of schooling a year, Attendance Officer Sloop produced the students, even if she had to take the parents to court to enforce their children's appearance in class. Four years after the two-room school was built, there were 121 students attending classes in Crossnore, double the enrollment of 1912.

She insisted that hiring only qualified teachers was essential to improving the education of children, and she set out to find teachers who could take students beyond the rudimentary schooling that was the norm in public schools. It was no easy task to convince college-trained young women to leave paved streets and city life for the back-woods of North Carolina. They found tough duty there, and not all could stand the physical strain of Crossore's brutal winters and simple comforts. One of Lingle's early referrals left after only one year because of the isolation. Mary Sloop persevered, however, and by 1917 the school at Crossnore had five "first-class teachers" teaching nine grades. The commencement exercises on April 11 of that year featured a student debate. Arguing in the affirmative that "women in North Carolina should have the right to vote" were Libby Franklin, Carrie Johnson, and Nellie Johnson. Speaking in the negative were three boys, Walter Franklin, Monte Johnson, and Otis Weld. Cordelia Franklin gave a music recital. The following morning, certificates of completion for the various grades were handed out by Lula Cassiday, one of the teachers. In a newsletter that Sloop wrote to her growing list of donors, she expressed her hope that within two years Cross-nore students would have a high school.

The success of the Sales Store was essential to the school's growth from year to year. Sloop continued to help older students with the cost of tuition at Lees-McRae and Berea. The demand for scholar-ships grew each year as promising students received all the education they could at Crossnore and begged for more. Meanwhile, the pro-ceeds from the Sales Store also paid a share of the salaries of teachers working a nine-month term after their regular state pay ceased at four and a half months. This money supplemented payments from parents who could afford the $1.50 monthly subscription fee required to offset the cost of the extended school term.

A most pressing need as the school grew was a place for the teach-ers to live. In the early days, when there were only two or three teach-ers, they stayed in the Sloop home. In about 1915, Mary Sloop wrote her growing list of benefactors that this could not continue. What Crossnore needed, she wrote, was a teacherage, and she asked friends to send the money to build one. The first building was a small frame cottage that was erected just up the hill from the school. It had a kitch-en, dining area, and a dressing room on one level. "The teachers slept

A building that the students called "Treasure Island" was the home of the early vocational classes and later became a dormitory for students.

on a large upstairs porch," she later wrote, "that in winter certainly provided full benefit of fresh mountain air."

At the same time that she sent out her appeal for money to build the teacherage, she reported that the Sales Store was providing money to purchase shop equipment for use in a manual arts course for the boys, and for sewing machines in the sewing classes offered to girls. The vocational programs became part of the curriculum after community volunteers built a modest two-story, weather-boarded frame building. Carpentry classes for the boys were taught on the first floor, while the girls' classes in "Domestic Science" were held on the upper floor. The building sat on a small square of land quite near the school. The area had once been a soggy bottom before the men used drag pans pulled by oxen to clear the ground and divert the water of a meandering stream into a new channel. The students called the building "Treasure Island," which was a popular title on the school's reading list when the building was completed.

Not long after, Sloop recruited a music teacher, and Berea College sent two helpers to teach music for a month, one of whom created a Crossnore chorus of seventy-five voices. "There has been too little music in the mountains," Sloop wrote in an early newsletter. "They are hungry for it and are beginning to distinguish between the right and the wrong sort." Some wanted piano lessons, and Sloop issued a plea for money to buy instruments. The world was consumed by the demands of World War I, and both money and upright pianos were hard to find. Some of those she contacted scoffed at her request. "So this cousin told the Wanamaker Piano man about it, and proved it to him, and now we have the pianos, and they have their daily gratitude, plus," she wrote. The school held a "Pie Supper" to raise half of the $150 needed to pay for the new piano.

The school also offered instruction in agriculture, horticulture, and basketry and had adopted the state requirements for standard

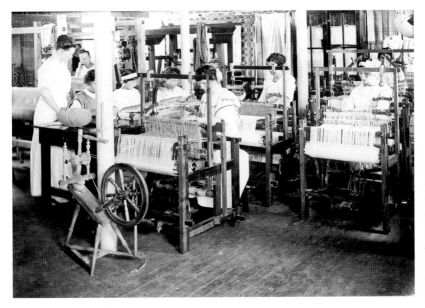

Crossnore's weaving instructors learned on looms like these at Berea College under the eye of the legendary Anna Ernberg, who is standing beside loom at left. Photo courtesy of Berea College archives.

academic instruction in the first seven grades. In addition, it had a teacher for a class on the Bible that was offered as an elective. This teacher's pay came entirely from the proceeds of the Sales Store and the pockets of contributors. "But the 'election' has been unanimous," Sloop wrote her friends.

The school was drawing attention throughout the county. Not the least of the enhancements admired by the neighbors were the electric lights in the classrooms. Electric power was rare in the rural reaches of the country, and widespread electrification of homes and business was still years away for most of the communities in the North Carolina mountains. Just as the Sloops were leaving Plumtree, the Reverend Edgar Tufts had been completing work on a power-generation plant driven by the waters of the Elk River. Electric power would reach Crossnore through a similar intervention by Eustace Sloop.

The 180 acres Eustace and Mary bought from Potter Brown when they built their house included land along the Linville River. There was one particular spot about a mile or so from the school where the banks rose steeply from the riverbed that looked to Sloop's eye like a prime location for a dam and power station. Sloop cut big timbers,

Reaching the dam required a long tramp through the woods to the river. Dr. Eustace Sloop made the trip regularly, even when snow and ice covered everything and made travel difficult.

laid them across the river, and built a dam with a millrace that directed the river's flow to a stone powerhouse, where he planned to install a turbine and a generator.

Electric power was not merely a convenience for Doctor. It was almost a medical necessity. Whenever possible, he performed surgery out of doors, but in bad weather or at night he was forced inside, with only the faint glow of kerosene lamps for illumination. He envied colleagues who were benefiting from electric power that privately owned companies had brought to the Carolina Piedmont by the late teens. The largest of them, Southern Power Company in Charlotte (later Duke Energy), had hydroelectric plants along the Catawba River from the mountain foothills west of Asheville to the midlands of South Carolina. The power from these plants was going to industrial customers, as well as to families living in cities and towns. Sparsely populated areas, such as the mountains, were left in the dark. Unless Sloop did something for himself, he knew it could be years before he had electric lights in his surgery.

When Sloop began his work, he had no money for equipment, but he remembered an old generator at Davidson College that had been stored away after regular power service reached the campus. He wrote his wife's brother William, who by this time was president of the college, and asked if it was for sale. Fifty dollars was the asking price, Martin replied, but he was certain it was not usable, and probably not even worth the cost of repair. Nonetheless, Mary Sloop insisted that her brother send the twenty-three-hundred-pound piece of machinery to Crossnore. After making repairs on his own—Sloop tested it with a battery he had on hand—he declared it worthy of his power station, where he had already designed and installed a turbine.

Working with his neighbors and his wife—Mary leaned their baby boy against a tree stump to keep him from rolling down the hill—Doctor set poles and stretched wire across the mile or so of rough country between his power station on the river to his house, where he had installed electrical circuits. His daughter, Emma, was about five years old when she flipped a switch and squealed with delight as the dull bulbs hanging in the rooms came to life. Soon after, Potter Brown, his neighbor, asked Doctor to run a line to his house. When that work was done, Mary told her husband, "Now, if you can do it for Mr. Brown, you can do it for me. I want electricity at the school." The pie supper that helped raise the money to pay for the piano also covered the cost of wiring the school. There was enough money left over to buy basketball hoops.

The Sloops shared as deep a concern for Crossnore's spiritual health as for their neighbors' physical and educational needs. At the outset, they worshipped with the Baptists in the old school building until, a year after they arrived, the congregation built a church high on a hill overlooking the school. Attendance required a stout heart and dedication: members had to climb about seventy steps from the flat by the road to reach the church's front door. Then, in 1916, the

Sloops were among a group of Presbyterians who gathered at a small chapel built on land donated by Potter Brown and paid for with $300 in donations that had come from Mary Sloop's solicitation letters.

The Sloops attended Sunday morning services with the Baptists, where about a hundred were in attendance. In the afternoon, they were among the seventy-five or so Presbyterians meeting at the chapel. A community worker who was paid out of the Sales Store receipts performed some of the ecumenical chores. (She may have been one of the laypersons commissioned by Walter Lingle's training program at Union Seminary.) She organized missionary societies at each church and led the weekly meetings of the Christian Endeavor Society, a nondenominational evangelical program for young people. She also taught the Bible class at the school, as well as Sunday school for the Baptists and the Presbyterians.

In 1918, the Sloops and their neighbors gained permission to organize Crossnore Presbyterian Church, and Doctor was elected as the first elder. He took charge of the Sunday school and also led the choir. The church's first pastor was called the following year, in 1919. He was Christopher McCoy Franklin, who was finishing his studies at Berea College.

If Mary Sloop had a model for the kind of school she wanted at Crossnore, it was Kentucky's Berea College, a nondenominational Christian institution that was dedicated to the education of the children of Appalachia. Students of school age were admitted to classes in the elementary grades or as a complement to the education they had gained in one-room schoolhouses like the one in Crossnore. They could then continue to earn a bona fide college degree with studies in Greek, Latin, the sciences, and literature. Moreover, the educational program included vocational training in mountain agriculture, carpentry, bricklaying, telegraphy, home economics, and health and hygiene. Tuition was free, and the costs were kept to a minimum, but every student, no matter how wealthy, contributed a minimum of seven hours of work each week at some job on the campus. The college's goal was to provide "thorough Christian education" and contribute to the "spiritual and material welfare of the mountain region of the South."

Each year, Berea's president, William G. Frost, set out through the mountains of Appalachia in search of young people eager for an education. On one of his trips, he interested the Sloops' friend Alexander A. Johnson in the school, and all ten of his children ended up there as students. Another recruit was McCoy Franklin, who came from a large, well-known family in the Crossnore area. Franklin had met the Sloops through their medical practice in the area, and he was deeply impressed with the world that they told him about beyond the mountains. Though he was nearly twenty-one when he met the couple, he could barely read or write. The encounter inspired him, and as soon as possible he enrolled at Berea. In the fall of 1914, he was one of seven students from Crossnore attending Berea, out of a total of thirty-one students from Avery County. He was in the first year of the school's academy, which started him at the fourth-grade level and sent him home with a college degree.

In a short time, the community of Crossnore had risen well above the modest circumstances of a few years before. The schoolhouse was the hub of all manner of activities. A Boy's Literary Society—for students and nonstudents—met there once a week for organized debates. Each grade received a weekly lesson in agriculture taught by a state-provided county extension agent. The third- and fourth-grade students developed a garden where they got practical experience. After the United States entered World War I in 1917, all the students turned out three afternoons a week for calisthenics. The older boys practiced drilling with wooden rifles. (While Doctor conducted physical examinations of the men drafted for military service, Mary Sloop raised enough money to provide a khaki-covered Bible to every Avery County man who served.) The school's domestic science teacher organized canning clubs to instruct homemakers in the proper methods of storing foods. She also left her classroom, traveling to other schools in the county to teach courses in home nursing, hygiene, and bread making, as well as to lecture on ways to prevent typhoid fever and tuberculosis.

The Sloops were helping to breathe life into a community where neighbors were beginning to learn to work together toward common goals. Some parents had built small cabins near the school and moved to the community so their children wouldn't have to walk

By the early 1920s, Crossnore had two general stores, a post office, a garage, and other busi-nesses. The photograph shows the 1913 school building, the 1920 school building (at right on hill), and the teacherage that was set in the woods. The Baptist church is on the hill on the left

through mud and snow to get to class. The post office had moved into a building of its own. The general store's new owner brought in a larger and better selection of goods. A cooperative cheese factory, one of three in the county, was organized in 1917, and production of ten thousand pounds annually was predicted. Mary Sloop wrote her friends that a woolen mill was expected, although it never material-ized. The legislature did approve $150,000 for building roads, and Potter Brown, a college-trained engineer, was put in charge of the work in Avery County. A dentist made regular stops at the school to treat anyone who asked for care. Mary Sloop paid half the charge of twenty cents per tooth for students who needed attention.

Not all of Avery County's citizens were thrilled with what many called progress. Mary Sloop had stirred up considerable resentment in her zeal for civic improvement. Most everyone knew about her campaign against moonshiners. She regularly called the authorities to account for lax enforcement of the laws against the making of illegal liquor. She also had men hauled into court for defying the truancy laws. Her own health and safety were threatened from time to time, but she pressed on in her efforts. Years later, she said she was sure that mountain men would not harm a woman, especially the wife of the doctor responsible for patching up the wounds of those who settled their differences with firearms.

There was a less lethal concern in the community about where all this change was headed, however. As various members invested more and more in the school, Sloop heard talk that some of her neighbors believed the Presbyterian Church would be taking over the school and all the improvements. Rumors of subversion by the Presbyterians could undo all that had taken place, Sloop believed, and she set out to the ease the fears of her neighbors over what they were building together.

The answer was a corporate charter, issued by the state in 1917, which established Crossnore School Incorporated as a nonprofit corporation that would be controlled by community representatives. At the outset, it would own the nearly twenty acres of land that had been acquired the year before by Eustace Sloop, Alexander Johnson, and Potter Brown, acting as trustees for the community's interests. The organizers agreed that the work of Crossnore School Incorporated, like the work of Berea Incorporated, would be "to promote the cause of Christian education and to maintain and operate a school or schools in which students may obtain a Classical, Mathematical, Scientific, Technical, Agricultural, Vocational, or general education." In short, Crossnore School Incorporated was to operate as a partner with the public school to expand and enhance the educational program. The original trustees were Eustace Sloop, Johnson, and Brown. Brown was later succeeded by Milligan S. Wise, a Berea Academy graduate and woodworking teacher.

The community was thinking ahead. Mary Sloop wanted more land on which to build a high school. She also yearned to create a

One of the first residences for boys at Crossnore was called the "Donkey Barn" because of its crude construction and accommodations.

demonstration farm where boys would gain practical experience in new farming techniques and that would allow students to learn the basics of gardening. In this, she might have been inspired by North Carolina's governor, T. W. Bickett, who in his inaugural address in 1917 had called for a six-month school term and regular instruction in agriculture and homemaking. The legislature complied with his request for the longer school term and appropriated $500,000 to build rural schoolhouses. It also enacted a statewide truancy law.

Avery County responded with a three-story brick high school in Elk Park that opened in 1919. Meanwhile, in Crossnore the students in the higher grades attended classes in a lean-to affair where lumber was stored at the back of the shop. It was called "the Wart" because it looked so out of place. Sixteen students who were enrolled in the ninth grade met in this crude room and sat at handmade desks. Unbleached muslin covered openings cut into the exterior walls for windows.

The community leaders knew that in order to build the kind of school they wanted, they would need more than free labor, donated materials, and the money Mary Sloop could raise from donations and the sale of used clothes. An early estimate of the cost of the building was $26,000. Other communities, such as incorporated cities and towns, were voting to increase their taxes to pay for schools. While Crossnore was not incorporated, the law allowed rural townships to impose a tax for schools if the voters approved it. The election was called, and it produced one of the curious tales that Mary Sloop loved to tell in later years. The deciding vote in favor of the tax was cast by the owner of a gristmill whom she had put in jail for refusing to send his children to school.

With the tax approved, the community began work. The plan was to build a consolidated school to serve all the students in the Altamont district, from the elementary grades through high school, which ended at the eleventh grade at the time. It was to have fourteen classrooms and be equipped with steam heat, drinking fountains, electric lights, bathrooms, laboratories, individual desks, and recitation benches. The site selected for the three-story frame building overlooked the crossroads at Crossnore on a level spot that locals carved out of the hillside with shovels and drag pans.

Construction began in 1918 as soon as weather permitted, even though the organizers had only $4,000 worth of wood and a promise of $3,000 in cash from the Avery County Board of Education. Mary Sloop was on the site daily. Her husband's sister, Lena, whose husband had died in 1914, had moved in with the family to help care for the Sloop children while their mother was out and about. Mary Sloop nursed every penny that came available. When money ran out, work stopped, to be resumed when she had enough funds to meet the weekly payroll.

Some workers, like Newton Clark, refused to take any pay. He told Sloop that he and his wife, Mary Jane, had agreed that he would donate his labor because of the importance of the school to the community. While they talked one day, Clark asked Sloop if Latin would be taught at the new school. Such a question from an unlettered mountain man caught her by surprise, according to the account in her memoir. Yes, she told him, Latin would be part of the high school course. How did he know of Latin? "Cause," he replied, "our folks from the Old Country writes to us that we're settled in this lonely place, and we've got to be sure to get young 'uns educated and that nobody is educated that don't know Latin. So we've always wanted 'em to have Latin, and I'm agoin' home and tell Mary Jane they're agoin' to have Latin."

Construction progressed in fits and starts. Sloop was just about to suspend operations when a letter arrived that contained a check

The school built in 1920 was large enough to accommodate hundreds of students from the elementary grades through high school. It produced its first graduates in 1921 and became accredited the following year. Students met a rigorous academic schedule that included foreign languages as well as vocational courses.

for $5,000. It was from William B. McGillican, a cotton broker in New Orleans who had heard about her work and was inspired by her story—as were others whom he had told about Crossnore. Three more checks—one for $1,000, one for $500, and another for $250— arrived a few days later. Work resumed, but the community was still short of what was needed. Sloop appealed to the school board, whose members refused to cosign a loan for the $10,000 required to finish the building. She then went to E. C. Guy, the head of the Bank of Avery County, and told him she wanted to borrow the money.

"On what security, Mrs. Sloop?" Guy responded.

"On my face," she replied. He laughed and approved the loan.

The school was still incomplete, the bank account once again

The school at Crossnore produced its first high school graduates in 1921. This faculty included Mary Sloop, who is at right in back, and the Reverend McCoy Franklin, the tall man near the center. Seated in the center of the front row are teachers Betty Bayley (Gillen) and Jean Busey (Yntema), two Illinois women who came to teach at Crossnore and encouraged Mary Sloop to appeal to the National Society of the DAR for support.

about empty, when Sloop returned to the school board for help. Again, she left empty-handed, but she was determined to see the project through. She traveled by horseback to Morganton, a commercial center down the mountain, where she boarded the train for Raleigh intent on a meeting with the state superintendent of public instruction, E. C. Brooks. After Brooks heard her story, he asked her to find the Avery County school superintendent and the Avery County attorney, who had just left his office after a meeting on another matter. She hunted them down in Raleigh and told them Brooks wanted to see them again. By the time they finished their second meeting with Brooks, they had agreed for the county to cover Sloop's debt at the bank and see that the school was completed.

On April 6, 1921, Gurney Franklin and Nell Johnson became the first graduates of the new Altamont Consolidated School, as it was called. Nell and her brother Monte had been students at Berea in the spring of 1920 when they got a request from Mary Sloop to return to Crossnore to complete their high school education and be part of the school's first graduating class. Monte chose to remain at Berea, but Nell heeded Sloop's call. About ten years earlier, Nell, like her brother, had been one of the children who had recited the 200 verses and received a Bible from Sloop.

At the graduation ceremonies, Nell Johnson recited a twelve-page paper, "The Art of Handweaving," that drew on skills she had acquired in the weaving department at Berea. Franklin's recitation was on fruit-growing in western North Carolina. Edgar W. Knight, a distinguished educator and professor from the university in Chapel Hill, delivered the main address. His attendance was remarkable considering the difficulties of travel to a tiny, isolated community like Crossnore. Knight's presence was also a testimony to the unique educational opportunity becoming available in the mountains.

The school had chosen its own colors—blue and white—and a motto: "By our own effort we hope to rise." In 1922, the school at Crossnore became the first fully accredited high school in Avery County.

4
Spreading the Word

Standing half a head taller than the other teachers at the Cross-nore high school the year it produced its first graduates in 1921 was McCoy Franklin, a muscular man with strong features and a full head of brown hair. No other son of the Avery County mountains better il-lustrated the fire that an education could kindle in a man.

In 1910, at the age of twenty-one, Franklin had broken with his father and left for Berea College with twenty-five dollars in his pock-et, a wooden suitcase on his shoulder, and a vision of what might lie beyond the family's farm over the mountains from Crossnore. In nine years, he completed the requirements for the elementary grades, earned a high school diploma, finished his studies at Louisville Theo-logical Seminary, and received a degree from Berea College.

Franklin was from one of the legendary families that had mi-grated into the Linville River valley from the northeast and settled there a hundred years or more earlier. It was said there was a direct relation to Benjamin Franklin's brother John. Will Franklin, McCoy's father and the patriarch of the clan, was tall, lean, and a bit stoop-shouldered. He wore a thin beard. He was a farmer and entrepreneur who operated a gristmill and a sawmill; he also traded the leather he tanned in his shop for shoes made by his neighbor Alexander John-son. Education was of no importance to Will Franklin. His son lat-er said his father told him that the only educated people he ever met were cheats and scoundrels.

The elder Franklin had mellowed a bit by the time his son McCoy returned from Kentucky with his pocket full of degrees. In the intervening years, he had lost another son to the flu epidemic that swept through military camps in 1918. Like his brother McCoy, the young sailor had left against his father's wishes, and their last words had been harsh. Will Franklin wished it had been different.

McCoy Franklin was just what Mary Sloop needed in the summer of 1921. The young man brought home to Crossnore an educated wife and a fierce calling to serve the Lord and to improve the lives of others in the community. He was called to be the first full-time pastor for the congregation at Crossnore Presbyterian Church even before he left Berea. When he arrived back home, he became the public voice of Crossnore, appearing in pulpits and on the lecture circuit all across the United States. (He claimed he only missed speaking in two states, Idaho and Oregon.) Over the next decade or more, his evangelizing for the Lord and for Crossnore would help raise the money that the community needed to meet the growing demands of the school.

It had taken almost ten years and thousands of dollars to build the new high school, which was far better than many of the others in the rural reaches of North Carolina. Once the school was opened and equipped, however, the needs seemed to grow, one on top of the other, both for Sloop and for Franklin, who in addition to his pastoral duties became the president of the board of trustees of Crossnore School Incorporated. Not the least of their challenges was accommodating the growing number of students who were drawn to the school and to the chance for a real education. Many lived miles from Crossnore and were unable to maintain regular attendance if they had to commute daily. The trek over trails and muddy roads was especially difficult in winter. Passage was so arduous on some routes that a sled with runners made from stout timbers had a better chance of passage than a wagon with wheels.

The first of the commuter students had appeared at the Sloop home and asked for a place to stay when the school had only a few classrooms. One girl offered to spend the winter sleeping on the broad porch that wrapped around two sides of the house. Instead,

An early school bus was a converted truck with its bed covered in straw. In this photograph, probably taken by Dr. Eustace Sloop, the "bus" is filled with the Sloop children and their cousins. Will, the Sloops' son, is the boy standing near the back of the truck. His sister, Emma, is seated on the front and all but hidden from view.

Sloop found her a bed in the attic of a nearby home. A handful of boys took up residence in the loft of a gristmill. They washed up in a cold stream and ate rations that they carried with them to Crossnore each week.

Sloop could hardly refuse aid to such eager learners. She had enforced the law to require attendance and had even coached children in ways to irritate parents who refused to free them from farm work so they could be in the classroom. She encouraged boys and girls to wail and cry when they were kept at home. If that didn't change their parents' minds, she later wrote, she told them to pout. "They were to do their work ... but were not to do it pleasantly; they were to go about it unsmiling and glum, with the air of injured innocence, the attitude of martyrdom. That almost always worked. The parents sent them back to school in self-defense."

Providing housing was an unexpected consequence of her efforts to boost attendance; Sloop had never intended to create a "boarding department," as it would come to be known. Like so many other things in Crossnore, student housing simply grew out of necessity, as was the case in a number of rural counties in the state. In the Helton community of Ashe County—another isolated mountain area—private citizens raised a thousand dollars to build a dormitory, kitchen, and dining hall. Crossnore's boys had to fend for themselves. After the first year in the gristmill, the older boys built a shelter they called "the donkey barn" because of its crude, open-air construction. Younger boys took their place in the loft at the gristmill.

It didn't take long for Sloop to realize that these temporary arrangements would not do. As the demand increased, she arranged for the boys to take over the upper story of the shop building they called Treasure Island. The girls were placed with local families until they could move into the original teacherage after larger and more spacious quarters for the teachers were built and became available. Eventually, the girls moved into a dormitory large enough to sleep thirty. It was built with money donated by a Charlotte textile man, Charles W. Johnston, who also was a benefactor to the Presbyterian orphanage at Barium Springs, near Statesville. Meanwhile, Sloop convinced the Men's Bible Class at the First Presbyterian Church in Gastonia, North Carolina, to send enough money to build a small dining hall nearby. All the residential students and the teachers living on campus took their meals there.

Sloop was eternally frugal. When one building was freed from its original intended use by the construction of something new, the old space was consumed by another mission, such as the conversion of Treasure Island into a dormitory first for teachers and then for the boys. When the new consolidated school opened, boys who had been rooming in the old schoolhouse were displaced by the need of the grammar grades for recitation space. Other former classrooms accommodated an office for a dentist and a nurse, as well as Mack's Barber Shop. "Mack is one of our manly boys, with such a sweet tenor voice, who came back to school after being out at work for years, and undertook to work his way through school," Sloop wrote in a broad-

During her trip through the mountains in the 1920s, Chapel Hill photographer Bayard Wooten took this picture of the rough condition of mountain roads. Photo courtesy of North Carolina Collection, University of North Carolina at Chapel Hill.

side entitled, "How Crossnore Spends Her Money." "He does it with his barber shop, which we give him free of rent, so long as he keeps the conduct of it up to the proper standard."

The new consolidated school opened just as forces in social and civic improvement were stirring beyond the peaks that surrounded the mountain communities, where little had changed in a hundred years. If Avery County was to benefit, then it would need better communication and access to the rest of the state. In the spring of 1921, Mary Sloop set out for Raleigh to try to do something about the sorry state of mountain roads, which were impassable in foul weather and all but nonexistent to points south and east. She arrived at the state capitol to work with another strong-willed woman, Harriet Morehead Berry of Chapel Hill, who was helping to craft a road-building program that would create the state's first modern highway system.

The 1921 session of the General Assembly opened in January with a new governor in office, Cameron Morrison of Charlotte. During his four-year term, he would push through a bond issue that would provide money to build hard-surfaced, two-lane roads to connect every county seat across the state. At his side was Heriot Clarkson, an influential Charlotte lawyer who knew something about the condition of mountain roads. Clarkson was one of the developers of Little Switzerland, a community of wealthy summer residents—most of them from Charlotte. Their homes perched at the edge of the Blue Ridge just below Spruce Pine, a thriving mining town not far from Crossnore.

Sloop left her entire family behind and literally moved to Raleigh for six weeks as the legislators haggled over the governor's road program. She went to work with Berry's Good Roads Committee to win votes for state approval to sell $50 million in road bonds. Sloop organized letter-writing campaigns, and day after day she tugged on the sleeves of members from the mountain districts to convince them that borrowing millions of dollars was the only way the state could move forward. In late February, during a public hearing organized on behalf of the bill, she was one of twenty speakers drawn from around the state who had been chosen to appear in favor of the bill. The presenters included businessmen, politicians, and community leaders, yet the *Greensboro Daily News* said Sloop's presentation was "incomparably the best," because she spoke "from tragic experience of the horrors of red clay roads."

The bill passed, and in the following decade hundreds of remote locations like Crossnore gained access to the world beyond. For Crossnore, it meant a new route through Avery County that connected the communities on the eastern side of the high mountain ridge that ran north to south. Her neighbors called it "Miz Sloop's Road," but it was nearly a century before that designation was formalized by an official highway sign on US 221 erected in Mary Sloop's honor—an effort led by her successor Dr. Phyllis Crain.

Sloop wanted good roads to provide markets for the potato crops that state agricultural extension agents began helping Avery County farmers produce once they discovered that the Irish potatoes grown in the North Carolina mountains were as good, if not better, than those produced in Maine. The road also gave farmers a way to get their cabbages—another cash crop—down the mountain to customers before they spoiled. More important, better roads made it easier for children throughout the township to reach the school aboard the buses that had replaced a horse-drawn wagon Sloop had commissioned to carry students to school.

By the early 1920s, the classrooms at Crossnore were offering opportunities for adults as well as children. Adults who had never completed their elementary education returned to the classroom and began work toward their high school diplomas. One graduate during these years was a woman who moved to Crossnore with her four children, kept house for her father-in-law, and graduated at the top of her class. Mary Sloop was looking over her grades prior to graduation and found her teachers had not issued a grade for deportment. She asked why and was told, "I would not presume to grade a woman on deportment who rears a family, cooks for in-laws and makes the best grades in school."

No member of the faculty touched more lives than the school's agriculture teacher, Thomas P. Dellinger. He was a Berea graduate who continued his studies at what had recently been renamed North Carolina State College (later North Carolina State University). Half of Dellinger's salary was paid from federal funds made available to the state through the Smith-Hughes Act. This 1917 federal law was designed to promote vocational and agriculture training, particularly in rural schools. Like McCoy Franklin, Dellinger was a Crossnore native who returned to improve life where he had been raised.

Dellinger built himself a small frame house that became a model for others in the community, and he worked with his students to find alternative farming methods suited to mountains where a tillable field was considered a godsend. The state extension service was promoting a future in poultry production, and in a few years Dellinger had more than fifty poultry houses on Avery County farms. The work of the students inspired their fathers to create the Mountain Hatchery Association, which found a market for eggs in the kitchens of the summer homes at Linville and Little Switzerland, and as far away as restaurants in Charlotte.

Just as at Berea College, Crossnore students were immersed in the standard curriculum as they acquired practical skills. The two went hand in hand to improve the lot of individuals and the community at large. Sloop believed that young men who became handy with a hammer and saw would build sound homes of their own and keep them in good repair. Girls who learned to sew and prepare nutritious meals would become better homemakers, with children who would be better clothed and fed. New farming techniques would open new markets and put more money in the pockets of farmers who for years had struggled to grow enough to feed their families.

Crossnore was even producing teachers. The school's teacher training department was one of two in the county. It enabled high school graduates to attend for a full year during the regular term and qualify for an elementary B state teaching certificate upon completion.

The vocational programs, the development of a hatchery, and the students who worked to pay their room and board became a compelling story for a gifted preacher like McCoy Franklin. After his return to the valley, he had worked with Sloop at the school and organized a half dozen churches in the area. In the summer of 1921, he became a Crossnore School Incorporated trustee and was named president of the board. The title was thought to enhance his prestige as he traveled across the country preaching the Gospel and telling Crossnore's story. While Sloop managed the day-to-day operation of the campus, Franklin raised the money that she needed to pay for more buildings, hire additional teachers, and underwrite the cost of housing and feeding students, many of whom arrived full of desire but with empty pockets.

She eagerly endorsed the new role for Franklin, telling him at one point, "So many of the people in North Carolina who could help us look on Crossnore as an old woman's hobby and they won't give me a thing. I am sure they will give to you."

Franklin stood about six foot two, but his most arresting feature was a smooth, rolling voice that he used to captivate his audiences. He could create vivid images of a crisp, cool mountain morning, or the crystal waters of the Linville River as it flowed over moss-covered rocks, or the dark shadows and fresh perfume of the tall pines that were repopulating the land. Congregations in New York, Pittsburgh, and Baltimore heard a preacher whose brogue suggested an unlettered mountaineer but who could express his theology with profound intent and entertain with a repertoire of bird calls that he had learned as a lad. He often told his own story of leaving home for an education and how he had used his training in the ministry since his return.

Franklin's ability to charm an audience caught the attention of a booking agent in 1922. He offered to add him to his stable of speakers and assured Franklin that he could make a weekly minimum of $1,000 on a tour of the country. Franklin turned him down, but he remained on the circuit. The National Reform Association sponsored some of his talks, and he appeared before DAR chapters. Some of his appearances included Chautauqua events in New England, where his $100 fee paid his expenses and produced an income for the school. When he was in top form, he could fill collection plates with cash for Crossnore and inspire his audience to ship trunks and boxes of clothes and other used belongings to the Sales Store. People who knew nothing about the mountains of Appalachia responded to his call for scholarships to pay the $2 a week needed to cover a student's living expenses.

Franklin didn't limit his visits to churches. He sought out young people to interest in the work at Crossnore. In 1922, the Camp Fire Girls of Baltimore "adopted" a Crossnore student and raised money for her support. "This girl will be sent to school as her New Year's Gift, and her annual tuition sent at this time," said a notice of the donation in *Everygirl's* magazine. A Boy Scout troop in Pennsylvania sent five boxes and one barrel filled with clothes later that same year.

Franklin formed the Save the Children Club, whose members contributed at least $1 a year. In return, they received a summary report on the work of the students, the buildings erected, and other improvements at the school. "It cost us $0.01 to mail the folder and most of the club members would send us $5.00 or $10.00 each year," Franklin later reported in a memoir.

A national magazine writer told Franklin's story in 1925, and she came back a year later to write about Mary Sloop. Mildred Harrington's feature in *American* magazine, titled "No Magician's Trunk

Ever Held Such Wonders as These!" recounted the tale of Hepsy, the trunk of old clothes, and how the money from the Sales Store had become the financial wellspring for a unique school. It was a theme that would be recounted many times by other writers over the years.

While Franklin was telling Crossnore's story in his travels to congregations around the country, Sloop began building a relationship with the National Society of the Daughters of the American Revolution, an organization that would be critical to Crossnore's future. The school's story had an intrinsic appeal to the DAR. It was located in a region where old-timers talked of knowing men who had served in the Revolutionary War. The grave of Robert Sevier, a hero of the Battle of Kings Mountain, was nearby. Crossnore's self-help program, its preservation of mountain culture through the weaving department, and the work of the Sloops to the upbuilding of the area all resonated with the Daughters.

Mary Sloop was encouraged to make an appeal to the DAR by Betty Bayley (Gillen), a young woman from Illinois who had stopped at Crossnore in the summer of 1919 while she was vacationing in the mountains with her family. During her visit, she asked Sloop if she could teach at the school after she graduated from the University of Illinois. Bayley returned in 1920 with another recent Illinois graduate, Mary Owings Graves. Sloop was so taken with Bayley's enthusiasm for Crossnore that she sent her on a speaking tour to promote the school and generate clothing donations. Bayley and McCoy Franklin were together in Champaign-Urbana, the home of the University of Illinois, when she met up with a classmate, Jean Busey (Yntema), at a showing of *The Little Shepherd of Kingdom Come*. The six-reel silent feature told the story of an orphan boy from the hills of eastern Kentucky who was caught up in the Civil War when brothers chose sides between the North and the South. Throughout the movie, Busey remembered, Bayley and Franklin kept saying to each other, "That looks just like Crossnore."

Bayley's fund-raising assignment left Crossnore without a teacher, so she recruited Busey to take her place in the classroom. Busey's degree was in chemistry, but Sloop assigned her to teach history and French in the high school, as well as reading to sixth graders. She lived in the teacherage with two others and stayed to the end of the term to see Crossnore's high school graduate its first class in 1921.

In November 1921, Sloop attended a meeting of the North Carolina DAR in Gastonia, where she told the members about her work at Crossnore. Before the meeting adjourned, the membership had endorsed the school and recommended it to chapters in the state as worthy of their support. A few months later, in the spring of 1922, the Illinois DAR learned about Crossnore from Busey, whose mother was a founding member of Champaign-Urbana's Alliance chapter. Busey made a presentation to the state meeting and talked about her experience as a teacher at the school. At the time of Busey's presentation, three more Illinois women with ties to the DAR were teaching at Crossnore. Busey didn't ask for money, but she repeated Mary Sloop's appeal for old clothes. Her mother's chapter in Champaign-Urbana sent money as well as six barrels of clothes and other items donated by chapter members. Bayley and Busey may also have been responsible for the donation of musical instruments from the university's band director, which allowed Crossnore to organize a band with eighteen members and a big bass drum.

Mary Sloop became a "member at large" of the National Society of the Daughters of the American Revolution in April 1922, when she attended her first meeting of the Continental Congress, the DAR's annual meeting in Washington, DC. She certainly had sufficient bona fides for membership through her mother's family, the Robesons of southeastern North Carolina. Colonel Thomas Robeson had fought at the battles of Moore's Creek, Stuart's Creek, and Elizabethtown. It is said that he paid those under his command with private funds. Robeson County was named in his honor.

She returned to Washington in the spring of 1923 for the thirty-third Continental Congress and reported, "A few days ago we graduated five boys and five girls, each one of whom is entering college and at his or her own expense. For when we graduate them and they are ready to enter a class in college they ask no man to give them a penny. They work their way through."

The development of Crossnore dovetailed nicely with the DAR's interest in education. In 1919, the South Carolina Daughters had cre-

The National Society of the DAR endorsed Sloop's program of education in 1922.

Uncle Gilmer sized up clothes for customers and then set a price for items purchased at the Sales Store.

ated Tamassee School in the mountain foothills of South Carolina with purposes and goals very similar to what Sloop hoped to accomplish in North Carolina. The Berry School for Girls in Rome, Georgia, a self-help school that had been founded in 1909, was on the organization's list of schools approved for support. At the time, there were about a dozen others that did not receive direct support from the organization but were endorsed as "approved schools." This imprimatur allowed institutions like Crossnore to appeal directly for support to DAR chapters, which knew through the endorsement that the schools were worthy of their attention.

The national DAR organization did send money to Crossnore—$500 in 1924—but the greatest benefit for Sloop was the opportunity to solicit help from one of the largest and fastest-growing women's organizations in the nation. The relationship was just as good as money in the bank. "I may say in the mountains that I am known as 'The Old Clothes Woman,'" she told the Continental Congress in 1923, "and that last year we were fortunate to sell twelve thousand dollars worth of old clothes for our school."

The Sales Store remained Sloop's treasure chest, providing most of the money for operating expenses and to cover expanding the inventory of campus buildings. Old clothes had produced enough to pay one-third of the cost of the high school building. Sales had paid half the cost of the teacherage, two-thirds of the cost of the concrete-block vocational training building, and half the cost of the girls' dormitory.

The store had regular hours four days a week and remained in the care of Uncle Gilmer and Aunt Pop. Just inside the front door, a turnstile admitted customers to the sales floor, where clothing was set out. There were no price tags; the place was too busy for that now. Instead, Uncle Gilmer sized up both the customer and the merchandise and tried to arrive at a fair match. Customers whose purchases amounted to as much as $3 were allowed to take home one of the "grab bundles" that were filled with an assortment of items. These hung by strings from the ceiling. The merchandise included both the old and the new. A men's civic club in Charlotte had recently sent along sixty suits for sale. They brought in $600. Nothing was given away.

H. V. Kendall of the *Charlotte Observer* visited Crossnore in the summer of 1926. In his report on the community and the school, he wrote, "Mrs. Sloop said that she made it a point never to give away any clothing regardless of how pitiful a tale might be put up. The mountain people, she explained, have to be dealt with firmly, and once the bars are let down there would be no let-up, either to the gifts or the stories of need which would be poured into her ear."

She didn't believe she was being harsh. "If I gave them all these clothes," she explained, "they'd have nothing in the world to show for the gifts and would not be helping themselves in the least." Kendall wrote that the sales had totaled $15,000 in the previous year, "and the residents of the section had put just that much into the improvement of their own conditions and the upbuilding of their community."

By the time of Kendall's visit, Crossnore had become an incorporated municipality. The legislature created the town in 1925 and

This photograph of the stores at the center of the village of Crossnore found its way onto a postcard. The expanding campus is up the hill and to the right above the store buildings.

One of the first substantial buildings erected on the campus was built to house teachers. It also served as the center of campus activities, and Mary Sloop had her office there from the 1930s until it burned in 1946.

named Milligan S. Wise, a Crossnore trustee and teacher, as mayor until an election could be held. The first board of alderman included Dr. Eustace H. Sloop, S. H. Franklin (McCoy's brother, who operated a garage), Charles Vance, Thomas P. Dellinger (the agriculture teacher), and Mack Dellinger. The sleepy crossroads that a decade earlier had only a broken-down log schoolhouse and a post office was now able to boast a restaurant and a bakery run by the Vance brothers, a theater that showed movies twice a week, and two grocery stores, one of which was a cooperative. There were two filling stations and Franklin's garage.

The town's most important industry was the school, which had grown beyond anything that could have been imagined a decade earlier. The latest addition to the campus—which now consisted of ninety-plus acres of land—was the teacherage, a residence hall large enough to accommodate up to thirty teachers. There also was a room for square dances on Tuesday nights with fiddles and a banjo for accompaniment. Talent shows were held on Saturdays in the school auditorium. Aside from the high school, the teacherage was the first permanent building on the campus. Everything else had been built with expediency in mind. This two-story building of concrete block was sound and spacious, and it featured two large porches off the front, one for each level.

Sloop moved her office into the teacherage. She had been named business manager of Crossnore School Incorporated in 1922 after Milligan S. Wise had held the job for a year. Sloop maintained the financial accounts and handled the correspondence that flowed into the school in the wake of Franklin's visits abroad. If Mary Sloop wasn't home tending to her family, she could be found at the teacherage.

One of the busiest places on campus was a building that arose through the growing affection of the ladies of the DAR for Crossnore. Finished in 1926 with the help of contributions totaling more than $3,000 was a building known as "the Shop," but it carried a plaque that read, "D. A. R. Building 1926." The carpentry class occupied the first floor, while the second story was scheduled to become the home of the new toy shop. Sloop planned to grub stumps of walnut and maple from the school land, which students would use to make toys. These would be added to a growing inventory of mountain handicrafts, the most popular of which were articles of hand weaving and hooked rugs made from scraps of fabric she harvested from textile mills in the Piedmont.

Seventy-five of the three hundred children attending the school in the mid-1920s in the first through the eleventh grades lived on the campus in the dormitories and other makeshift living spaces. Most of them worked at various jobs to cover the cost of their room and board. Despite the challenges, students remained as eager as ever to attend. While the overall attendance rate for Avery County schools stood at 66 percent, attendance at Crossnore was the highest in the state, at 96 percent.

In 1925, the high school had twelve graduates, and all of the students were headed to college. One of them was Emma Sloop, the daughter whose future had inspired her parents to improve education in Crossnore.

5

The Weaving Department

As Mary Sloop carried her story about Crossnore to civic clubs, church groups, and DAR gatherings in the mid-1920s, she often arrived with napkins, stoles, and other items from the looms of the Crossnore weaving department. The handicraft of Thomas Dellinger's boys in the carpentry shop did not travel well, but her luggage easily accommodated woven items like the coverlet that she and her daughter, Emma, presented to the wife of President Calvin Coolidge in 1926.

The creation of the weaving program was as natural an extension of the school's vocational training as any of the courses in practical skills for men that she appropriated from Berea College. As soon as space became available in the new high school, Sloop installed looms and hired teachers to give women, young and old, an opportunity to learn to weave and earn an income. In time, the school's weaving program would become a signature, in much the same way that Berea was known for its Fireside Industries.

Crossnore's first weaving instructors—a teacher named Clara Lowrance and a young Crossnore woman named Zada Benfield—were both Berea-trained. Lowrance was one of the first classroom teachers whom Sloop enticed into the backcountry to teach when the school had only two or three classrooms. She was from Texas, a Presbyterian, and possibly one of those sent to the mountains by the Reverend Walter Lingle at Union Theological Seminary when Sloop appealed to him for help. Lowrance had learned to weave in a summer course at Berea. Benfield, by contrast, had grown up in Crossnore and was introduced to weaving during a year at Berea in the precollege program.

The school's new looms were made by the boys in the carpentry shop using a design that Sloop borrowed from Berea. Instruction was open to all, not just the young people at the school. In addition to the twelve looms that students worked with on the campus, another six were placed in the homes of older women. As was the case in Kentucky, the handiwork of the weavers was offered for sale through the school. An able weaver could make as much as seventy-five cents a day.

"The work [out in homes] has a three-fold effect upon their lives," wrote Forest Selby in 1921 in a review of the weaving department's first year. "Their coming in contact with the teacher and the school changes their outlook and ideals; they find life very different when they handle a little money of their own, and the children feel a difference also; the beauty of the product, made under the guidance of trained teachers, creates a desire for better things in their own homes. The homes soon look better and become more attractive and comfortable."

Sloop told Selby that weaving was a way "to keep alive an almost forgotten art; to cherish in the young people of the mountains a reverence for this art; to provide a means of livelihood and pleasure for women and girls; to furnish homes with beautiful and lasting material." In short, weaving combined all of the elements for uplifting the community that she had cherished since her earliest days in the community. It was an art form that refreshed the senses, exercised the body, and helped add a few coins to a pocketbook.

Crossnore's weaving department began to attract attention as Americans from outside the region developed a new appreciation for the warmth and beauty of homespun fabrics, the smooth finish of a wooden bowl, and the soft shine of hammered copper. Mary Sloop quickly found herself in

Zada Benfield and Clara Lowrance

league with other like-minded women who were devoting themselves to a revival of mountain handicrafts.

Down the mountain in Asheville was Allanstand Cottage Industries, which had been founded by Frances L. Goodrich, a social worker in the schools of the Women's Board of Home Missions of the Presbyterian Church. Allanstand operated the region's oldest weave room—a sales store had opened in 1908—and Allanstand weavers were producing items that were popular with the growing number of visitors and wealthy summer residents who filled Asheville and the surrounding area during the tourist season.

Asheville was also the home of Edith Vanderbilt, the widow of George Vanderbilt, whose wealth had created Biltmore Estate. Before her husband's death in 1913, Edith had founded Biltmore Estate Industries, whose weavers and woodworkers figured in the early days of the handicraft movement. In the late teens, she promoted agricultural clubs for young people, supported "moonlight" literacy programs for adults, and touted products made in the Carolinas. For a time, she ran the North Carolina State Fair in Raleigh. She and Mary Sloop may have met in Raleigh in 1921, when Sloop was there promoting the governor's road program and Edith spoke to an extraordinary joint session of the state legislature. She appeared that day wearing a suit made from Biltmore homespun.

The new roads paid for by Governor Morrison's bond program meant the shops in Asheville that could offer Crossnore's woven goods were only a couple of hours away from Crossnore by car. Business was booming in the mid-1920s. The well-heeled guests at Asheville's Grove Park Inn arrived in late May and stayed until September. Visitors played golf and tennis, swam in the mountain lakes, rode horseback through the mountains, and enjoyed the cool evenings. So many Floridians spent their summers in Hendersonville, a bustling community south of Asheville, that a candidate for governor made a campaign stop there one year.

In the summer of 1925, Mary Sloop attended a meeting in the city at which she and others made plans for an exposition of mountain arts and crafts that would feature weaving, pottery, and woodworking for two days in August. The weavers who demonstrated their work

WEAVING
DEPARTMENT
Crossnore School
Crossnore, N. C.

Hand-Woven Household
Furnishings and
Sport Materials

Mrs. N. W. JOHNSON,   - - -   Director
Mrs. CLYDE PERREL,   -   -   Assistant
Miss DORTHEA McLEAN,   -   -   Assistant

By the mid-1920s, the weavers at Crossnore were turning out a brochure full of items that were offered for sale to friends around the country. The weaving department's director was Mrs. N. W. "Aunt Newbie" Johnson, a Crossnore woman who learned to weave on the school's looms. Photo courtesy of the Southern Highland Craft Guild.

came from Crossnore and from the Appalachian School in Penland, a boarding school run by the Episcopalians. The sister of the Penland school's founder, Berea-trained Lucy Morgan, had started a weaving department at about the same time that Sloop was installing looms in the high school in Crossnore. Morgan's weaving department became the foundation of what would become the Penland School of Crafts.

The Asheville exhibition was a first for Crossnore. It was successful, and a fitting end to Clara Lowrance's tenure with the school. She had been at Mary Sloop's side for about a dozen years. In that time, she had seen Crossnore grow from a small school with rudimentary classroom offerings into a bustling educational and vocational enterprise that was training hundreds of young people and adults. Mrs. Lillie Clark Johnson, the wife of Newbern Johnson, took her place in the weaving department in the spring of 1926. Everyone in Crossnore and throughout the world of weavers would come to know her as "Aunt Newbie." She was from a large local family and well-known to Mary Sloop. A sister, Leota, was one of the girls whose education at Lees-McRae had been paid for with money raised from the early clothing sales.

Mrs. Johnson personified the reason Mary Sloop had created a weaving department at Crossnore. It was organized not just to revive a dying art but also to be a platform to raise standards for the entire community, especially women. Lives could be transformed, she

The weaving department at Crossnore expanded rapidly in the 1920s, with dozens of looms in a building on the campus and others installed at the homes of women in the community. Mary Sloop saw weaving as a way to restore a dying mountain craft, as well as a way for women to earn money of their own. Photo courtesy of the Southern Highland Craft Guild.

believed, and Mrs. Johnson's story was a vivid example. She had not finished high school and married by the time she was sixteen. She enrolled in the weaving class when it was in its second year and she already had three children at home. She proved to be an able student. At the end of her first year, in 1923, Clara Lowrance listed her as an assistant, and she soon qualified for a certificate of instruction from the state Board of Vocational Education.

"Let me tell you what she did in those days," Mary Sloop wrote about Mrs. Johnson in her memoir. "She would get up early in the morning, milk, get breakfast, wash the breakfast dishes, dress the children, take them to her husband's mother's home and leave them there, and then walk a mile and a half to the school, where she would arrive at eight o'clock. All day—until six that night—she would work at those looms. Then she'd go get the children, take them home, feed the stock, milk, help work in the garden, cook supper, do her housework, get the children to bed, and then sit down to read in order, as she said, 'to improve my education.'"

The Crossnore weaving program would never have succeeded without the help of George W. Coggin. He supervised the vocational education courses funded under the Smith-Hughes Act for the state Department of Public Instruction and took a special interest in Crossnore. Even before the first looms were installed at the school, he was working with Crossnore students who were studying weaving designs. By the mid-1920s, Coggin had qualified the school for salary subsidies by slipping the weaving program into a special category of job training intended for industrialized textile operations like the huge cotton mills in the Piedmont. With Coggin's endorsement, checks came to Crossnore School to cover three-quarters of the pay of the weaving department's top instructors. Smith-Hughes's money paid half of the salaries, and another fourth was paid by the county school system. Crossnore's fund-raisers, Mary Sloop and McCoy Franklin, came up with the money to cover the difference. Coggin also helped Crossnore get labels for its woven goods made at a textile mill in Lexington, North Carolina, and became an unofficial promoter of Crossnore's products.

Coggin must have been impressed with the vitality of the Crossnore weaving department. In its second year, the weaving students included thirty boys and girls of high school age and four married women. By the fall of 1924, there were thirty-eight students working on the campus looms, while women weaving at home kept eleven more looms busy. Not all of the weavers could be at the looms at the same time. Some worked as they had time and slipped in to help finish long warps that were fifty to a hundred yards long. Mrs. Lowrance, and later Mrs. Johnson, kept a log of the workers' hours and assisted student weavers in perfecting their skills. Students often put in two hours a day after they finished their regular academic classes.

Crossnore became the largest ongoing weaving program under Coggin's review. In 1925, he convinced Sloop to send one of her weavers, Ann Johnson Stanley, to the Sandhills of North Carolina, where she taught weaving at a training school for girls run by the state at Samarcand. The program only lasted for one year.

In just five years, the weaving department had become a thriving enterprise. In 1926, it generated $3,000 in revenue. Not all of that was profit. The money had to cover the cost of materials and the pay to weavers. Wage earners received ten cents an hour, while others were paid by the piece. Crossnore's woolen coverlets sold for $25; baby blankets were priced between $6 and $10. The demand for Crossnore's work went well beyond the region. When a reporter for the *Raleigh News and Observer* visited the school in the summer of 1927, weavers were filling a $1,100 order from a hotel in Yellowstone National Park. The school's catalog included rugs, scarves, towels, and blankets, as well as coverlets or bedspreads in popular old patterns such as Martha Washington and Lee's Surrender.

In her travels and visits to large groups, Sloop praised the work of the weaving department and called the weavers working at home her "hidden heroes": "You help us to produce the result when you enable us to sell their finished products. So, WHO WILL BUY?" The brochure containing this question included photographs of the popular patterns and a price list.

Like everything else at Crossnore, the weaving program seemed to be constantly in need of more space. Sloop moved the looms from the school building as attendance grew there and installed them in a two-story concrete-block building that was supposed to support the school's budding farming program. Those plans had to be abandoned when Sloop's money ran out, so with the help of friends in the North Carolina chapters of the DAR, the building was refitted to accommodate twenty-four looms on the bottom floor and a woodworking shop above.

The solution to the space needs of the weaving department came in the school's most unusual building. Built at the edge of the main road that passed through town, it was a huge structure, sixty feet by thirty feet, with two connecting wings. Like the old clothes in the Sales Store just a few hundred feet away, it, too, was made of recycled materials—in this case logs from old barns that McCoy Franklin's father, Will, had salvaged from his property and another farm nearby.

During the 1920s, while his son was president of the Crossnore School Incorporated trustees, Franklin became the Sloops' primary

Mary Sloop began her work with girls in the Crossnore community by teaching them to sew. By the 1930s, sewing was one of the regular chores of Crossnore girls. They repaired clothing and some made products for sale, such as the Susie Crossnore doll.

builder. He first turned his hand to building Crossnore Presbyterian Church, where his son was the pastor. On a steep hillside overlooking the valley at Crossnore, he created an enduring example of mountain masonry. Franklin worked from plans drawn by a Greensboro architect, but he incorporated his own artistry with the careful placement of the worn, disk-shaped stones from the Linville River. They arrived by the wagonload—two hundred wagonloads, by Mary Sloop's count— and Franklin selected each one with care. He placed them both vertically and horizontally to a pleasing effect, especially in the arches over windows and doors. Clearly, he finished the interior with his son in mind: nearly a hundred years later, most preachers required the use of a raised platform to accommodate the pulpit that Franklin built of stone and proportioned for a man as tall as his son.

From 1929 until it burned in 1936, the largest building on the campus was the Weave Room, a huge structure built from logs salvaged from the barns of area farms. It was built by Will Franklin.

Franklin started work on the church in 1924, and the inaugural services were held on August 8, 1926. Shortly thereafter, he began his next project, a cottage-style hospital for Eustace Sloop's medical practice.

The hospital had been completed when Franklin began work in 1929 on the Weave Room. It was the largest structure added to the campus since the main school building was finished in 1920. The building hugged the hillside along the road. Windows filled the sides and flooded it with light. The building was large enough to accommodate nearly forty looms, as well as the hooked rug department, where students—mostly boys—worked. There also was space for the sewing classes for girls that had been a staple of the Crossnore curriculum from the beginning. The building was easily accessible to tourists and travelers on the new highway that connected Newland to the north and Spruce Pine to the south. Sloop especially liked the

log construction. She believed it incorporated the romance of the mountains and provided an appropriate backdrop for the handicrafts offered for sale.

Cash contributions from the DAR chapters in Charlotte helped offset the cost of building materials, including the large hewn logs that Franklin had hauled in from nearby farms and installed as the walls of the new structure. He told Sloop some of the timbers came from a barn once owned by the notorious McCanless family, whose sons included a gang of bank robbers who ran with Frank and Jesse James. The James brothers were said to have visited the farm on nearby Three Mile Creek when they were on the run from the law. Franklin also brought in logs from a barn built by his grandfather.

Will Franklin was at work on the new Weave Room when his son, Mary Sloop, her daughter, Emma, and the manager of the Crossnore weave room, Mrs. Newbern Johnson, rode over the mountains to the

Students in the 1930s outside of the log building that housed the Weave Room and the sewing department.

Weavers Cabin at Penland for a meeting with others eager to maintain the legitimacy of mountain handicrafts, whose market was being eroded by goods brought in from outside the region. They left two days after Christmas 1928 as a blustery cold front moved in from the west. After everyone had arrived, it began to snow. The next morning, the mountains were covered in white, prompting some to wonder if they might be trapped for days.

They huddled in the Penland Weavers Cabin, which had been built of hand-hewn logs pulled in by the husbands of Morgan's weavers. It sat on a high ridge near the Appalachian School, the boarding school that Lucy Morgan's brother, Rufus, had opened at about the same time that the Sloops were trying to bring education to Crossnore. Earlier in the year, at a meeting of the Conference of Southern Mountain Workers, Olive Dame Campbell of the John C. Campbell Folk School in Brasstown, North Carolina, had talked to Morgan and others about getting a group of "craft-minded" people together. Morgan had issued the invitations, and she waited nervously as the weather closed in. All in all, those who got to Penland before the snow fell represented the best of those who were part of the movement for quality mountain crafts.

Mary Sloop posted a sign at the entrance to the campus to direct summer visitors and tourists to the Crossnore Weave Room.

One of the first to arrive was Allen H. Eaton of the Russell Sage Foundation. The foundation was interested in the welfare of people in the southern highlands, and Eaton had sponsored the first exposition of mountain handicrafts a few years earlier in Knoxville, Tennessee. The others sitting around the fireplace included the contingent from Crossnore, Clementine Douglas from the Spinning Wheel in Asheville, Berea president William J. Hutchins, and representatives from Cedar Creek Community Center in Tennessee and Allanstand Industries in Asheville.

The group spent the next two days talking about how they could band together to promote the mountain arts and work cooperatively to earn money to support their efforts. They heard from Hutchins, as well as Mrs. Campbell. Sloop talked about the broad benefits that the Crossnore weaving program had brought to the community. Talking together, they discovered there were as many as forty craft centers in the southern mountains that were producing weaving, hooked rugs, basketry, pottery, hammered copper, hearth brooms, and other articles. A conservative estimate of the total income of these known outlets was put as $125,000—not an inconsiderable sum when even the best items sold for $25 or less.

On their second day, they endorsed a plan to organize a group to develop and promote regional handicrafts. Of primary concern was the proliferation of poorly made products and cheap souvenirs that filled roadside stands and could be found in stores catering to tourists. They talked of forming an organization that would keep standards high and enable each center to develop resources and build a market beyond its immediate area. Some, including Crossnore, already had experience with a broader market. Crossnore's weaving was in the homes of DAR members all across the Northeast. Morgan herself would soon leave for a selling trip to New Orleans.

Five months later, in April 1929, at the annual Conference of Southern Mountain Workers in Knoxville, the Southern Mountain Handicraft Guild (later the Southern Highland Craft Guild) was formed, with Crossnore School as one of the founding members. In three years, guild membership grew to include twenty-five centers, twelve individuals, and nine friends. In 1933, one of the guild's meetings was held at the Weave Room in Crossnore, where Eaton reported on an exhibit that had opened at the Country Life Association meeting in Virginia. It had then gone on to the Corcoran Gallery in Washington, DC, and the Brooklyn Institute of Arts and Science. Of the six hundred pieces in the exhibit, twenty-three had been made by Crossnore weavers.

As Crossnore weavers assembled pieces for the Southern Highland Handicraft Guild tour, Mary Sloop was distressed by news she received from George Coggin. The state subsidy supporting salaries in the weaving program was shrinking as part of severe budget cuts brought on by the state's financial crisis. State and county salary subsidies had diminished from three-fourths in the early years to two-thirds by the mid-1920s. Now Crossnore, Penland, and other schools could expect government sources to make up no more than half of the salaries of weaving instructors. Sloop wrote Coggin in early June about her hope that the demand for woven goods by the summer tourists would improve her attitude.

"The school is having a very hard time now," she wrote. "I sometimes wonder what it is going to mean."

6

Eustace

The small cottage hospital that Will Franklin built for Dr. Eustace H. Sloop was a beauty of a building, to which he devoted the same attention to detail that he had lavished on the Crossnore Presbyterian Church. It featured gabled end sections connected by a center portion with space for a combination examining room and surgery, twenty beds for patients, and ten bassinets for newborns. Most important, it was clean and well lighted, and on opening day in the summer of 1928 it brought medical care in the Sloops' part of Avery County into the twentieth century.

While his wife had set about to build a thriving community, one that centered on the busy campus spreading out on the hill above the hospital, the man Mary Sloop lovingly called "Doctor" had spent his first two decades in the mountains doing what he had intended when they first arrived: he was providing medical attention to people whose lives literally depended on whether he was there or not.

In the early days, during their time in Plumtree, the two doctors had worked as a team. Their skills were evenly matched. The high scores they had received on their licensing exams were identical. "We figured we were pretty good doctors," Mary Sloop wrote in her memoir. "We had health, we were both tough as pine knots, and we could take a lot of licks." The challenges were considerable. Mounted against their medical training, simple instruments, and rudimentary medicines were poverty, ignorance, disease, and living conditions that had not improved since the days of the early settlers.

Once the family moved to Crossnore, Mary began investing her time in community projects, while Doctor pressed on with his medical service. He encouraged patients to come to his office, which was a small frame building connected by a raised walkway to the Sloops' house. When an office visit was not possible, he traveled on horseback, in all kinds of weather and at all hours of the day and night, to the out-of-the-way cabins back in the hollows. There were times when he returned to his home on bitterly cold nights with his stirrups encased in ice. Mary used a hammer to break his boots free.

Neither of the Sloops had been trained as surgeons, but that didn't keep them from practicing general surgery, which they performed under the most primitive of conditions. If possible, Doctor postponed surgery until fair weather. He then set up his operating table under the best apple tree he could find. He believed the tree provided some cleansing effect, but he never fully tested the theory. Mary Sloop recalled these occasions, saying, "Doctor said I have not quite made up my mind yet, whether apple tree is antiseptic or aseptic but I have never had an infection operating under an apple tree." When he was operating outdoors, he usually had a gloved and robed attendant waving small branches above his patient to keep away the bugs.

The weather didn't make allowance for emergency calls. As a result, Doctor worked in the dirty and unsanitary conditions he found in the mountain cabins. Once, during surgery on a child who was laid out on the family's kitchen table, his work was interrupted when an old hen that had slipped in through an open door took flight and landed right on the girl's abdomen, cocked its head, and stared into the open wound. Reduced to working by the light of a lantern in many instances, it was no wonder that as soon as he could Doctor began planning a way to bring electricity to Crossnore.

Eustace Sloop was more than a medical doctor: he was a polymath with an affinity for the physical sciences. He fabricated a thermometer and barometer and for more than fifty years supplied the weather service with readings twice a day. He brought with him to the mountains a large camera, with which he recorded images of the daily life at Crossnore. Some of his pictures showed an appreciation

When weather permitted, Dr. Eustace Sloop preferred operating out-of-doors and under an apple tree if one was nearby. He operated under these primitive conditions for twenty years until Garrett Memorial Hospital opened in 1928. Photo courtesy of North Carolina Collection, University of North Carolina at Chapel Hill.

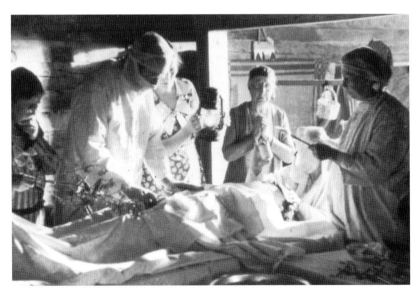

This photograph, probably taken by Bayard Wooten of Chapel Hill during her visit to Crossnore in the 1920s, illustrates the conditions under which the Sloops performed their surgery in their early years in Avery County.

Dr. Eustace Sloop had a stone dam constructed on the Linville River. The millrace into the generator house is just below and to the right of Randall Pyatte, Dodge Hoilman, Burney Pyatte, and Milt Pyatte.

for the art of photography as well as its utility. He bought and maintained one of the first automobiles—a Ford Model T—that came into the backcountry. Astronomy was second nature to him. He knew his way around the night skies as well as he knew the paths and roads around Crossnore.

Nothing quite equaled his study and dedication to establishing electrical service to his home, his office, and, in time, many of the homes in the Linville River valley. The log dam on the Linville River and the installation of a power generator was his first major undertaking. When a flood washed out the dam in the 1920s, he rebuilt it, this time out of stone. The power station that housed his first generator required daily attention, and he bore the scars of electrical burns he suffered while tending to its proper functioning. The generator was a behemoth of a machine, weighing more than half a ton. It was mounted on a heavy sled in the belly of the powerhouse and was driven by a large, inch-thick leather belt attached to the turbine in the millrace. From time to time, the belt would grow slack, and Sloop would have to drop into a small chamber, crossing on a board over the rushing water, and slide the generator along a skid to regain the proper tension.

Sloop's practical genius confounded experts at General Electric, who told him that an amateur could not refit the aged direct-current generator that he had acquired from Davidson College to operate as an alternating-current generator, which would allow the station to serve more customers. Rather than take the word of the manufacturer, he ordered a small forge from Sears, Roebuck and Company, and using what he learned from technical manuals, he made the metal rings that GE would not sell. He then wound them with copper wire, using one of the teachers boarding in the Sloop home and later his daughter, Emma, to assist with the final wrapping of the core. Their small fingers could fit the tight space that he could not reach with his own large hands.

Electricity was just the beginning. Next, he installed a network of telephones. For a time, the Sloop home served as an exchange for fourteen telephones out in the community. A water system for the school followed, with water pumped from the river to the campus more than a mile away. The Crossnore water system, using water from wells, served the campus and the town until well into the 1960s.

Mary Sloop supported her husband's every endeavor, as he did hers. Together, they made a formidable team. Since his patients paid very little for his services, she kept the family expenses to a minimum by sewing clothes for Doctor, herself, and the children. Outfitted in shirts and trousers made of khaki, and wearing heavy boots and leather leggings that reached almost to his knees, he looked more like a forest ranger than a physician. The rugged clothing came in handy on his rounds in the rough country, as he often walked beside his horse, mounting only when he had to cross a stream.

In the early years, the family lived off a small dowry that Mary brought to the marriage after she sold her interest in her father's Blowing Rock home to her brother. She didn't complain when every spare dollar went into the power system Doctor was building, so long as one of the power lines ran to the new schoolhouse. Neither she nor her husband cared much for storing up wealth. Even though Doctor kept careful records of each patient's visit, logging fees of fifty cents or a dollar into his ledger, he then often proceeded to forget about collecting the charges. He didn't enforce payments of past-due amounts that he was owed. "Dad just hated to ask his patients for money," his daughter, Emma, later said.

When Crossnore was incorporated, Doctor was named to the original town council to serve until regular members could be elected. His longest service to the community was as chair of Crossnore School Incorporated. During his forty-plus years on the board, he would open the session and then turn matters over to his wife, Crossnore's "business manager." She carried the trustees through the business at hand while her husband nodded off to sleep.

Some believed he suffered a form of narcolepsy. Most likely, Doctor was simply taking advantage of the quiet time to catch a nap. He seldom slept more than four hours out of every twenty-four and preferred taking the late shift at the hospital. He began his office hours in the late afternoon and often worked until after midnight. He rose late and frequently got his first meal of the day around noon, at his sister's house on his way to the hospital. Despite his unusual routine, he remained athletic and healthy. Nothing pleased him more than clasping his hands behind his back and skating across the ice in the wintertime.

Together, the Sloops helped organize the Crossnore Presbyterian Church, where Doctor was an elder and director of the choir. He was devoted to the church, and his reputation for a deep Christian faith was enhanced in the early days by those who saw him riding along with his eyes focused on a book in his hands. Many took it to be the Bible. In fact, he was studying technical data on electrical systems. Despite the distraction, his horse always carried him home, even when he fell asleep in the saddle, which had been custom made to handle his large frame.

Will Franklin used a design brought to him by Mary Sloop to build the Crossnore Presbyterian Church. The basic building materials were wagonloads of rock from the Linville River and chestnut wood from the surrounding forest.

His faith was a sustaining comfort and the Bible a constant companion. Doctor led a Sunday School class from the church's early days until he was no longer able to make it into the warmth of the sanctuary that he had seen rise, stone by stone, under the hands of Will Franklin. Even though Doctor was a man of science, he took the Bible literally. One who attended his classes said that he was "so earnest in his leadership and so literal in his acceptance and interpretation of every phrase in every verse." He called the choir to practice at odd hours, when he wasn't tending to the demands of his patients. In the years when the church did not have a regular preacher, he filled in at the pulpit.

A houseparent on the campus in the early 1940s who arrived with a more liberal religious disposition than what she found among the Calvinists in Crossnore was taken with Doctor's theology. "He is a beautiful old man with the peace of God in his countenance," she said, "and it may do me some good to sit in his presence each Sunday and listen to the exposition of the old-time religion."

Mary Sloop cut a wide swath through the community, stalking moonshiners and calling to account the parents who didn't send their children to school. She infuriated many of the neighbors. There were some who wished good riddance to such a meddlesome woman. She even exhausted the patience of her friends and supporters. Newland banker E. C. Guy helped Crossnore School through many difficult times when the campus bank account was down to its last dollar. Mary Sloop became a constant presence in his life, seeking advice and extensions of the obligations owned his small bank. She called on him so often that he finally gave instructions to his daughter, Martha, that when Mary Sloop called at dinner time, Martha was to lie and say her father was not at home.

Meanwhile, Doctor came along in her wake, calming angry voices and soothing tempers with his easy manner, light disposition, and wry sense of humor. "He's the quiet kind," Mary Sloop once said of her husband, "but he's got twice as much sense as I have—I'm mostly mouth. He should have the credit for a lot of things I get credit for doing. But Doctor would not have it that way. He'd rather stay in the back of the hall and let me take the bows from the stage."

Despite Mary Sloop's penchant for upsetting men who plied illicit trades in the county, Doctor traveled with impunity. He was a big man who stood head and shoulders above his short, stocky wife. A full beard added to his formidable presence. Like his wife, he respected the integrity and the customs of his patients, even when they defied common sense. At the same time, he looked for ways to turn quaint notions about medicine to his advantage. When a patient told him that he had heard a wound wouldn't heal if used bandages were put in a fire to burn—the instruction Doctor had just issued to prevent infection—Sloop didn't dispute the mountaineer's wisdom. "Oh," he said, "that's only if you watch it burn. You shouldn't watch the bandage burn, and then it will be all right."

The Sloops were able to manage their busy lives and raise two small children with the help of Doctor's sister, Lena, who was a young widow when she first came to stay with the family during the summers not long after they arrived in Crossnore in 1911. She eventually moved to Crossnore to live full time with her brother and his

Dr. Eustace Sloop opened Garrett Memorial Hospital in 1928, and it remained in use until the late 1990s, when Avery County's Cannon Hospital opened. The early building was the work of Will Franklin, whose creative stone masonry is part of the Crossnore Presbyterian Church.

wife. In 1919, she remarried but stayed on in Crossnore and taught off and on at the school. Her husband was Theron Dellinger. He ran a small store that included the post office, where she was postmistress. She relinquished the job to her husband in 1930, and he remained Crossnore's postmaster for the next thirty years. Theron and Doctor together strung most of the lines for the Crossnore power system, and he was available to help in its maintenance, going out on dark nights when a line went down. The Dellingers' daughter, Rachel, was one of the first babies born in the hospital in 1929.

As the Sloop children grew older, Emma and her brother, Will, spent a portion of their summers with Mary Sloop's family in Davidson. Emma said years later that her mother sent them there "hoping a little bit of culture would rub off," because the children "were speaking just like the mountaineers." Emma's upbringing was further polished during a year at a prep school following her graduation from high school. The tuition was paid by one of her mother's DAR friends, who also helped her enroll at Mount Holyoke College. She later transferred to Duke University and got her medical degree at Vanderbilt University. Her brother became a dentist.

Emma was away at college when construction began on the hos-

Dr. Eustace Sloop still used his horse when his Model T could not carry him into the rough country.

pital. Work was able to begin after the Sloops received a $5,000 donation from a Mrs. E. N. McWilliams of Norfolk, Virginia, who made the gift in honor of her mother, whose name was Garrett. Not much else is known about the namesake of Garrett Memorial Hospital. The organizers also received a smaller donation from the Duke Endowment, which was just beginning its work in support of health care in the Carolinas when the hospital was chartered in July 1928 and began accepting patients. With an office in the new hospital, Doctor was more accessible to patients and also closer at hand to the daily activities of his wife, who spent much of her time on the nearby campus of the school. In addition to his office and the patient ward, Doctor had a room for a small X-ray machine and a room for nurses. The food for patients and staff came from the school's dining hall. A laundry that served the hospital and the campus was in the hospital basement.

Space was at a premium. There was no waiting room, and patients seeking medical attention usually loitered around the front door. There was one nurse on duty, but Mary Sloop recruited high school girls to assist her husband and help with patients. Those with regular assignments at the hospital lived in spare rooms on the hospital's second floor. Some of them took to this early introduction to nursing and continued their studies after they graduated from the high school.

By the 1930s, the new paved roads in the mountains put the city of Asheville—the hub of commerce in western North Carolina—within easy reach of Crossnore, and each Tuesday the Sloops headed down the mountain for a ritual visit. Doctor carried a list of ingredients he required to prepare medicines for his patients. Mary Sloop had her shopping list, too. Since Doctor was not an early riser, the two often didn't begin their two-hour drive until the afternoon. A campus worker usually squeezed into the single bench seat of the Model T with them. They often arrived in the city just as clerks were preparing to close their stores for the day. All three shopped furiously and then met for dinner at the S&W cafeteria, the Sloops' favorite restaurant. The car then headed back to Crossnore in the dark.

Denise Abbey worked at Crossnore for nearly a decade, and she made the trip with the Sloops from time to time. "The purpose of the workers in the car," she later wrote, "was to keep Doctor awake. So one told stories, asked questions, eventually sang every song possible in order to survive the drive. It was bad enough in good weather, but in heavy rain, so common in the hills, or in winter snows, it was a real trial for all concerned."

On occasion, if there was time, the trip to Asheville included a movie. A few days later, Mary might be found at the campus dining hall telling the gathered students, teachers, and staff about what she had seen on the silver screen. If a motion picture was one that she particularly enjoyed, she would have those in the room rolling in laughter as she acted out the parts and recalled her favorite lines from the show.

Doctor had only the help of a single nurse to attend to all the medical tasks of his practice until the mid-1930s, when his son, Will, and then his daughter, Emma, returned to Crossnore to work with him. Will, a dentist, opened his practice in the hospital, where Emma, a physician, worked alongside her father—something she had done since she was a child helping to administer ether in her father's surgery.

7
The Faculty

In the early years, Mary Sloop relied heavily on young people with a missionary spirit who were willing to become teachers and share the primitive living arrangements in the mountains. Through her contacts in the Presbyterian Church, she recruited graduates of Davidson, Flora McDonald, and Queens colleges, as well as universities and colleges in Illinois, New York, and Ohio. Berea College supplied instructors in weaving, carpentry, masonry, agriculture, and manual courses that were an important part of the vocational curriculum.

By the 1930s, Crossnore required a broader array of skills and talents. Sloop needed houseparents to supervise the children in the dormitories, cooks for the dining hall, a manager for the laundry, and day and night firemen who kept the coal stoves stoked and the buildings as warm as possible in winter. She could keep two stenographers busy taking dictation for the thank-you letters and other correspondence that filled the mailbag at the post office. She had a bookkeeper to manage the accounts. At the center of it all was Mary Sloop.

"She seems to be the One and Only Authority," Grace Sperry Burns, a housemother, wrote in a letter to her daughter. "Everything has to pass over her desk, every decision through her lips. Hence an interview with her is almost a burlesque, because she is talking to half a dozen people at one time, in two rooms. Young and old, male and female, come to see her and she tries to accommodate all of them. If she weren't humorous about it, it would be awful."

Mary Sloop could most often be found at her desk in the administrative offices near the only telephone on the campus.

With two dozen or so employees in the 1930s—a number that would swell to almost sixty a decade later—the campus was the town's largest employer and most important enterprise. For the Johnson clan, it was virtually a family business. Among those working at Crossnore from the extended family of Alexander Johnson, a trustee and the Sloops' long-time friend, was his sister-in-law, Mrs. Newbern Johnson, who ran the weaving department. One of her sisters, Cora Clark Nunan, was a housemother in the Big Boys Dormitory, while her husband, Russell, a Davidson graduate and former Crossnore teacher, was away studying for the ministry at Union Theological Seminary in Richmond, Virginia. One of Johnsons' sons, Corwin, made regular trips with his truck to pick up the clothing shipments that arrived at the train depot in Ashford, twelve miles down the mountain in McDowell County. Another son, Obie, a Berea graduate, handled building maintenance and taught woodworking. He also called the weekly square dances and organized the folk dancing and singing performances at the DAR meetings. His wife was the campus dietician. The Sales Store, an essential source of revenue, continued under the management of "Aunt Pop and Uncle Gilmer," who were almost as well-known as Sloop herself. They caught the attention of every writer for flatland publications who found his or her way to the mountains. They were Johnsons, too.

The greater Crossnore family included people from all over. Somehow, they just seemed to find the place, often by word of mouth and institutional advertising through the DAR and the Presbyterian Church. Roger Q. Bault was finishing at Wooster College, a Presbyterian institution in Ohio, in the late 1920s when he learned about Crossnore. He came to teach school, married a local girl, and subsequently became principal of the high school. He built a home on the campus grounds and recruited his brother Robert to work on the buildings erected in the 1930s. Robert married a teacher in the high school named Bertha Bell, who was a graduate of Carson-Newman College and taught Latin. They lived in an apartment on campus. Mary Naomi Foster was from Connecticut. She was a teacher and then became Mary Sloop's secretary. She enticed a classmate from Mount Holyoke College, Vivian Little, to come to Crossnore.

Denise Abbey was from Long Island, New York, and a senior at Barnard College in New York City when she heard about Crossnore. She later wrote that Sloop was looking for graduates "who might be interested in working at Crossnore for what amounted to room and board, $10 a month when the exchequer could afford it, and 'boundless goodwill.'"

Abbey arrived in the summer of 1933 to become Crossnore's truant officer. (Sloop wrote Abbey's mother with assurances of her safety.) Sloop teamed her up with a teacher, Aubrey Chisholm, and the two set off in a car, riding as far as they could over the rutted roads and then dismounting to hike to the head of the hollows in order to conduct the annual school census. It was much the same job that Sloop had done herself twenty years earlier when she made sure every child eligible for an education came to school.

Abbey found a world she had never imagined. "These remote cabins were in the direst straits," she later wrote. "Half-chinked cabins, the surrounding hard ground gullied and washed away, the fields with scant corn and cabbage growths, a few wormy apple trees, and half a dozen or more big-eyed solemn children in rags, with a gaunt mother and even gaunter father. Yet they never failed to offer us something, an apple or two, a drink of fresh water from the spring."

Abbey became Sloop's utility infielder during the five years she was on the campus. She assisted the houseparent for the older boys, started a chapter of the Campfire Girls, taught swimming in the summer, and helped string beans and peel peaches during the canning season. She was a gifted writer, producing a script for a dramatic presentation of Crossnore's story. It was called *At the Rag Shakin'*, and it related Sloop's conversion of used clothing into cash to build a school. She also produced a short script about the families that bartered food at the dining hall in exchange for credit at the Sales Store. Another of her assignments was to talk with the old folks around the area and gather all the information she could about its history and people in preparation for application for a DAR charter for the Crossnore chapter that was granted in 1934. Abbey finally hung a sign on her office door that read: "The Undertaker: She Undertakes Anything and Buries Her Mistakes." Sloop laughed and told her that her predecessor, Jean Emily Maxwell, had called herself "the office goat" and even received mail addressed "Dear Miss Goat."

The attraction of Crossnore to young people like Abbey clearly wasn't the money. Sloop paid what she could when she could. In the mid-1930s, houseparents received between $10 and $15 a month. Some of them were employed as teachers at the school and worked on campus in exchange for free room and board. One year in the mid-1930s, the total monthly payroll for twenty-three employees was $315. That included wages for the Bible teacher and the public school's athletic coach, who only worked eight months out of the year. The pay of the workers in the weaving department was subsidized by Smith-Hughes funds and income from the sale of weaving and hooked rugs.

The Sloops didn't draw any income. Throughout all her years at Crossnore, Mary Sloop was reimbursed for her travel expenses only. Moreover, the paying customers of Eustace Sloop's power company subsidized the cost of the electricity that the campus received without charge. (By 1930, his Linville Valley Power Company had grown to 750 customers.) Doctor also provided free medical care. In 1934, he performed fifty operations on boarding children, most of them tonsillectomies and the like, and paid for the anesthetics himself.

Some of the adults who applied for jobs on campus were as much in need of help as any needy student who showed up at Mary Sloop's office door. In her own way, she had created a locally subsidized welfare program that was designed to give aid in any way it could. Georgia Lunsford was living in Asheville with her six boys and an unreliable husband when she learned Crossnore needed someone to run the campus laundry. The pay was ten dollars a month, plus room and board for her children. She found when she arrived at the campus, however, that in addition to her work in the laundry, she also was expected to be a housemother in the Little Girls Dormitory.

Washing and drying the bedding and clothing for two hundred people was exhausting work, even with the assistance of teenage girls who were assigned to help her in the laundry. Each morning, after the children in her dormitory were off to school, Lunsford headed to the laundry, which was located in the basement of the hospital, where a low ceiling and overhead pipes made it difficult to move around with heavy loads. In good weather, the wash was hung outdoors to dry; in winter or when it rained, everything was hung inside. After a year of this demanding schedule, Lunsford's health failed. A younger woman took her place as housemother, and she moved into a spare room near the furnace in the basement of the teacherage. She eventually returned to Asheville, but Sloop allowed her sons to stay on and finish their education at Crossnore.

Denise Abbey tutored one of Georgia Lunsford's boys. He was struggling with his schoolwork, and over the summer Sloop had asked Abbey to see what she could do. Both teacher and student be-

Davidson College graduate Robert Woodside came to Crossnore as a teacher in the 1930s and devoted his life to the school, first as a teacher, then as principal of the high school, and later, after Mary Sloop's death, as director of the campus.

came frustrated with their progress. One day, after Joe had finished work on the farm, showered, and gathered his schoolwork, he showed up for his lesson. "Miss Abbey," he said, "I figured something out. You can't teach me anything. I got to learn it." Abbey recalled, "From that moment on, everything changed and Joe went on to be a senior and graduate."

The mother of another Joe, Joe Powlas, became the dietician at Crossnore under similar circumstances. In 1933, she was a widow, living in the Piedmont section of North Carolina with a couple whose son, Dwight A. Fink, was a teacher at Crossnore. They told her that Sloop was looking for a dietician to replace Pina Hill, who had held the job for several years. Powlas applied for the job, even though she had no prior experience as a cook or as someone expected to manage a dining hall feeding two hundred people a day. She moved into a room on the campus, leaving her son behind in Salisbury. He joined her two years later, after she had married Obie Johnson. Joe lived in the dormitory with the other boys and saw his mother and stepfather only occasionally, usually when he was at the dining hall for meals.

The operation of the school was the responsibility of the county board of education, but the lines between Mary Sloop's campus and the county-owned school often became blurred. Robert Woodside was a Davidson graduate who taught social studies. When he wasn't in class, he ran the campus print shop, which turned out all manner of printed materials, such as application forms, regulation sheets, and the like for campus activities. The print shop produced the *Crossnore School Bulletin*, a newsletter written entirely by Sloop. It was published quarterly and began with a circulation of 3,000, which quickly grew to 14,000 by the late 1930s. A decade later, the *Bulletin* was being mailed to more than 27,000 readers. It had nothing to do with the academic program and everything to do with keeping Sloop in touch with the school's friends and benefactors.

The *Bulletin* was created while the community was in turmoil over the dismissal of the Reverend McCoy Franklin as president of Crossnore School Incorporated. In March 1933, the Crossnore trustees fired Franklin following a dispute over the legitimacy of a fundraising letter that Franklin had mailed to potential contributors. The matter mushroomed into a bitter public feud that left the Crossnore community deeply divided. Board members received death threats. One writer threatened to burn down the school if Franklin was dismissed.

Franklin had only recently returned to the campus when the trouble began. He had been absent for a year after working himself into exhaustion and moving to Florida to recuperate at Penney Farms, a retreat for ministers established by the department store magnate J. C. Penney. Before his illness, Franklin had been the public face of Crossnore before church congregations and public audiences across the country. He was the very personification of what education could mean to mountain children. By the late 1920s, he had a following of sorts, including a board of directors that included Sloop's brother at Davidson College and some of the pastors of the large congregations in the northeastern United States where he had been invited to preach. The directors basically lent their names to Crossnore. The control of the campus remained with the board of trustees. Franklin was a vigorous and energetic man—he advocated "breaking a sweat every day"—and his fund-raising included appeals on behalf of the campus, as well as his ministry at Crossnore Presbyterian Church.

In March 1929, Mary Sloop retired from management of campus affairs after Franklin urged her to step aside in favor of a younger person. There was no indication she opposed the move, and it was endorsed by the trustees, one of whom was her husband. She was in her mid-fifties and probably eager for some relief. She had been engaged on behalf of the school and the community for more than fifteen years, often neglecting the needs of her own family in the process. When Franklin made his proposal, her children were out of school and settled in their college studies. Her work on their behalf was done.

She moved out of her office in the teacherage, turned the checkbook over to Franklin, and retreated to her home. Though disengaged from daily duties, Sloop maintained the title of business manager, even though she did not conduct any business on behalf of the campus. Office workers began answering mail addressed to her if the subject concerned campus affairs. The presumption of this action did raise her ire, and she asked the postmaster to put any mail addressed to her in her husband's box rather than hold it for the campus pickup. Though retired from duty, she never really left the campus business behind, and she remained in touch with her friends and supporters through correspondence. She did spend more time sewing clothes for her husband, whose patients continued to be slow in paying their bills. From the bit of money she did have, she paid the wages of a stenographer whom she kept busy from eight-thirty in the morning until five in the afternoon.

Franklin returned to the campus from Florida with his health restored. As he resumed his duties, the trustees returned the school's finances to Mary Sloop's control but left him in charge of campus affairs. Money was dear. Franklin asked for permission to cut campus workers' pay by 10 percent and reduce the number of students accepted for the dormitories if that was required.

The trustees fired Franklin nine months later. At issue was whether a solicitation letter he had mailed was raising money for the campus or for Crossnore Presbyterian Church's Opportunity Club, a fund he had established to support his ministry. Franklin subsequently sued Crossnore School Incorporated and Mary Martin Sloop, claiming he was owed $18,000 in unpaid salary and expenses. The case went to the state supreme court twice and ultimately turned on the legitimacy of a contract that Franklin said the trustees had signed. The case never went to trial. It was settled for a single payment of $1,500 to Franklin after he left Crossnore for Tennessee, where he established a busy preaching ministry. At one point in his new career, he served as mayor of the town of Madisonville. Franklin died in 1989 on the way out of his house to tend his garden.

Mary Sloop never forgave Franklin for transgressions that she believed threatened the integrity of the school, set members of the community against one another, and challenged the veracity of her word and that of the trustees, including her husband. In the memoir that she wrote in 1951, she made no mention of Franklin, even though twenty years earlier she had heaped praise on him and his work in the brochures and broadsides that came off the Crossnore printing press. She never again released control of campus affairs.

The *Bulletin* filled a void left by the loss of Crossnore's roving ambassador, and it proved to be the most effective fund-raising tool at Sloop's disposal. For only pennies per copy, the quarterly newsletter expanded the reach of Sloop's fund-raising as it carried Crossnore's story to mailboxes all across the country. She cultivated a mailing list maintained in a cabinet full of index cards that carried the names and addresses of anyone who had donated clothing or other goods to the Sales Store, made cash contributions, provided scholarships, visited the campus, or mailed a letter of inquiry. She saw that information on each "friend" was updated regularly, with notes indicating replies by telephone, thank-you notes, or personal visits.

Forty years later, a member of the campus staff pulled a card from

By the 1930s, houseparents in the dormitories at Crossnore often had two dozen or more children under their care.

the file for a one-time donor to the Sales Store who had not had any contact with the campus in years. He questioned the value of keeping such information and began calculating how much had been spent on mailings over the years. The next day, an attorney representing the estate of this very donor notified the school that his client had designated that Crossnore receive a $55,000 bequest.

In Sloop's day, the *Bulletin* was as good as money in the bank. She was an engaging and fearless writer who used a keen sense of drama and attention to detail to describe every dimension of Crossnore's story. She included accounts of children struggling under desperate conditions and Crossnore's efforts to guide them to a new life. There were stories of triumph as she related news of graduates who had excelled at college or in adulthood, as well as occasions of absolute embarrassment. Some readers might have shed a tear after learning that children were wearing sandals in the snow because stout shoes weren't available, or felt outrage upon learning that boys re-enacting a scene from a western movie had hanged a classmate from a tree limb. (He was taken down without serious injury.) The *Bulletin* always closed with an appeal for donations to the Sales Store, clothing for the children (especially shoes), sheets and towels for the dormitories, plates and eating utensils for the dining hall, and equipment and supplies for the office. Sloop also never failed to make an appeal for scholarship subscriptions. The scholarship program had begun under Franklin and remained an important part of Sloop's fund-raising. Scholarships of fifty dollars a year covered part of the expenses for a third of the boarders or more. The program was the only remnant of Franklin's connection with the school.

Getting the *Bulletin* published and to the post office was everyone's responsibility. Any available staff member and students down to even the youngest children were recruited to fold the printed sheets in thirds and then pass them on to stenographers, who typed out the addresses. Preparation could take days. As late as the 1940s, when circulation reached its peak, the best students in the high school's typing course would be assigned to add the addresses to *Bulletins*. The newsletter then had to be sorted, bundled, and carried to the Crossnore post office by a deadline that Sloop always pushed to the limit.

Those with the most challenging jobs were the houseparents, who often were single men and women. Each one could be responsible for twenty or thirty children at a time. They saw that the children got up and out of the dormitories in the morning, arrived on time for meals, and performed their campus jobs before the evening meal. They supervised a two-hour nightly study hall and managed baths at least two or three times a week before the lights went out at 10 p.m.—earlier for the young students. Women often mended the clothes of the children in their care. Some of the men coached athletic teams. It was exhausting work, and the only respite from the around-the-clock care came during the Christmas holiday, when students went to stay with families or other responsible adults who answered Sloop's call to have a child or two in their homes for the season. During the school year, the houseparents got some relief from older boys and girls who were assigned to them as "monitors." Their job was to

The campus dormitories were simple buildings, usually put up without the aid of architectural plans. The sides were covered by slabs of bark from the chestnut trees until a blight decimated the species and the American chestnut disappeared from the forest.

help the younger ones find their clothes and get properly dressed at the start of the day, as well as to usher them to church and campus functions.

The houseparents lived in modest apartments in the dormitories that were only a little larger than the rooms that accommodated up to four boys and girls in bunk beds. A widow who arrived in 1942 to be the houseparent for the Little Girls Dormitory wrote her family that her room had a dresser, a chest of drawers, a rough homemade table, a bench to put things on and another to sit on, a small rocker, and a bed. There were no curtains for the windows. She had a blanket but no pillow or sheets. She found a coil spring for an extra bed in the closet. But, she noted, her girls had even less to call their own. They kept their spare clothes in piles at the foot of their beds.

The houseparents were young and old, and they came from a variety of backgrounds. Some were teachers in the school. The job attracted retired teachers and widows, women whose sense of purpose was renewed in the care of children. More than one young mother, widowed and divorced or simply abandoned by her husband, came with small children in tow. The job provided a home and meals for their children. Some chose to return to school, earn their diplomas, and leave Crossnore eligible for better jobs.

In the 1930s, the houseparent in the Middle Boys Dormitory was a retired minister whom the boys called "Pop" Childers. He was responsible for twenty-five boys between the ages of twelve and fourteen. Naomi Greene was a widow who looked after fifteen youngsters in Little Boys Dormitory in the early 1930s. With little more than compassion and common sense at their command, Childers, Greene, and the others counseled the children in their care. During the Depression, when Sloop took in many orphans, the houseparents had to deal with the children's deep feelings of loneliness, abandonment, anger, and fear. They didn't try to fix the problems they encountered. Most often, their job was simply to make a crude system work as best they could. "Ma" Greene, as the boys called her, kept order with the aid of a rubber shoe sole that gave out a loud crack when she slapped it into her open palm. She never used it on any of her boys, but the threat of a spanking was enough to bring order to a room.

One night, a new arrival in the Middle Boys Dormitory refused Pop Childers's command to take a shower. Baths were required on Wednesdays and Saturday. This was a Thursday, and the boy was covered with grease and mud. When the boy ignored Childers's second order to bathe, Childers told four boys to tackle the newcomer and carry him to the showers. They had him subdued and under the water when Childers told Joe Powlas, "Here, Joe, you take this rag and this Old Dutch Cleanser and I want you to scrub him clean. And I will stand here and have a prayer."

While Sloop was a constant presence on the campus, she didn't interfere in the running of the dormitories. From time to time, she met with the houseparents in her office to review schedules, upcoming events, and just to talk. The sessions were often a jumble of conversations, with Sloop interrupting the meetings to take a phone call or ask her assistant for a file on a student. Though they came from different backgrounds and circumstances, the staff members became Sloop's disciples. Her dedication inspired others, a former houseparent wrote: "She has saved many a boy and girl, and put them into a decent way of life, which makes me reverence her and her enterprise, and I'm more than glad to be in the group who are helping her."

The houseparents tried to hold down the mischief and enforce the rules. Sloop was especially fussy about table manners: No more than one piece of bread at a time, left arm and elbows to be kept off the table. Chewing gum was just short of a cardinal sin; Sloop considered it a nasty habit that suggested sloth. Smoking apparently wasn't much of a problem. Children had so little money that cigarettes were a luxury. Older boys and girls were chaperoned as closely as possible. Romances developed despite rules that only permitted "alone" time while children were walking back to campus after church or Christian Endeavor meetings.

The houseparents handled discipline in their own way. One night, Roadman Hollander and Joe Powlas pulled a prank on a particularly sour teacher who had stayed over in her campus apartment after the close of the school term. They waited for her to leave for the movie theater and then put a headless mannequin, which they had made by stuffing straw into a man's shirt and trousers, in a chair just inside her room. Before they left, the doused it liberally with ketchup. When she returned, Joe later wrote, "all hell broke loose. I had never heard such screaming in all my life. Roadman and I doubled over in laughter." They also doubled over for a spanking but considered it a just punishment. The next day, the teacher packed up and left.

Serious or repeat offenders were sent to Mary Sloop. Those who were called to her office to answer any charges, or for poor performance in school, approached with trepidation, fearful of what they would find. In fact, Sloop frowned on corporal punishment, although it was practiced with regularity at the school. Instead, she counseled gently, heaping guilt upon the offender, who left her presence believing that the only road to redemption was to make her proud.

"I don't believe a harsh way of punishment is correct," Sloop would later say. "If I can't affect a child's conscience and make him do right because it is right, we haven't accomplished much."

When her gentle persuasion didn't work, Sloop simply expelled repeat offenders. She had too many other children eager to be at Crossnore to waste space on a troublemaker.

Sloop's ability to delegate authority seemed to work well. Visitors to the campus marveled at the warmth, efficiency, and friendliness of those they met. The campus and all the children always were well groomed whenever the DAR "grandees," as one housemother called the dignitaries, were due for a visit. A prayer, the recitation of the pledge of allegiance, and the singing of the national anthem were part of the routine at the evening meal and essential when any Daughters were present. Sloop treated her guests like royalty and assigned one of her best pupils as an escort during unannounced visits. These assignments were eagerly sought. The visitors usually left a generous tip with their guide.

Joe Powlas remembered the DAR matrons arriving in large LaSalles and Packards, which were often driven by chauffeurs. They were large-bosomed women, heavyset, and draped in fine clothes with broad sashes denoting their official capacity. Joe was recovering from the removal of half of his lung and couldn't work at a regular job, so Sloop chose him for guide work. One of his guests was a Daughter from Tacoma, Washington, who returned from year to year. Joe always showed her around, and she always gave him a dollar. He knew her as "Miss Olds" but didn't learn until 1977 that she was Mave Olds, heiress to an automobile fortune. When she died, she left $10,000 to the Presbyterian Church that Powlas was pastoring in rural Kentucky.

8
The Boarding Department

The boarding department at Crossnore School began in the early 1920s as a convenience for students who lived too far away to make the daily commute and maintain their studies. All that had changed a decade later, when nearly two hundred children from "six years to six feet," as Mary Sloop would say, were living in the dormitories perched on the side of the mountain. The children were there out of necessity—they simply had no other place to go.

Most lived in Crossnore only during the school term from August to May, but the campus was never empty. A large number of children, sometimes as many as eighty or more, lived on the campus all year. Those who stayed at the close of the school term were children without a family member or volunteer willing to take them in during the summer, when school was not in session. The children worked at jobs on the campus, assisted the staff that prepared meals, and performed the constant maintenance that was required to keep the Crossnore buildings habitable. Others had jobs on the school farm, which had grown to include 160 acres. Some washed hospital linens in the laundry, while others worked in Sloop's office.

The mission of Crossnore School Incorporated had changed to such an extent by 1934 that Sloop and the board of trustees amended the charter to describe Crossnore as a "child-caring institution, providing a home and industrial training for boarding pupils under its care." Special efforts would be made, the revised charter read, "that this home receive orphan children, deserted children, those for any reason without a home or a suitable housing and home who need to leave their homes for a better education, but have not the means to so do it." They also adopted a new name: "Crossnore Inc., a home for mountain children."

There was some hope that the campus program might qualify for assistance from the Duke Endowment, which provided financial aid to orphanages in the Carolinas. Sloop was disappointed to learn, however, that although she had many orphans living on campus, her institution did not qualify for aid because it remained open to all children, regardless of their family situation.

The population of Crossnore began to swell in late August of each year as adults and children made their way to Sloop's office in the teacherage, which also served as the campus administration building. Sloop held forth in a small corner room with an opaque interior window that was almost always open so she could talk with her secretary in the room next door. The space was small, a bit shabby, and devoid of frills and color. She greeted each arrival with warmth and respect from behind a desk that was always cluttered with papers. The one telephone on the campus hung on the wall within easy reach.

Some of the boarders came because living on campus was more convenient than slogging through mud and snow in the winter. There usually were a few students who had been enrolled by parents who hoped that the discipline and self-help regimen of Crossnore would help their sons and daughters improve their grades and undergo an attitude adjustment.

More often than not, however, children came to Crossnore because they needed a safe home, regular meals, and a roof over their heads. Sloop assessed the case of each child who came before her. There weren't any stories that she had not heard many times before, and the common theme was poverty. Of the 192 students admitted in 1934, only 66 came from families that could afford to make even a modest tuition payment. Those with means were charged four dollars a week, but only 10 of the nearly 200 students could afford that. The most that 37 families could pay was twenty-five dollars for the entire session. Sixty percent paid nothing. Out of 192 children in Sloop's care, 125 were orphans. That number was greater than the enrollment at some of the established orphanages in the state.

Since the mid-1920s, when the boarding department began in earnest, Crossnore had become the refuge of more and more mountain children who had been abandoned or whose care had become too much of a burden for aunts, uncles, and grandparents. The Great Depression made things worse, especially for motherless children whose fathers struggled to find work nearby and usually failed in their efforts. They were then forced to leave the mountains in search of a job. Crossnore was their only option for child care.

All in all, the boarders ranged in age from as young as six up to boys and girls in their teens. A few were in their early twenties. The class of 1935 included a thirty-six-year-old mother who enrolled in the high school and lived with her daughter, who was a student in a primary grade. The older ones were young men and women who had left school early or who never got a chance at an education and were now intent on earning a high school diploma. The only real qualification for admission was that a student be eligible for school.

Providing habitable housing was an ongoing struggle. The make-shift dormitories like the "donkey barn" gave way to larger buildings in the 1920s, but even these were built with economy in mind. A decade later, the situation was even more acute. Crossnore's future depended on providing a safe and secure place for children in need. When Sloop ran out of room, she became unrelenting in her requests to friends and supporters for help.

Speaking to the North Carolina state meeting of the DAR in the early 1930s, Sloop said students were sleeping two to a bed. A dormitory built in the early 1920s that had been designed to house thirty girls had eighty-four children under its roof. During the evening study hall, the older girls sat on the edge of their bunk beds and wrote on tablets balanced on their knees. She said the boys would rather sit on the floor of their dormitory than on their beds. Before the meeting adjourned, the state regent, Mrs. Sydney Perry Cooper, had gathered enough support to make building a dormitory for the older girls a priority of her administration.

Sloop's implied contract with the DAR was that if the Daughters would provide the buildings, she would take it from there by paying the staff, buying the food, and keeping children clothed and safe using other sources of funds, mainly the proceeds from the Sales Store. Over the next quarter-century, her partnership with the DAR would flourish as Sloop moved from her early reliance on contacts in the Presbyterian Church to reliance on the women's organization. Sloop and Crossnore became known to women from some of the wealthiest families in America.

Construction of a dormitory for the older girls began in the spring of 1933. The new building was to be a distinctive residence hall that Sloop later said set the standard for the campus buildings that followed. The foundation was of river rock, and the sides were covered in chestnut bark. An arched entry built of rock led to the main floor, with a large chestnut-paneled living room whose centerpiece was a stone fireplace. Sleeping rooms for the thirty-six girls and their houseparents were in the two-story wings on either side. The North Carolina Daughters raised most of the $8,000 needed for construction, with help from chapters in New York, Massachusetts, New Jersey, and Connecticut.

The dormitory was dedicated in an elaborate ceremony in honor of Mrs. Cooper on December 16, 1933. The occasion in the dead of winter attracted not only the top echelon of the state DAR but also the national society's president general, Mrs. Edith Scott Magna of Massachusetts. The DAR royalty processed into the building accompanied by music from the Crossnore school orchestra and an array of American flags carried by an honor guard of students. It was high ceremony, with poetic recitations, patriotic speeches, prayer, and the singing of the national anthem. The building was put in the care of the Crossnore DAR chapter, which was just about to receive its charter. Sloop introduced some of the local craftsmen who had built the dormitory. Using the mountain vernacular, she presented "Uncle Bod Franklin, Uncle Jones Dellinger, Uncle Alex Johnson, and Uncle 'Newt' and his two brothers." Their courtesy titles were included with their names in the official report to the Continental Congress.

At the time, North Carolina had more than sixty DAR chapters and a membership of nearly twenty-five hundred. None were more

This postcard image of the dedication of Crossnore's Cooper Building featured the leadership of the National Society of the DAR. Sloop's longtime supporters Mrs. William Henry Belk and Mrs. Ralph Van Landingham are in the front with President General Mrs. Edith Scott Magna. Photo courtesy of North Carolina Collection, University of North Carolina at Chapel Hill.

involved at Crossnore than the chapter in Charlotte that included among its members Mrs. Ralph Van Landingham, the state chairman of the DAR's approved schools. An energetic civic volunteer, she was the wife of a successful cotton broker. Her interest in Crossnore was enhanced by her familiarity with the area. The Van Landinghams owned a home in the summer resort colony at Linville less than ten miles away. Linville residents were some of the best customers for Crossnore weavers, and Van Landingham had recruited support from five chapters that provided money to build the imposing log Weave Room. During the campaign to raise money for the dormitory, Sloop brought young people from the campus to perform mountain dance and songs at the Linville clubhouse.

Mrs. Van Landingham always accompanied a delegation of state and national DAR officers that periodically toured the campuses of the dozen or so schools on the organization's approved list. One regular visitor to Crossnore was the national schools chairman, Mrs. William H. Pouch of New York, who later would become president general. She took a special liking to Crossnore, and a flagpole was dedicated in her honor, as well as windows in the campus chapel built in the 1950s. The travelers also included the state officers, including Mrs. William N. Reynolds of Winston-Salem, whose husband ran the R. J. Reynolds Tobacco Company, and Mrs. William Henry Belk of Charlotte. Her husband's department stores were scattered throughout the Carolinas.

The opening of the new DAR dormitory relieved what had become a desperate situation for the older girls, but the overcrowding for the boys was just as bad, if not worse. Forty to fifty of the older boys lived in a two-story concrete block building with twelve small rooms on each floor. It had been the school's shop building before being taken over by the weaving department. It had a furnace and a modest hot water system that was inadequate for regular bathing. There was a common room with a large table and some straight-backed chairs. The boys slept in cubicles with barely enough space for two bunk beds that Sloop had salvaged from the government. In the winter, the coal-fired furnace fought a losing battle with the bitter cold. The younger boys lived in the rough frame building that had once been the shop for the carpentry class.

For many years, the first task of a new boy in the dormitory was to literally make his bed. He was given a mattress cover and told to stuff it with straw. This style of homemade bedding continued into the late 1930s. Sloop eventually convinced textile manufacturers to ship cotton waste to the campus and received bed ticking from others. The

A delegation from the DAR and their student escorts. The woman second from the left is Miss Dean Van Landingham, and in the middle is Mrs. William Henry Belk. The two women were early and dedicated supporters of Mary Sloop.

One of the first chores for new arrivals at Crossnore in the 1930s was filling mattresses with straw. Photo courtesy of North Carolina Collection, University of North Carolina at Chapel Hill.

girls finished off the manufacture of cotton-filled mattresses in the campus sewing room.

Sloop had more than comfort and basic needs in mind when she begged her correspondents for improvements in campus housing. Her big boys were going to become fathers with homes of their own—and soon, she said. She wanted them to learn about living in a proper home before they left Crossnore. "I've long since learned that when a boy does not experience the satisfaction and influence of living in a home of comfort and attractiveness, he will rarely make the effort necessary to provide such a home for his own family."

The addition of the Cooper Building relieved conditions for the older girls, but housing was such a serious problem in 1935 that Sloop reduced the number of boarding students to 154. Even with the lower count, 22 of the youngest boys lived in the former shop building.

Soon, the population began to grow again after donations came in

Apples harvested from nearby orchards were a staple in the Crossnore pantry. Along with peaches, they could be canned and preserved for use throughout the year.

for new dormitories for the youngest boys and girls. Mrs. George Negley Reed, a Daughter from Oil City, Pennsylvania, paid for a dormitory for little boys that was named in her honor. (She had earlier given money to acquire land for the campus farm.) Mrs. Geraldine Fleshman Pratt of North Carolina, another friend from the DAR, was the major donor for a companion dormitory for the youngest girls. It was dedicated in honor of Mrs. Pratt's mother, Mrs. Nina Peffer Fleshman. By 1939, there were again about 200 children boarding at Crossnore.

The mountainside filled with new buildings in the 1930s. One by one, they appeared on the hillside, stair-stepping one after the other up the steep slope. As soon as Sloop had pledges of support, she quickly choose a location for the new building, cleared the brush and any trees out of the way, and brought in the drag pans to level the ground for the foundation. She didn't bother with the expense of professionally drawn plans—apparently the only buildings that came from an architect were the church and the hospital—depending instead on the construction experience of local carpenters. Once

Mary Sloop economized on provisions for the campus dining hall by exchanging credit at the Sales Store for produce and other staples brought in by area farmers from their gardens.

a building was in place, it was linked to the rest of the campus by a narrow dirt path covered in cinders pulled from the coal stoves that provided heat.

No sooner had Sloop begun to relieve the housing shortage than she was faced with overhauling the campus food service. Like every other building on campus, the kitchen and dining hall had begun as something else. The old building was once known as the "donkey barn" and had been converted into a dining hall with help from a Bible class at a Gastonia church. Over the years, it had been enlarged several times. By 1938, Sloop's insurance underwriters were telling her the building was a fire hazard and a threat to nearby structures. It would have to be replaced, they said. At the time, the kitchen was preparing meals for about 230 students and faculty members, as well as patients in the hospital.

Feeding everyone was simply another of Sloop's miracles. In the early 1930s, Pina Hill was the cook, although Sloop called her the "dietician" in her correspondence with Mrs. Van Landingham of the DAR. For monthly wages of fifty-five dollars, Hill cooked a hearty breakfast and an evening meal for all the students and the campus staff. Eight months of the year—when school was in session—she had a paid assistant, but most of her kitchen help were students who prepared the vegetables, peeled potatoes, and did other chores. The older boys handled the large pots on the stove. They assisted with the daily baking of biscuits and cornbread—the staples of a Crossnore meal—and waited tables at mealtime. Sloop estimated the cost of a meal at ten cents per person.

Keeping the kitchen stocked with food consumed a large part of the budget. Milk came from the school's dairy farm, which also occasionally provided meat for a meal. String beans, a mountain staple, were harvested in the fields beside the Linville River. There also were apples and peaches from nearby orchards. Any fruits and vegetables not eaten at harvest were canned and stored for winter. Of constant concern was the monthly bill from the Waldensan Bakery in Valdese, which supplied the school with loaf bread. At times, the books were so out of balance that shipments would cease until Sloop could find cash to restore Crossnore's credit.

"We substituted potatoes, increased quantity of beans, made biscuits for breakfast, cornbread for supper," Sloop wrote in her memoir. "We did without bread. The children missed it. They wanted bread and molasses for breakfast. We kept telling them that if they prayed to God to pay that back bill, and if they behaved so well that God thought their prayers ought to be answered, that we would get bread."

Early on, Sloop discovered that the school's demand for fresh food might benefit local farmers who were eager to sell their crops. Since she was usually short of cash, she established a barter system. Farmers delivered cabbages, lettuce, potatoes, sorghum molasses, canned items, and beans to the kitchen, where they were given credits that they could use at the Sales Store. Thus, a bushel of potatoes could become a new silk dress or shoes for the family. One year in the early 1940s, this exchange saved $7,000 on the grocery bill.

Like she did with so many other opportunities, Sloop used bartering for food as an exercise in what she called "adult education." "We knew that we must not take poor food and give our good clothes in return," she wrote in one of her quarterly newsletters, "so we arranged to have lessons given to them. A teacher was found who would even go to their homes to teach a neighbor [how to improve their gardens] and let the neighbor pass it on. The incentive to get the better clothes and more of them made everybody willing to profit by the lessons. Now, we have lots of good gardeners and lots of good canners, and we can exchange lots of good produce for the clothes."

The center of activity in the kitchen was a huge coal-fired cookstove that had been donated to Crossnore in the 1920s by a Statesville druggist, who was said to have gotten it from the Richardsons, a family of devoted Presbyterians in Greensboro whom Sloop knew from her years in Davidson. Lunsford Richardson was a pharmacist who experimented with various patent medicines. While the Sloops were getting established in Crossnore, Lunsford's son, Smith, who had started at Davidson while the Sloops were there in medical school, had begun selling one of his father's patent medicines, an aromatic salve, throughout the mountains. Vicks VapoRub became a national sensation during the flu epidemic in 1918, when annual sales tripled to $3 million. The stove at Crossnore was said to be the one that Lunsford Richardson had used to prepare the first batches of his popular cold remedy, and there were claims that for years it emitted faint odors of the curative.

It took Sloop nearly three years of fund-raising to get the money for the dining hall, and as soon as she had enough to buy materials she enlisted the older boys taking classes in masonry and carpentry to begin construction. They dug the foundations, poured the footings, laid the rock, and began raising a building ninety feet long and thirty-six feet wide. It was large enough to seat two hundred and fifty for a meal. A second story had sixteen rooms for student housing. Sloop's friends from the North Carolina DAR chapters contributed to the building, which was completed in December 1941. By that time, four more kitchen fires had threatened the safety of the campus. At the time, the school was $7,200 in debt, most likely on a note that Sloop had negotiated with her ever-faithful banker, E. C. Guy, in Newland.

The story of Crossnore's wobbly finances was becoming too familiar, Sloop told her correspondents, but she had faith in the Lord that the dining hall would be built and paid for just like all the others on the campus. "We would put up a building, get into debt, then work out of debt," she remembered. "Build another and get into debt again. Faith? Yes, it was faith, but we tried hard not to impose on the Lord."

Sloop recalled: "When our creditors just had to have their money, we would go to the bank and borrow it. Then, we would take those bank notes to the Lord and ask him to help us pay them. The checks would come in and we would get out of debt again."

Sloop's buildings were as simple as they could be. The floors were unfinished lumber, the walls barely deflected the winds of winter, and the furnishings were spare. "The bareness is shocking," one new housemother wrote to her family soon after she arrived on the campus. She was placed with the youngest of the girls and ached for some relief to the dullness of their living quarters. "The furnishings are adequate, but very cheap. The floors are bare and by night littered and dusty. There is not a single bright or pretty thing in any of the houses, though all are well lighted."

The first Belk dining hall, with an accompanying building to house the staff, opened in the early 1940s and could seat more than two hundred at each meal. The upper story had dormitory rooms, and the attic was the "Bird Cage" where Christmas presents were stored until the holiday celebration.

Mary Sloop didn't hide the extent of Crossnore's pressing needs or the challenges that hung like dark clouds over the future. She was honest and frank with the children and the staff and asked that their prayers for help be added to her own. When times were bad, she wrote her friends, "we go to the dining hall and tell the children just where we stand." She explained: "We tell them that we have tried and that they have done their part. They have peeled and they have to cook. Now, we must ask the Lord to give us more vegetables, more food, before they get too hungry."

If anyone doubted in the durability of her faith or took issue with her philosophy for building an institution, Sloop would tell them about the struggle to build the dormitory for the little boys. She had begun saving for the building after the trustees told her she was not to commit the school to any more loans. She was deeply moved when one of the youngsters who were sleeping two or three in a bed stopped her one afternoon and said, "Miz' Sloop, we ain't never agoin' to get our new dormitory." The boy's frankness brought a prompt response. "Oh yes, we are," she said, "and we're going to begin work on it right now." She sent the boy to get the others with instructions to meet her, with tools in hand, at the spot chosen for the building.

They cleared brush and worked through the afternoon until the bell rang for dinner. Before they left to wash up for the meal, Sloop gathered the boys around in a circle for a prayer. She told them to pray for the Lord to provide the money for the building as soon as he thought best. "And also," she said, "we'll ask Him to teach us to be worthy of a new dormitory, to behave so well that people will want us to have a dormitory. And we'll get the money."

Each boy prayed earnestly. When the last had spoken, Sloop saw one of them pull his hand from his pocket. In his fist was a penny. "Here's you some money to start on," he said.

Months passed. Sloop was returning to campus one day when she heard a shriek as she approached her office. A woman came running out with a check for $6,000 that had just arrived in the mail. It was from Mrs. Reed, who designated that her gift help build the Little Boys Dormitory.

9

The Children

Roadman Hollander was one of the boys who stood in that prayer circle with Mary Sloop to ask the Lord to help build a dormitory for Crossnore's youngest boys, aged six to eleven. His journey to Crossnore was not exceptional, but during his eight years on the campus he would become one of the best known of Crossnore's students and the only one for whom a campus building would be named.

For Sloop, Roadman personified the very essence of Crossnore. He was bright, eager, earnest, and reverent. He was eight years old and full of promise when he moved into the dormitory with the other younger boys in 1934. His story was not unlike those of many of the children who found their way to Sloop's office to apply for admission. His family lived in a far corner of Avery County, and Roadman and his two sisters had lost their mother. Their father turned to Crossnore for help in raising his children, as others in his family had done.

"And they came," Sloop wrote, "two sisters and a tiny brother, underweight, puny looking, but with snapping dark brown eyes that never missed a thing, and a brain behind that that registered." Roadman needed medical attention, and he was lying in a bed when a nurse asked his name. He gave it, and she corrected him. Isn't it Rodman, she asked? No, he said, his name was Roadman, explaining that his mother was away from the house when she went into labor. "So she just laid down and had me in the road, and when my daddy came he laughed and named me Roadman, and I'se been Roadman ever since."

In Sloop's stories, Roadman was the idyllic child. He absorbed every lesson, in school and at church, and was a willing and cheerful helper on the campus. He was elected by his dorm mates to represent them on a campus council. His singing voice captivated audiences entertained by campus singers and dancers, and Roadman eagerly performed for visitors and guests. Anything that was good for Crossnore was good enough for him. For Sloop, Roadman personified the Crossnore motto of "noblesse oblige," which she interpreted to her students to mean doing right because of the nobility they carried within them.

Roadman moved into the new dormitory that he had asked for in his prayers. "We're all fixed in our new home," he told Sloop the evening after he and the others had carried their belongings up the hill. The sight of the boys earlier in the day was a lasting memory for Sloop. "What a motley line it was," she wrote. "Big bundles, little bundles, bulging bundles and oozing bundles. Up the hill they came, faces aglow and eyes shining." It was only a short time before Roadman aged out and had to move again. This time he joined the Middle Boys, whose dormitory was as shabby as what he had known before. He began his prayers anew, sending notes to Sloop when she was away on trips. "We boys hope you have a good trip," he once wrote. "We pray for you every night. But something's the matter with our prayers. Nobody gives us a better dormitory."

In May 1940, Roadman was admitted to the hospital in Banner Elk with a ruptured appendix. He said he knew he was dying as he said goodbye to two roommates who accompanied him. The funeral was held at Crossnore Presbyterian Church, and the fourteen-year-old was buried in the family cemetery near his home in the Roseborough community. In the days afterward, Sloop wrote her friends about building the dormitory that Roadman had prayed for. When the boy's father heard about her plans, he paid her a visit and gave her ten dollars to start the building fund.

It took more than ten years, but Sloop finally raised the money she needed to build a simple wooden-frame dormitory for the Mid-

CROSSNORE SCHOOL, INCORPORATED

CROSSNORE, N. C.

THE STORY

OF

ROADMAN

He was a little chap for his 7 years and far from healthy looking. We found his tonsils must come out. As he lay on the hospital bed (He had never seen such a white bed) the nurse came to take his history. He felt very important. The bed was all white, the nurse was in white and she was going to write something about him. "What is your name, little man?" she said and prepared to write. "Roadman Hollander" he answered. "Rodman you mean" corrected the nurse. "No, it's not neither" he answered very positively. "Mammy was up on the mountain pickin huckleberries and she got sick and started home but she couldn't get quite to the barn, so she just laid down and had me on the road, and when Daddy come he named me Roadman and I'se been Roadman ever since."

Never has there been a child on our campus that so won the hearts of young and old and visitors too. Teachers noted that he had an unusual brain and manner. Three different ones who taught him prophesied that he'd be President of the United States some day, which was their way of saying that Roadman was an unusual child. But he didn't grow as he should, nor did he ever look healthy.

Appendicitis overtook him at 12 years. Once more he was prepared for an operation. Again he spelled out his name to a white-robed nurse — "R-o-a-d-m-a-n". But he couldn't take it. He rallied on the afternoon and then went down. Two older boys were in the room with him. They noticed that the nurse came in and out frequently and then the doctor came. They were alone. Roadman mustered all his strength and said — "I know I am going to die tonight but I am not afraid and I'm not going to be yellow," and quietly he went out. There was a beautiful funeral service in our village church. The big tears filled the eyes of all those school children, but not a sound. They took him away to his mountain home in an isolated corner of our county and laid him to rest on top of a lonely peak beside his mother who had died before Roadman came to Crossnore.

I told the children that some day we would have the money to build a good dormitory, a real home for Middle Boys, at Crossnore and name it for "Roadman". The father heard of it and brought me $10. as the first gift to the Roadman Home. Each year since, we have thought we could do it, but failed. Now we have started it! There were some cinder blocks left over from the splendid new dormitory we have just finished for the big boys — 15 and 16 years old. So we have excavated, poured the foundations and started the walls. The $10. didn't go very far but it helped. It seemed like a sacred beginning and we believe more will come. That big load of cement and brixment came, and had to be paid for. The workmen "brought in their time" last Friday afternoon — Day before yesterday, opening the mail, with a hope in my heart, I noticed a check. 'Twas from a very young business man. It paid the Roadman bill — and you will help us with the next one — won't you?

Roadman had two older sisters who came to Crossnore with him. They graduated, then became Registered nurses — good ones too. What might Roadman have become? Let's let his spirit carry on in the dormitory for Middle Boys that we are building now at Crossnore — *THE ROADMAN HOME.*

MARY M. SLOOP

dle Boys, and she named it in Roadman's honor. It would be the last of the buildings from that era to be demolished more than fifty years later.

As the hard times of the Depression bore down on families everywhere, life was especially tough on people in Avery County. Forty-three percent of all families in the county were on relief in 1934, and farming was reduced to small gardens and a little livestock. The number of children in need of a home and an education became almost overwhelming, and that year more than half of the children living on the campus were orphans. There were others, like Roadman, who had lost a mother or a father. Some children had parents, but their homes were not fit because of neglect or abuse. The plight of little boys troubled Sloop the most. It seemed someone often took in motherless girls, she said, "but the little boys are not wanted." Sloop observed, "To know that you are not wanted is the cruelest thing that can happen to a little boy."

Crossnore applicants came from all around. A sixteen-year-old boy asked for a bed so he could enter the first grade. Another teenager arrived from a West Virginia lumber camp, where he had been living with a brother. He came because there was no school at the camp. A young man who had been working in a Civilian Conservation Corps camp asked if he could live at Crossnore so he could finish high school. "No iron had touched his very worn clothes," Sloop wrote. Another CCC boy told Sloop he had a fourth-grade education, but she discovered he couldn't read at all. Some had been in trouble with the law. A teenage boy was about to be sentenced to a term in the state's training school when his lawyer arranged for him to enroll at Crossnore. She took him in, and he became a leader in his class. "When a sixteen-year-old boy comes to school to take first grade work, you know that he has determination that is a match for his lack of 'opportunity,'" she wrote. A teenager arrived from Florida and convinced Sloop to take him in while he worked off the cost of his room and board. Toward the end of his first year, he told Sloop about his brother, who was admitted the following year. Their sister soon followed.

There were other sibling groups, like Roadman and his sisters. One year, a widower asked Sloop to find a place for his five children, who ranged in age from seven to twelve years. The county welfare office had encouraged him to place his children in an orphanage. Instead, he chose Crossnore and used the modest payments he received under a government program called Aid to Families with Dependent Children—part of the new Social Security Act—to cover part of the cost of their tuition. Fred Hawkens and his brother, James, arrived on the back of a Nehi soft drink truck, along with two other boys the driver had picked up on his way up the mountain.

Others were dropped at the door. Joe Powlas was living in the Little Boys Dormitory when an older man appeared one night and declared he had spoken with Sloop about his grandson, whose mother had died the week before. The boy's father was dead, too. "I ain't got no money for his keeping," the man declared, "so you don't need to send me any bills." He turned and departed, leaving behind a boy he called Charlie. Everything the child owned was stuffed into a small paper bag, and the grandfather was gone before anyone thought to ask the boy's last name. Charlie wouldn't tell them. He was so traumatized that he didn't speak for weeks. Finally, one night, after he finished a serving of ice cream, he said, "I never thought it could be so good, I never thought it could be so good."

Sloop was a strong woman who had stood down hardened mountaineers, some of whom probably wished her dead, or at the very least gone from Avery County. At the same time, she couldn't say no to people in need, even when her decisions stretched Crossnore beyond its capacity. One Saturday in August in the mid-1940s, she was registering boarders for the coming year when she was told two hundred children had been admitted. That number was higher than the year before, but it was still early in the afternoon, and she looked out her office window and saw a crowd of parents, guardians, welfare officers, and children still waiting to see her. "How could we stop?" she wrote later in a newsletter. "They were standing around thick, all depending upon us for the solution to their problems. What could we do with 240 children and only 200 beds?"

She kept working and adjusted her room assignments. The older boys moved into an unfinished building that was hastily outfitted with bunk beds that Sloop had recently purchased for ninety-nine cents each at a War Assets Sale. The mattresses were were donated by an Asheville doctor who had acquired two dormitories in a real estate deal and sent the surplus bedding to Crossnore. There was no heat in the building, temporary flooring, and no windows. The building did have two working bathrooms. She installed the teenagers in it, figuring they were stronger and better conditioned to withstand nights when the temperature would drop to freezing or below.

The boys called their temporary home "Fresh Air Camp." Meanwhile, Sloop waited for the normal attrition to reduce the excess population and bring the number of boarders back in line with Crossnore's resources. She knew from hard experience that some children would leave within a few weeks because they were homesick, or because they found that they weren't suited to the discipline and regimen she imposed. Some just ran away. Crossnore wasn't bound to go after them, although their absence was reported to family or authorities. One boy who returned after taking his leave told Sloop, "I never run away; I just take off." Mostly, she counted on common sense to turn the runners around. A boy who was constantly leaving without permission finally came straggling back, his feet blistered from walking the roads. "Miz Sloop," he said, "I've decided that a fella is pretty lucky when he has a good bed to sleep in and all he wants to eat. I won't run away again."

Many children came empty-handed but burdened with the baggage of their troubled lives. Sloop's response was to embrace each new arrival as if he or she was her own. "She was surrounded by an aura of love, an aura of acceptance," recalled a boy who arrived at Crossnore in 1940. "You went close to her and you were covered." She then turned the children over to the houseparents, who coped as best they could to ease the pain of the twenty or more children under their care. Most often, the children kept their personal stories to themselves.

Campus life was closely regulated. During the school year, the campus was awakened at 6:30 a.m. by the clanging of a bell mounted atop one of the buildings. It was a gift from a Pennsylvania family that had used it on their farm to call workers in from the field. When the rope broke, a boy climbed a ladder to the rooftop and attacked it

Saturday was cleanup day on the Crossnore campus. Younger boys and girls were detailed to clean up trash—and leaves in the fall—as part of the minimum of fifteen hours per week that they devoted to campus chores. This photo is from the 1930s.

with a hammer. One housemother wryly observed that the rigid daily schedule of the entire campus was totally dependent on the accuracy of one clock kept by a teenager. Another clanging of the bell called everyone to breakfast. It was as hearty a meal as Sloop could provide and usually consisted of oatmeal, bacon (when available), and plenty of biscuits and gravy.

The school day occupied the children until 3:30 p.m., when the boarders trooped back to the campus and reported for their assigned jobs. Some took part in music lessons or extracurricular activities, such as football and basketball. Sloop loved music, and piano lessons had been available for those who wanted them since the school's earliest days. There was also a glee club and a dramatics society. After the evening meal, announced by the ringing of the bell, the houseparents enforced an evening study period that lasted until bedtime at 10 p.m.

Everyone worked fifteen hours a week, even if their tuition was paid in full. Sloop believed that the school's self-help component developed students' confidence, useful skills, and self-esteem. There were practical reasons as well, not the least of which was keeping a herd of youngsters occupied during their off hours. Boys and girls alike reported to the Weave Room. Girls were the weavers, while boys used scraps of material from the Sales Store to make hooked rugs. Some of the older boys headed down the road to the farm, where the school's dairy herd grazed in a pasture. The dining hall depended on the beef cattle and the bounty of an apple orchard.

Students were a main source of labor in the dining hall. Younger children peeled potatoes and prepared vegetables in the afternoon. The larger boys were assigned to handle the heavy pots and bake as many as a thousand biscuits in a day. Each of the long tables where children sat for meals was served by one of the girls, who had to rise early to be on duty for breakfast. One girl was assigned as a housekeeper for the Sloops. Job assignments rotated every two months.

Child labor was not only instructive, it helped relieve Crossnore of routine expenses. Children kept the campus clear of trash and debris, and they shared in upkeep of the landscaping. Sloop loved wildflowers, and she seldom disturbed the growth of any shrub or tree. As a result, the campus paths wound around any living thing that obstructed a direct route. Some of the older girls assisted in the office with filing, correspondence, and other administrative chores. Boys in the carpentry classes were involved in routine maintenance of the buildings and were assigned to major building projects like the dining hall. Girls filled the sewing room in the afternoon, mending and making clothes for the children on campus. The campus print shop produced the quarterly newsletter that was folded, bundled, and mailed out to thousands of readers. Student workers at the hospital assisted the nurses and doctors. As a result, Crossnore regularly produced candidates for nursing school. That was the career path of Roadman Hollander's older sisters.

The children were an unending source of inspiration. Sloop didn't talk down to young people; she brought them into her confidence. Each week—often it was on Friday evening—she would appear in the dining hall at the close of the meal and speak about whatever was on her mind.

Occasionally, her message was nothing more than an animated report on a recent trip or a review of the movie that she and her husband had seen that week during their trip to Asheville. At other times, her message was serious, such as a request for prayers to relieve an immediate financial crisis or for Crossnore's future. "Silently, we took our place in the large circle," Joe Powlas later wrote in his memoir, *Somewhere along the Way*, "and each person bowed his head and asked for God's blessing upon our school. There wasn't a dry eye among us."

Children who had seen the worst that life could throw at them heard, often for the first time, that they were something of value. They were God's children and had been put on Earth for a purpose. "She made us feel important and worthwhile," Fred Hawkens later wrote. "Never had I heard such inspiring words and they seemed to be directed right at me. 'Stand up straight,' she would say, 'and face the world with dignity and grace.' Sometimes she would throw in some advice. She told us to hang our socks up at night and never put them in our shoes. To this day, I still hang up my socks at night."

Donors of the annual fifty-dollar scholarships reinforced Sloop's message of self-worth. In the early 1930s, Sloop had about thirty-five scholarships. The number had tripled by 1940. Sloop saw to it that students given scholarships connected with the donors and wrote letters telling their benefactors about themselves. The donors responded with notes of encouragement. One day, Sloop found a girl reading a letter as she sat in the living room of the Middle Girls Dormitory. "My scholarship lady says she is going to send me a new dress if my report at mid-term is good," she told Sloop. "Give me my books. I want to do good."

Sloop also could scold. Grace Sperry Burns, the housemother who arrived in the winter of 1942, saw Sloop for the first time when she appeared in the dining hall at the close of the evening meal. "The head of the school came in, with an airy greeting to all—a fine pleasant-faced woman of advanced years—walked to one side of the room and began a long harangue about some of the problems that were getting out of hand and needed correcting. It was quite dramatic. She spoke like a Calvinist, especially when she inveighed against lying and deception and avoidance of church and Sunday school."

The huge log Weave Room burned in 1935, and Mary Sloop immediately set about building a replacement. On a chilly Sunday afternoon in October, she and children began retrieving rocks from the bed of the Linville River. The result was the building that came to be known as Homespun House.

The young people were a resource that Sloop and Crossnore would draw upon when everything looked bleak. On October 9, 1935, Sloop and Mrs. Newbern Johnson were attending a DAR meeting in West Virginia, accompanied by student weavers and a carload of weaving for sale, when they got word that the Crossnore Weave Room had burned to the ground. It was a devastating loss. Literally overnight, the school's largest industry was destroyed. Twenty-five looms and $15,000 in materials and finished goods were reduced to a smoldering ruin. Only the furnace room survived. There was no clue as to the source of the blaze.

Within two weeks, Sloop had mobilized the students to start work on a new building. The air was cold in late October, but while workers cleared away the rubble and spread the crushed rock of the old foundation on the road below, Crossnore children formed a rock brigade at the Linville River. It was a Sunday afternoon, and they shed their shoes, took a place in the shallow, cold water, and began hand-ing rocks one by one to classmates at the riverside, where the stones were loaded on wagons and hauled to the campus. Like the hospital, the new building would be built of river rock on a site just around the hill from Garrett Memorial Hospital. Sloop used $300 that had been donated on the spot by the West Virginia DAR to begin the reconstruction of what she called "the new industrial building."

She spent the cash on cement, and work commenced on not just one building but two, although together they didn't compare in size to the old log structure. Each was one and a half stories, with an excavated basement. One would be for weaving, and the other was to be for carpentry, but it would later be transformed into a sewing room. Masons worked through the winter and left fires burning overnight to prevent the mortar from freezing. In the meantime, Mrs. Johnson contacted Berea College and arranged for the purchase of new looms and replacement patterns. She also restocked her supplies of yarn. While construction was underway, some of the new looms were placed in homes around the community. She put ten of them in her own home, where weavers worked any hours they could. She had unfilled orders and was eager to build up a good inventory by the time of the DAR annual meeting in the spring.

The new buildings had been in use for about a year when they were dedicated in the spring of 1937, along with the Reed and Fleshman dormitories for the youngest of the boys and girls. The carpentry department now had space for storage of lumber, a shop, and an apartment on the upper floor for one of the married couples that worked on the campus. It was designated the Bullard-Sloan Building in honor of two donors, W. Irving Bullard and Dr. Henry Sloan of North Carolina. Once again, the president general of the DAR and a contingent of North Carolina DAR dignitaries participated in a grand ceremony.

Missing from the usual DAR representatives was Mrs. Ralph Van Landingham, who had recently died. One of her last contributions to Crossnore was a Thanksgiving dinner that she had personally delivered in her big car and a truck the year before. It was served up to the houseparents and children who remained on the campus when the others had gone home to family for the holidays.

Mrs. Johnson called the new weaving room Homespun House. "Like the other buildings on Crossnore's campus," she said at the dedication, "[it] was built by mountain people with local materials." The new building reaffirmed Crossnore's weaving program. "From a few workers making a few things, the work has grown to accommodate weavers who come five days a week, others who hook rugs, finishers and those who prepare materials."

In an invocation written for the occasion, Denise Abbey said, "The rivers gave their rocks for me / the hills gave their chestnut wood and bark / the coves sent their people to build me / the elements have christened me and made me one with the fellowship of Earth."

On the same day as the dedication of the buildings, county school officials broke ground for a new high school to be built on a piece of land across the hill from the dormitories and the campus dining hall. It was paid for with money from the Works Progress Administration, and it relieved the crowded conditions at the old school, which had opened more than fifteen years earlier. Along with a replacement elementary school added later, the complex was designed to accommodate seven hundred students and reflected what was becoming the Crossnore style of architecture. It had a rock foundation and was covered with siding of chestnut bark. Classes for the elementary grades continued in the school building that opened in 1920.

Campus life remained confined to strict boundaries, and the "dormitory children," as they were known among the locals, did not venture off the campus without permission. Once a week, if they had a few pennies, the young ones could visit the village to buy candy. Seeing a motion picture was allowed for those whose grades qualified them to see the features in Theron Dellinger's modest theater. Other entertainments included the weekly square dances in the large living room of the Cooper Building. Occasionally, on Saturdays and Sundays, houseparents took their charges on hikes or overnight camping trips to Hawshaw Mountain. Some of the older boys were allowed off campus on the weekends, and they hitched rides out on the highway to spend time with friends and family.

Houseparents and assorted staff members made Christmas as

Crossnore High School was built with money from the Works Progress Administration during the 1930s and remained in use until 1968.

exciting as they could. Throughout the year, they set aside special deliveries of clothing, toys, and other items in the "Bird Cage," a space in the attic of the dining hall that was enclosed in chicken wire. A few weeks out from the campus holiday celebration, the houseparents sorted through the collection and found gifts for their children, marking each selection with a name. Just before the campus emptied for the holidays, everyone gathered in the dining hall for a special meal.

"The dining hall was beautifully decorated with candles, evergreens, bells, etc. and in the center was a huge Christmas tree with colorful lights and just 'oodlings' of snow and icicles," recalled Mamie Shirley Church, a teacher in the late 1930s. "Underneath the tree presents were piled high not to mention the ropes that were strung diagonally across the room and were simply hung full—just like you hang out clothes—of the most exciting looking and queer shaped packages."

A young boy might get a box of marbles, while a girl his age got a doll. Sloop reported one year, "The older boys are rejoicing in some boxing gloves." If there were more gifts than could be used on campus, Sloop packaged the remainder and sent them to Sunday Schools at churches elsewhere in the county. That evening, there were bonfires and sledding—any smooth board would do—if there was snow on Christmas Tree Hill, a cleared knob above the campus.

For Sloop, the most important off-campus activity was Sunday worship services. Some children attended the Baptist church that was close by, while the others lined up outside of their dormitories in time for the half-mile walk to Crossnore Presbyterian along an old road that hugged the hillside across the valley from the school. It rose gently from town and continued along a steep ravine to a rise and a wooden bridge across the highway. A stone arch marked the entrance to the church grounds on the other side. Children attended Sunday School and then filled the seats in the sanctuary for the 11 a.m. service. Some of the campus girls, along with staff members, sang in the choir. In the mid-1930s, Thelma Church, Mary Sloop's administrative assistant, played the organ.

The separation of affairs between the Presbyterians and the school remained as strong as it had been on the day that the community endorsed the charter establishing the nondenominational character of Crossnore School Incorporated. Nonetheless, there was no mistaking the tilt toward Crossnore Presbyterian Church, where the Sloops worshipped. Sloop demonstrated her faith daily, and she was not shy about engaging crowds of people in prayer. The Lord was often the salvation of her work, as far as she was concerned, and she was eager to give thanks. She opened the door for the unchurched who lived on the campus, children and adults alike, but she did not impose her faith on those who weren't ready.

Young Jack Haim arrived at Crossnore in 1941. His story was perhaps the most unusual of any of those who found their way to the school in those days. Jack was a Jew. His family had left Italy as the alliance of dictators Benito Mussolini and Germany's Adolf Hitler

Mr. Lewis Aldridge and his son, Talton, often played on Saturday nights in the living room of the Cooper Building. Mary Sloop included Talton in a group of students she took to New York to perform for prospective donors.

made it clear that his family's future was threatened. The Haims left their home in Genoa for Switzerland and then Cuba before reaching the final stop in their journey, New York City. Jack was an only child and newly settled in New York when a Daughter recommended Crossnore to his parents as a place where he could thrive. He arrived on the bus with his father, who introduced him to Mary Sloop and then left him in her care. Jack didn't know anyone in this strange country. He spoke three languages, but none of them was English.

Haim recalled more than seventy years later that he and his father had walked up the hill to Sloop's office, where he was expected. "She got up, came to me, looked at me and gave me a hug. Even though I was scared, suddenly I felt as if she was my grandmother, even though I had met her two minutes before."

Haim never learned how his father connected with the DAR, although his arrival coincided with Mary Sloop's work with a committee to find homes for refugee children from England, which was then under threat of invasion by Germany. She called them "our English refugee cousins," explaining, "All of us in this corner of the mountains are 'descended' from the British Isles, mostly England." The project of resettling English refugees never happened. Crossnore's limited space prevented her from bringing the fifty English children to the campus.

Sloop introduced Haim to the Crossnore family like any other child. His roommates in the dormitory struggled with his strangeness, but he found an overall acceptance and learned English, albeit with a mountaineer's accent. On Sundays, he lined up with the rest of the boys in his dormitory and made the hike to the Presbyterian Church, where he prayed quietly in Hebrew as the Christians recited the Lord's Prayer. He remembered: "They never tried to convert me. One of the most amazing and impressive things I have never forgotten. They had a rare opportunity to convert me. I have a strong feeling that Mary Martin Sloop had an influence on that."

The war in Europe had already begun to affect families in the mountains of North Carolina. By the early weeks of 1940, Sloop reported that four of "our big boys" were in military service. One was already in England. He had left Crossnore with $2.37 in his pocket and thumbed his way to Canada to enlist. He ended up in an article in *Look* magazine about American expatriates serving in the Canadian armed forces.

Many more students would follow this vanguard of four in the months ahead. Sloop embraced patriotism as fully as she did her faith. The national anthem was sung often, and students pledged their allegiance to the flag of the United States with regularity. When America entered World War II, Sloop reported, "We are still saluting the flag one hundred percent at Crossnore, singing 'God Bless America,' and trying every day to be prepared to offer Uncle Sam our strong bodies, keen minds, trained hands, fine characters, and loyal service, no matter when and how he needs us."

10
Over There

Nothing thrilled Mary Sloop more than to report on the accomplishments of Crossnore's young people. She frequently recounted the number who had gone on to college, finished nursing school, or opened a business. One of her favorites was Clarence Taylor, whom she called one of the "grist mill boys." He was in that group of teenage boys who had slept in the attic of the mill before Crossnore gained its first crude dormitory, called the "donkey barn."

Taylor graduated from the high school, went to college, and returned to teach math at Crossnore. In the late 1920s, he migrated to Newport News, Virginia, for a job in the shipyards, but he was out of work when Sloop hired him as foreman on the construction of the Cooper Building, the new dormitory for the older girls. When that job was completed, Taylor became the director of a CCC camp and later traded in his college ROTC credits for a commission in the army. He was sent to Fort Knox, Kentucky, to become a tank commander with a gold leaf on his collar. Sloop would later write fondly about "our major."

By the late 1930s, Sloop was writing more and more about Crossnore graduates who were in uniform. One was on a ship that had searched for traces of Amelia Earhart, the American flyer whose plane disappeared over the Pacific in 1937. "He is now head diesel mechanic on the biggest submarine Uncle Sam owns," she wrote in the summer of 1939. A year later, she told of four more of her "boys" who were in the army. Malone Street was already in England wearing the uniform of the Royal Canadian Engineers.

Military service came early for the men of Avery County. Sloop believed the number of local young men in uniform demonstrated the inherent patriotism of the mountain culture and the lessons they had learned at Crossnore. "Here in our mountains we believe in our country, our form of government, our duty to benefit mankind, our desire to be of service," she wrote. "These boys and girls are the splendid material put into our hands, the clay for the potter, but there must be a potters' wheel; that wheel must be manned, that 'pottery' must be housed." In short, Crossnore was doing its duty, but it required help from others to operate successfully.

There was another reason for the high number of enlistments. Military service offered steady pay, a significant enticement to men who had been out of work for a long time. Many teenagers switched to an army uniform after the state of North Carolina began phasing out the CCC camps in the late 1930s. That may have been why Avery County was third in the nation in terms of the proportion of its citizens who volunteered for military service once the nation began rebuilding its armed forces in 1940.

Sloop reported that campus jobs had prepared the volunteers and draftees for immediate service. "Forest knew his keyboard, and they took him right into office work; George had handled supplies and the quartermaster got him; Robert had longed to be a doctor and so asked to be connected with the medical work and will soon be ready for service in Walter Reed; Jess had worked in the kitchen a lot and right into the kitchen he went."

A year after the United States declared war on the Axis powers in December 1941, Sloop began receiving cards and letters from military camps around the world. Nearly a hundred young men from Crossnore were in the service—that number would swell to five hundred by the end of the war—and serving in all branches. Some of their names had already appeared on casualty lists and among the missing and prisoners of war. As she wrote in the summer of 1942, "H. L. went down with the Reuben James, Billy was on the Wasp, Jess was at Corregidor, and Zeb at Wake Island." At the time, five Cross-

After the Sloop's frame home burned to the ground in the early 1940s, Dr. Eustace Sloop designed a stone house reminiscent of Frank Lloyd Wright's Prairie Style of architecture, with broad windows and a flat roof.

nore girls were second lieutenants in the Army Nursing Corps. One of them was on foreign duty. Sloop closed her quarterly newsletter with the salutation, "Your mate in service."

The demands of the war brought some new challenges to Crossnore, but it mostly exacerbated long-standing ones—inadequate staffing, insufficient housing, and lack of money to pay the bills. These greeted Sloop each day as she arrived in her office, often at 7 a.m. Her habits hadn't changed over the years. Doctor ferried her to and from their home in his car, a sporty 1936 Ford V-8 coupe. They now lived in a house built of block and stone that was rather modern in design, with a flat roof and spare, straight lines. The frame house they had moved into in 1911 burned in the early 1940s. Mary Sloop reported on virtually every incident of consequence on the campus in her quarterly reports, but she never wrote a word about her personal trials, such as the home she and Eustace had lost to fire.

The Sloops were in their sixties—Mary was nearly seventy when the war began—but they remained as active as ever. Doctor usually worked nights at the hospital, while their daughter, Emma, who had returned with a medical degree in 1937, saw patients during the day. A woman doctor was unusual, and ailing men and women would huddle around the door late in the day in order to be seen by her father. Emma's brother, Bill, was a dentist with an office at the hospital. Mary fussed with the duty nurses who allowed her husband to indulge his sweet tooth from stashes of candy. She said he was overweight, a condition that she suffered from as well. She scolded him on winter days for skating on the ice that formed on a small pond the town had built at the foot of the hill as a water supply for the hoses should a fire break out on campus.

Despite his age, Doctor never hesitated to make the rounds to the dam to check on the power station or the often-unreliable pumps that supplied the campus with water. A water and sewer system had been installed on the campus with help from the Works Progress Administration, which also paid for a sewage treatment plant in the town. The power company occupied his time as he struggled to keep up service on lines that often needed repair. A large power company serving the corner of eastern Tennessee, whose lines approached the edge of his own service area, supplied extra power when the reduced flow of the Linville River cut the hours of operation of his turbine. The fee for his residential customers was a minimum of one dollar a month.

Advancing age didn't keep the Sloops from making their trips to Asheville. A horrific storm moved into the mountains in the summer of 1940 just as they were headed out for the weekly shopping trip. As they got down the mountain, they found flooded creeks and rivers threatening homes and towns. Washed-out bridges would leave some communities separated from their neighbors for weeks. They were on their return at night when Doctor pulled the car to high ground, where he parked alongside other drivers who had been told the road ahead was impassable. As they discussed their prospects for supper, a man hurried up to the cluster of automobiles and asked if there was a doctor around. Eustace was without his instruments, but

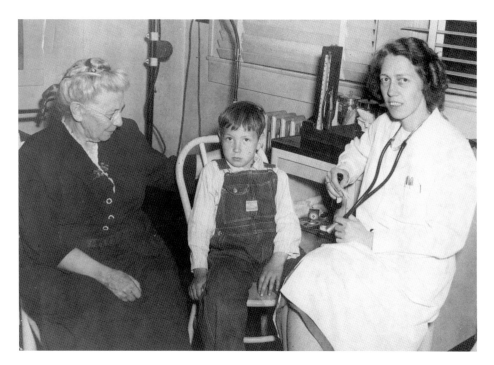

The Sloops' two children followed in the family business. Emma, here with her mother and a young patient, became a medical doctor and practiced with her father. Her brother, Bill, was a dentist and saw patients at his office in the hospital.

he followed the worried farmer back to his house, where he found the man's wife about to deliver a baby. A short time later, the family had a new daughter, and the Sloops and the other drivers were feasting on a harvest of fresh corn they had pulled from the farmer's field.

The ordeal was not over. The Sloops spent the night in their car and awoke the next morning to drivers dining on peaches taken from one truck, milk they had drained from the tanks of another, and crackers and cheese they had purchased at a filling station. The caravan then moved on. Sloop and the other drivers shoveled through one landslide, only to retreat when they reached a landslide that was too much for their hand tools. They drove back down the mountain, made their way to Asheville, and headed to Crossnore by another route. When they got back to Avery County at 2 a.m. the next night, they found the Linville River had flooded the valley, but the campus buildings on the hillside were undamaged. Doctor's dam had suffered a minor crack but was still standing, unlike two others upstream that the floodwaters had washed away. Mary was met by a man who had arrived at the campus with four children. "The floods had ruined his farm, taken out fences, barns, and left his fields littered with rocks," she reported. She said the man told her, "I've got one more at home and I hope you can make room for her. There's nothing for her to eat and our one-room school house was washed away and broken up." She also heard a young boy tell his father, "Daddy, Crossnore must be a mighty good place because the flood didn't hurt them a bit."

It had taken years of personal sacrifice, fierce determination in the face of daunting challenges, and a deep and abiding faith in the Lord, but the Sloops had transformed the community and indeed created a "good place." They had built an impressive educational and medical complex that was supported by thousands of people from all across the land. Garrett Memorial Hospital, with annual support from the Duke Endowment's contributions to rural health, had expanded to twice the size of the original cottage-style building. The hospital attracted patients from miles around and had a staff of professional nurses supplemented by girls from the campus.

The town drew its financial strength and life from both the hospital and the busy campus, where a staff of about fifty adults looked after more than two hundred boarding students. An intrastate bus made regular stops. Locals and visitors ate at two cafes, and the movie theater drew big crowds on the weekend. There were general stores open all week. The Crossnore Sales Store, open Thursday through Saturday, attracted crowds of customers, especially when word circulated that new shipments of donated clothing and other goods had arrived. On Saturday nights, it was hard to find a place to park a pickup on the street.

The holdings of the trustees of Crossnore School Incorporated now included about 250 acres of land, which reached from the town to the large dairy farm across the highway that spread out toward the Linville River a mile away. There were more than a dozen buildings on the campus. That count did not include the new high school, a modest gymnasium, and the 1920s-era school building with class-

When donations dwindled, Mary Sloop often began work for a new dorm using the energy and enthusiasm of the older boys living on campus.

rooms for students in grades four through eight. The primary students met in a new schoolhouse that was near the high school. Altogether, more than a thousand students attended classes on a campus that served about a third of the students in Avery County.

The high school building had been promised to the county as part of President Franklin Roosevelt's New Deal. When it was slow in coming, Sloop had someone drive her to Charlotte to check on the paperwork at a regional office there. After a two-hour wait, she was told the application was at an office in Raleigh, which was another three hours away by car. She rode on, found the proper office, and announced she would wait until the papers were signed. Finally, at around 6 p.m., the official who was dodging her visit approved the project after fielding several calls from his wife, who was holding supper for him. "And that's how Crossnore got a high school," Sloop wrote in a later account. Included in the project was money for a playground large enough to accommodate a playing field for soft-ball and football. It was built on a flat area at the top of the hill beyond the campus dormitories.

The high school opened just as Sloop was expanding the Cross-nore curriculum to include business courses for graduates. The new program began in 1935 with supplemental funds from the state's trades and industries division of vocational education. Students learned rudimentary bookkeeping, typing, and dictation. More than forty young men and women were enrolled at the end of the pro-gram's first two years. For Sloop, it was a logical extension of the vocational training begun twenty years earlier, except now she was preparing young men and women for future jobs in the cities rather than on the farm. The business students got practical training in the Crossnore office. They logged in packages for the Sales Store, pre-pared thank-you letters to donors, helped with the bookkeeping of boarders' accounts, and typed Mary Sloop's letters.

The Crossnore Business School, with tuition of fifty dollars a year, was run by the Sloops' son-in-law, Emma's husband, Dwight A. Fink. He was from Salisbury, North Carolina, and had a degree from Cataw-ba College. He'd also done graduate studies at the University of North Carolina and the University of Pittsburgh. The courses he supervised helped develop basic skills, although there was no degree or certi-fication that came upon completion. Sloop said it was "two years of splendid training." She wrote of the graduates, "No matter what they do to make a living or to make a home they are better fitted for it. This course, as it now stands, is equal in mental training to two years of college." If students couldn't pay the tuition, they were expected to settle accounts as soon as they got a job. In 1944, one former student used his army pay to cover a hundred dollars in unpaid tuition.

The postgraduate courses added some stature to the campus, but the new program also increased the demand for adequate hous-ing and meals. Campus buildings that had been erected hastily and on modest budgets in the 1920s were showing their age by the early 1940s. The floors in the old teacherage, where Sloop had her office, were creaky and warped. The condition of one dormitory was deplor-able, according to the mother of a twelve-year-old boy. "The morale of the boys in that dormitory is very bad from what I noticed, and it isn't to be wondered," she said. "They get up in a cold, drafty building, get dressed for schools in the cold. They return in the evening to a cold building. Because of the draftiness of the building, I requested John not to take baths there. We house farm animals in better buildings.... I am unable to shake off the depressing conditions in which these boys are living. I know I am not the only one who feels the need of a very speedy action in this matter to avoid grave and even disastrous consequences." Not long after Sloop received the letter, these boys were squeezed into temporary quarters in the Big Boys and Little Boys dormitories.

Shifting students among the dormitories occurred from year to year as the national emergency changed the makeup of the student body. There was a greater demand for accommodations for younger children whose parents had found jobs in the mills and factories down the mountain. At the same time, older boys liable for military service all but disappeared from the campus. "So girls are having to do things boys used to do that don't require too much muscle," Sloop wrote. "The monitors for the younger boys have been big boys, and a girl can hardly interest and manage the twelve and thirteen year olds, but they have succeeded with the two younger groups."

Viola Duncan attended the fifty-first DAR Continental Congress with Mary Sloop in the spring of 1942. She was a junior in high school, and she told the Daughters about her job as an assistant housemother for fourteen- and fifteen-year-old girls. Traveling with them was Clarice Burleson, another junior. She was the evening cook at the dining hall, and she nightly baked cornbread for 250 diners.

Sloop kept her students updated on the war news. Some used their pennies and nickels to buy Defense stamps. The paper trash on campus was bundled and saved. Sloop even conducted blackout drills as the war crowded into the students' daily routine.

Complications due to the war that troubled every community and every household seemed to be compounded at Crossnore, where resources had been thin for some time. The public school lost teachers who were called to military service. The *Bulletin* was late for delivery one year because Robert Woodside, the teacher who ran the print shop, had been called into the navy. Crossnore had a shortage of cooks, and Sloop accepted students for the dormitories even though she had no houseparents for the little girls, ages six to eight. "The only solution to that problem is to put two of our oldest and most reliable girls in charge of these, letting them divide the duty hours between them," she explained. Food supplies were curtailed after farmers found they could get cash for their butter and produce and no longer needed to barter at the kitchen door. Rationing and economic uncertainty meant there were no Christmas gifts for the children in 1942.

Young men and women who had spent their formative years at Crossnore and were now in uniform often came back to visit. Sometimes, this happened before they left for assignments overseas. Sloop recounted one day in 1942 when Will and Blanche met in her home. He was a captain. She was an army nurse. They "chatted of what had been and would be, and as she left, he said, 'Good-bye Blanche, I 'spec we'll run across each other there somewhere. The world's not so big after all."

The war was not merely a fact for Sloop, it was a teachable event for all the youngsters in her care. "What a lesson in COURAGE," she wrote of her two visitors. "Somewhere over there. They are going out to fight for freedom and often—to maintain a wise World Peace. That's what we are trying to prepare for here in Crossnore—to train them not only to do—but to think it out—to realize right now that education and training carry with them responsibility and influence."

The constant turnover in staff and the shortage of adults to look after two hundred or more young people created concern. Sloop worried aloud to her readers that the limited supervision was creating problems. "Is it due to 'war unrest?'" she wrote in the spring of 1942, when the war was not going well for the Allies. "We can't say, but we do know that the result was been distressing." The campus struggled with shortages of everything from food to children's underwear. Sloop found hope in small measure. In the same broadside in which she lamented low morale, she reported that at least no child had to wear sandals in the snow because of a shortage of shoes.

Nothing diminished the pride of Crossnore for its men and

women in uniform. Girls on campus received letters from their boyfriends in service, who made it back to campus when they could. Late in 1943, Sloop wrote, "A blue jacket on the campus means a furlough for one of our sailors, or a khaki uniform reminds us that this love of Crossnore brings them back. Imagine the thrill of hearing Fred say that for months he had been a tail gunner for the RAF and had flown as far as Cairo, had been in 29 battles and had not had a scratch though he acknowledged that he had shot down enough Nazi planes to have been decorated three times. No wonder we reminded him, that he had been spared for some great good." She found Augusta Peak, a sergeant in the WACs, in a photo accompanying a story in the *Saturday Evening Post*. Her assistant from the 1930s, Denise Abbey, wrote from Italy in 1944, where she was "handling secrets for Uncle Sam." She remembered Carl, who was killed when his plane crashed. He was buried at Crossnore, and three of his fellow pilots flew over in formation as the funeral was underway.

Seventeen of the more than five hundred former Crossnore students who served with the armed forces in World War II gave their lives in service to their country. Five men attained the rank of major, and one went on to the rank of colonel. Two received the Silver Star for bravery in the Pacific. One was awarded the Distinguished Flying Cross. Women wore the uniforms of the WAVES and WACs. One woman in the WAC helped General Dwight D. Eisenhower set up his office when he took charge of the European Theater, and Crossnore nurses tended wounded in every theater of conflict.

Even before the war, Sloop's continual demand for money and materials to pay for new buildings and improvements had led some to question the ongoing need for the boarding department, especially with the advent of paved roads and state-owned school buses that carried children to school. Sloop took exception to such talk. Consolidation of public schools had left many children in fringe areas that were away from good roads and a school bus stop. "Many children in the county walk two miles to a bus or school, but the little folks don't stand that well with their insufficient clothes and indigestible food, and so they miss many days during the school year," she wrote in 1941.

Crossnore was and would remain a "home for mountain children," although Sloop wrestled with whether she should accept more children from outside of the mountains whose parents were willing to pay the four dollars a week charged for room and board. She remained faithful to the charter and returned to more urgent appeals for scholarships from her correspondents among the DAR and elsewhere. She was unrelenting in her appeals and aware of her nagging persistence. (She signed one newsletter "your troublesome beggar.") Yet she was not going to abandon children and ignore the many tragedies that forced parents to leave their children at Crossnore as they struggled to get on their feet again.

Sloop managed to hold the campus together—and even expand it—during the war years. The dining hall was completed, largely with student labor, and she built a recreation hall with money donated by the New Jersey DAR. It was dedicated in honor of New Jersey's regent, Mrs. Raymond C. Goodfellow. When the building was completed early in 1944, there was a ceremony in which seventy children carried small flags at the head of a procession of DAR officers. A larger flag had been found among the donated clothing, but when it was hung on the front of Cooper Building, the organizers discovered it had only thirty-four stars.

What Sloop wanted most for the campus was an infirmary. Seriously ill children were treated at Garrett Memorial or taken to the hospital in Banner Elk. Yet the campus had no place for others whose conditions didn't require a hospital bed but who were unable to attend school because of mumps, measles, or other ailments. The situation became particularly acute one year when the hospital nurse called Sloop to say the hospital was overrun with twenty-nine cases of mumps. She couldn't take any more. Others who got sick had to remain in the dormitory, where a houseparent may or may not have been available to look after them.

Sloop wasn't going to impose on the hospital like that again, and in the spring of 1945, when the end of the war in Europe was in sight, she began a campaign to raise the $10,000 she said she needed to build an infirmary. One technique she had used earlier—asking every reader of the *Bulletin* to send a dollar—may have paid off. By the

The campus infirmary was built in the late 1940s and named for a former teacher who left money to aid in construction.

summer of 1945, she had $2,000 in the bank, earmarked for the infirmary. That was only a fifth of what she needed, but one evening after school opened that fall she rounded up all the students, pulling even the dishwashing crew off their sinks, and everyone headed up the hill to a spot across from the playground that she had chosen for the infirmary.

"Before we start, we are going to dedicate the land," Sloop told the children as she recounted that night for Legette Blythe. "We gathered around the lot, there were some trees there, and every boy lined up, big and little. All the shovels, picks and mattocks had been collected, boys stood there with them, and we had our little service. Aunt Newbie (Mrs. Johnson) offered a prayer. I will never forget it. We were to earn our part by our service to God, by dedicating our heart and our lives to God. The children were impressed. Then we began our work. We were going to do our part as far as we could. We sang good old gospel hymns, and then went back to work, dishes and such."

By the spring of 1946, the older boys had excavated the topsoil and were down to the hardpan. Dynamite was going to be necessary to go deeper. "In this country," she wrote, "we use that for everything from a white pine stump to a wedding." Money continued to come in. "About once a week for six weeks, we got a $1,000 check; every one of them marked for infirmary; from different parts of the country. It made us remember that we had asked God to send us the money. We worked through the summer and in the fall we had an infirmary that could take care of 29 cases of mumps."

The new building had a ward for girls and one for boys, as well as space for a nurse and an assistant. There was also room for four small apartments. Asbestos shingles were used for siding in place of the chestnut bark that Sloop loved so well. It was no longer available, since blight had destroyed the American Chestnut trees in the Appalachian forests. River rock formed the foundation. The infirmary was named in honor of Alta M. Malloch, a former teacher at the school who had left a bequest to Crossnore to help underwrite the cost.

While the infirmary was under construction, so was a new Sales Store. Neither project was quite complete in April 1946 when fire destroyed the campus administration building. The loss was just as devastating as the fire that had claimed the Weave Room. While the building was old and in need of repair, it had provided rooms for the older girls taking courses in the business school. It had also served as headquarters for Sloop and the campus support staff, and as the storage building for all the school's records. "It was the center of the campus," Sloop wrote in a report on the fire in the summer issue of the *Bulletin*. Nearly all of the early records, such as financial information and minutes of trustee meetings, were destroyed or damaged in the fire. "Every day we think of something else valuable or useful that was burned," she said. "It must be rebuilt. The same site will do, and a pretty one it was. We will manage poorly without it this winter."

The day before the fire, Sloop said a car carrying five children, three mothers, and an infant had arrived. The mothers asked if she could take the children in. For people from miles around, Crossnore had become more than a school. Children arrived weak and malnourished and left healthy and strong. They enrolled uncertain about

The campus administration building opened in 1948 after a fire destroyed the old teacherage and consumed most of Crossnore's records. The upper story of the new building was used as housing for older students enrolled in the Crossnore business courses.

their future and developed ambitions to learn and even to attend college, despite the dim prospects for further education. Somehow, Sloop told a senior finishing that fall, she would see that her desire to succeed realized. "I don't know how and you don't but there will be a way," she wrote, recounting the conversation. "God doesn't give us such feelings if there isn't any way possible."

That summer, Sloop faced the challenge of rebuilding the administration offices, outfitting the infirmary, completing plans for a campus gymnasium, and dealing with a pressing need for more beds. Donations of used clothing had slacked off as people responded to calls for emergency relief in postwar Europe. The need for space had become even more urgent as returning servicemen, ready to pick up where they had left off, asked her to take them in so they could get their high school diplomas. The regular dormitories were packed, but Sloop consented to let the young men use an old, discarded shack that had once been home to the middle boys. "I put on a very bold front and handed it over to the GIs with a real air," she told the DAR at their annual meeting in 1947. "Boys," she told them, "you will find this much more comfortable than a fox hole." And that's what they called it. Sloop was said to have been about to turn away one pleading former GI who was eager to finish his high school education when she told him he could share the bed of the night watchman, who would be on his rounds from dusk to dawn.

Crossnore even accommodated a few students crippled by polio. The first cases appeared in 1947 in nearby Linville, and Dr. Emma Fink treated patients suspected to have the disease. Major treatment centers were opened in Hickory and Greensboro, where the entire community turned out in 1949 to build a polio hospital in a matter of weeks. A few students crippled by the disease attended Crossnore in 1947 and 1948. They taught themselves to shower sitting in a chair, and finally standing up. On icy days, their mates carried them to and from the dormitory. One of the boys was Harlan Boyles, who was later elected state treasurer of North Carolina.

It was as difficult a time as Crossnore had experienced, but now there was a new condition that Sloop had not encountered in her earlier efforts to pick the pockets of donors around the nation. She turned seventy-three in the summer of 1946, and people were beginning to talk about Crossnore without Mary Martin Sloop. She was as certain of the future of the campus as she had been a quarter of a century earlier, when the first two graduates had been handed their diplomas in the high school that many believed would never be built. Each day, she saw evidence of the need for a safe haven for neglected children, a home for those without homes, and a place where hope could be turned into reality. "A mountain child without a home. That is the acme of suffering," she said. And just as the Lord had made possible teachers, housing, food, medical care, and opportunity, he was not going to desert Crossnore at this time.

"If God called me to this work," she wrote her friends, "and you and I believe that he did—won't He provide a successor? Did you ever see a worker in His vineyard whose place was not filled?"

11
Transition

In the early fall of 1951, with the shoulders of the North Carolina mountains wrapped in fall colors, the leaders of the National Society of the Daughters of the American Revolution and sixty Daughters arrived on the Crossnore campus, the first stop on a tour of DAR-approved schools. The women spent the night in dormitory rooms vacated for the occasion by the students, who doubled up in beds or slept on pads on the floor. During their stay, the women took their meals in the campus dining hall, experienced a pageant called *The Romance of Crossnore* that was written and performed on their behalf in the new Crossnore gymnasium, and dedicated three buildings, including a dormitory for the girls that was named for Mary Martin Sloop.

The naming of the dormitory in her honor came as a surprise to Sloop. But it had been a year of surprises. Earlier in the year, the Golden Rule Foundation had named her American Mother of the Year. She learned of her selection when a reporter interrupted Mary and Doctor during their weekly meal at the S&W Cafeteria in Asheville. The award was presented in New York City, where Mary and her daughter, Emma, were put up at the Waldorf-Astoria. She was welcomed by the wife of the mayor, sat for a portrait, and received lavish praise. Mary suffered all the fuss with humility and simplicity. The black dress with a collar of white lace that she wore for public affairs was one she had purchased at the Crossnore Sales Store.

One of the last large dormitories built on campus was dedicated in honor of Mary Martin Sloop in the fall of 1951 during the tour of approved schools by the leaders of the National Society of the DAR.

It had been forty years since the Sloops arrived in Crossnore with all their belongings piled on a sled, their saddlebags full of medical instruments, and their hearts filled with hope. In those four decades, they had survived skepticism and outright opposition from their neighbors, lived modestly as they raised two children who had returned to serve at their side, and endured deprivations brought by two world wars and a devastating economic depression. Yet laid out on the hill rising from the village where Eustace Sloop's hospital had doubled in size were seven dormitories with beds for more than two hundred students, a campus infirmary, the Homespun House weaving room, a music building, a new administration building, and a handsome gymnasium that was a war memorial gift from the Allen family of Charlotte. When she was introduced in New York, it was said that Mary Sloop was the "mother" of three thousand children, a rough estimate of the number of youngsters who had been under her care over the years.

Mary Sloop was chosen as America's Mother of the Year in 1951. Students greeted her on the steps of the high school upon her return to the campus. At right is Sloop's son-in-law, Dwight Fink, principal of Crossnore High School.

Mary Sloop remained involved in every detail of campus life. Her second home was the administration building, which was built on the site of the old teacherage, right in the heart of the campus. Every day, she could be found in her small cubicle, just eight feet square, where she managed campus affairs from a crowded desk set at an angle in one corner. In the evening, when Doctor arrived in his car to pick her up for the drive home, he often found her asleep in her chair. At her elbow, according to one report, "would be a list of children she hadn't been able to place tonight, but who she hoped somehow could be squeezed in—tomorrow."

She was nearly eighty years old, and securing the future for her incomparable institution was a burden as heavy as the needs of the children who applied for help. There were many who had helped make Crossnore what it was at mid-century, but Crossnore only existed because of the determination of this caring and faith-filled

The Allen family of Charlotte donated the money for a campus gymnasium as a memorial in honor of their son, David A. Allen, a navy officer who was killed in action March 19, 1945, aboard the U.S.S. Franklin *when the carrier was hit by a Japanese suicide bomber.*

woman who had provided direction and encouragement, and who had reminded all that prayer did make a difference. She was the engine that drove Crossnore, and she believed that her job was not finished—at least not while buildings were deteriorating and children remained in need of food and shelter and education. She was in a race with time, she had told the Daughters in 1947. "I would be a slacker to turn my work at Crossnore over to others if the buildings on our campus were not permanent ones. I am not a young woman, and so you and I must hurry."

Crossnore now required $100,000 a year to pay its bills. Much more was needed if Sloop's plans for permanent buildings were to be fulfilled. Only a third of the annual budget came from students whose families could afford the six-dollar weekly fee for room and board. Sloop squeezed some of the balance out of Crossnore's enterprises, but she depended most on the charity of others to make it from year to year. The DAR had become Crossnore's lifeline, and some years the school received as much or more from the Daughters—individually and through chapters—than the schools owned by the DAR itself.

Every dollar that Sloop received was used to its fullest extent. The administration building served dual purposes, like just about everything else at Crossnore. On either side of the central section that included the campus offices were wings to house a dozen or so older boys and a like number of older girls. Under the eaves were small apartments for campus workers. The building was finished in 1948 and named in honor of Mrs. Katherine B. Reynolds of Winston-Salem, a former president general of the DAR and a steady friend. Her personal gift of $10,000 had allowed Sloop to begin construction of a dormitory for the older boys.

The new music building had once been the campus laundry. It was transformed for a modest $2,600 with the addition of a second story that provided an apartment for the teacher and two studios with four pianos where students received their lessons. Sloop was agitating in the *Bulletin* for a new bell tower, and the campus needed an incinerator, she said. She proposed to combine the two projects, with the incinerator chimney incorporated into the tower, but she dropped that after donors objected. A proper bell tower was erected, and not one but three bells, including one donated by Southern Railway, were received to replace the old farm bell that had been pounded beyond repair. Another bell came from a private chapel owned by one of Sloop's classmates from Statesville Female Academy. It weighed 350 pounds. All in all, in the years after the war Sloop put up five buildings for a total cost of about $75,000.

Time was chasing more than Mary Sloop. Aunt Pop and Uncle Gilmer, the couple who ran the Sales Store, were almost as well known as Sloop herself. They had been with her since the beginning. The new Sales Store, built in 1947, now carried their names, and they were in their places, Aunt Pop behind the counter and Uncle Gilmer assisting customers, six days a week when the new building opened. Two years later, Aunt Pop died. Uncle Gilmer remained on and worked with his daughter-in-law, but the business suffered. Income dropped from $13,000 a year to $6,000. A new manager was hired, creating some ripples in the community but reversing the slump in sales.

The Sloops lost their oldest friend in the community when Alex A. Johnson died in May 1949. He had recruited the couple to move to Crossnore, and his family had been active partners with the Sloops over the years. The family still retained a presence on campus. Perhaps the best known was Alex's son, Obie, who was in charge of keeping the campus buildings in repair. On Saturday nights, he called the square dances. Thousands of children had learned mountain ballads

Obie Johnson organized dance teams to perform traditional folk dances at special events, including the annual Continental Congress of the National Society of the DAR.

and traditional folk dancing from Obie Johnson. For a boarder to be chosen to perform with Johnson's dancing troupe at the DAR's Continental Congress was considered a special honor.

Alex Johnson had only missed one meeting since the nonprofit corporation was formed in 1917. The board asked one of his sons, Lambert, who lived in Saint Augustine, Florida, to sit in place of his father. The other board members included Eustace Sloop, chairman since the beginning; Milligan S. Wise, another working companion from the 1920s; and E. C. Guy, the Avery County banker, who had become a member in the 1930s. Joining them in the 1940s were a High Point hosiery manufacturer, who regularly shipped socks to the children, and the former principal of the high school, R. Q. Bault. By the early 1950s, Bault was on the faculty at the University of Florida. Sloop also recruited the Reverend T. Russell Nunan, who was the pastor of a large Presbyterian congregation in Greenville, Mississippi. Nunan was one of the Davidson College graduates Sloop had brought to Crossnore in the late 1920s to teach at the high school.

Additional trustees reflected Crossnore's close association with the DAR, especially the North Carolina chapters. Mary Sloop's generous and wealthy friend in Charlotte, Mrs. William Henry Belk, became a permanent member, as did another benefactor, Mrs. John S. Wellborn of High Point. The state DAR regent, the state chair of approved schools, and their counterparts with the National Society were made ex officio members.

By the 1950s, one-fourth or more of the annual cost of operating Crossnore was paid through the support of the Daughters. Box after box of clothing arrived at the campus from chapters across the country. Many of the scholarships were underwritten by Daughters, especially those in North Carolina chapters. The scholarships now accounted for more income than the Sales Store. Wealthy members responded to Sloop's repeated calls for donations to erect new buildings, and members remembered Crossnore in their wills. For several years, a modest trust fund managed by the DAR had contributed about $1,600 annually. The DAR's national office in Washington, D.C., had even provided jobs for young women who had finished the Crossnore business courses.

The board met but once a year, usually in the summer. Eustace Sloop would open the meeting with a prayer and then turn the balance over to his wife. Even after forty years, Mary Sloop was not a board member. She remained Crossnore's business manager, the title she had assumed in the 1920s.

With the enlarged board came more formal financial accounts. The fire at the administration building had destroyed most of the records, but those that survived show the board left all financial matters to Mary Sloop. She made sure that trustees approved her requests for major changes, such as extending bank loans, erecting new buildings, or making adjustments to the charter. Otherwise, she spent money when she had it and stopped spending when she didn't. Available records indicate she didn't bother to prepare an annual budget, and the balances at the end of the year came out of the checkbook or whatever happened to be at hand. For example, the annual accounting for clothing sales and the value of bartered goods came from numbers Uncle Gilmer penciled into a pocket account book. To get anything more accurate would have incurred "unnecessary expense," Sloop said.

If a dollar didn't increase Crossnore's capacity to serve more children, Sloop didn't spend it. Buildings went up without the benefit of architectural plans and included a minimum of conveniences. That had been satisfactory in the 1920s, when the first buildings were nailed together and Sloop was begging for the state of North Carolina to pay attention to Crossnore. By the late 1940s, she found she could do without some of the visits of officials from Raleigh.

The state welfare department was obliged to inspect Crossnore's buildings to ensure that they were safe and sanitary. After an inspection visit in the summer of 1946, Sloop was told she had too many children assigned to each room and had to cut in half the number living in many of the dormitory rooms. "What?" Sloop wrote. "Leave one half of all those War Asset beds empty, turn away half the children we were preparing to take, do just half as much good in this needy section as we planned to do?"

The inspector had excused the overcrowding in the Big Boys Dormitory, where four boys were assigned to each room. She told Sloop that because those rooms had no doors and each room opened into a hallway and a living area, there was no way to calculate the "air space" required for each boarder. Sloop took the inspector's waiver in that dormitory as the answer to her problem in the other building with the same arrangement of rooms. She removed the doors and sold them to pay the bill for the war-surplus bunk beds. (She had purchased 151 beds for 99 cents each.) It did prompt a plea to readers of the newsletter to send door curtains.

As much as Mary Sloop praised the DAR and embraced its participation, the DAR's periodic evaluations, conducted to qualify Crossnore as an "approved school," could be meddlesome, especially to someone impatient with the opinions of people from off the mountain. In response to a survey of the school in 1951, Sloop argued that Crossnore did not need the added expense of a social worker whose training would be "rigid and hardly suited for a country school and dormitory life such as Crossnore's." Her own training as a doctor, her knowledge of the mountain people and how they lived, and her close contact with the houseparents made such a position unnecessary. Likewise, she saw no need to pay for surety bonds for those handling the school's money. "I would hate to spend the money for such a procedure," she wrote.

The attention of outsiders to Crossnore had always been a mixed blessing. In the early years, Sloop had cultivated the flatlanders' stereotypes about the lives and culture of the mountaineers. She was a well-spoken southern lady, with an accent of the sort often heard in the parlors of the Old South. For Sloop, the word "lamp" had two syllables (lay-yamp); supper was pronounced "suppah." Yet she often fell into using the mountain dialect when relating her encounters with the locals. It fed on the popular notion of mountaineers as simple, unlettered folk who were untouched by the cultural changes of America's melting pot.

Visiting magazine and newspaper writers picked up on this and included her most colorful stories in their accounts. In the years after World War II, regional and national publications once again discovered Crossnore after Bill Sharpe, a publicist in the state news bureau in Raleigh, included an abbreviated account of Crossnore in a broadside he mailed to reporters around the country. Soon after, Crossnore's story appeared in the *New York Herald Tribune* and the magazines *Pageant* and the *Saturday Evening Post*.

The articles read much the same. They related Sloop's account of Hepsy, the old clothes, and the benefits of the Sales Store. They told of Sloop's fights with moonshiners, her struggles to build the school, and the remarkable changes that had taken place in a neglected corner of the world. A few writers made their way to the campus and talked to Sloop herself. She complained that others drew too heavily on the article written by Mildred Harrington that had appeared in *American* magazine twenty years earlier. One very thorough journalist, Judith Crist of the *Herald Tribune*, sent a query to Sharpe asking if the clothes at the Sales Store were dry-cleaned before they were put out for sale.

He replied with a quote from Sloop: "Our clothes naturally come from a good class of homes. Most of them have been dry-cleaned and pressed before reaching us, and we do not do anything further to them. There has never been a report of any trouble." Writing Crist, Sharpe said, "To paraphrase, I'd say: These are good clean clothes from good clean people."

Some Daughters took exception to the story by Crist and one in the *Saturday Evening Post* that included little mention of the DAR's support of Crossnore. Shortly after Christmas in 1948, Mary Sloop received a letter from a Texas Daughter who wrote, "It was with amazement and indignation that I see no mention of the work of the Daughters to help you in your work of maintaining Crossnore." She said she had recently shipped fifty-six pairs of shoes, all of which had been repaired at her expense, but would not be sending so much as a T-shirt until she got satisfaction. Sloop wrote her immediately to explain that every writer was told about the DAR support, but she had nothing to do with what appeared in print.

Sloop's selection as Mother of the Year attracted the most attention to Crossnore. She was pleased when the North Carolina Federation of Women's Clubs chose her as North Carolina's Mother of the Year. The elevation to American Mother of the Year was almost more than she could take. Doctor said he had to stay home to look after the hospital, so Emma accompanied her to New York City. A welcoming committee of dignitaries and uniformed Boy Scouts met the two at the train station. Someone thrust a bouquet of roses in Mary's arms. With the photographers' flashbulbs popping all around, she said she felt like an antique movie star.

At the luncheon in her honor, attended by four hundred guests in the Waldorf-Astoria's Starlight Room, she sat at a table with actress Peggy Wood, who was the star of the CBS television show *Mama*, based on the Broadway hit *I Remember Mama*. Just before the program began, she whispered to a newspaper reporter, "I'm scared. I haven't been scared before, but I am now. If only I didn't have to make a speech." She held court in a hotel suite, where an artist pulled her away from her visitors to sit for a portrait. Mary fell asleep in the chair. She was invited to appear on television, but only if she could talk about Crossnore. She told one reporter, "In the mountains they think I am a mighty poor mother to have only two children. But you see, I had an invalid mother to take care of. I wasn't married until I was 35."

In addition to meeting the mayor's wife, she had tea with the wife of the publisher of the *New York Times* and paid a call on Mrs. William H. Pouch, a former national chair of the DAR's approved schools committee and a regular visitor to Crossnore. Her only disappointment in the trip was failing to catch even a glimpse of America's military heroes Dwight D. Eisenhower and Douglas McArthur, whose residences were in the Waldorf-Astoria Towers.

Mary Sloop's story about Crossnore was published in 1953 and subsequently issued in four languages besides English.

Edward Aswell, a top editor at McGraw-Hill Book Company, saw Mary Sloop on television and headed to the hotel to catch her before she left for North Carolina. He asked her to do a book. "Law's a-me," she told him. "I don't have time to read books and goodness knows I couldn't write one if I had time! I wouldn't know where to start." He was completely charmed. The two parted with Sloop's agreement to work with him on an autobiography. Aswell immediately called Legette Blythe, a biographer and novelist from Charlotte. "You've got to go up to see her," Aswell told Blythe, "and with her do a book about her tremendous work up there in the hills. I'm sending you a contract in the next mail."

Sloop never explained how Aswell had nudged her out from behind stubborn reticence to tell her story. Three years earlier, she had brushed off the notion in a letter to Betty Bayley Gillen, who as a young teacher had helped her win the support of the DAR: "I don't wish to see any autobiography about myself and the thing that would make it sell would be things I wouldn't want to tell about the people and enough of that has been done anyhow."

Blythe found her just as humble when he and his wife and daughter arrived in Crossnore at eight o'clock on a Friday night and met Sloop at her "coop of an office," as he called it. "Immediately I got the feeling that she was sincere, that she really didn't see why the publishers had been so anxious to have a book done about her and her amazing work in the North Carolina mountains."

Sloop was nothing like Blythe expected: "I had found instead a very young lady of 78 with a zest for living, a forward look, an enthusiasm for youth, and complete confidence in today's youth." Seated there at her desk, she told stories about her life in Crossnore, adding emphasis with her voice, eyes, and waving hands as she took on the part of the characters she had known over the years. Blythe was sure she would have made a fine actress if medicine had not been her calling. "There is nothing of the sham, the hypocritical, about Mary T. Martin Sloop. She's as plain and simple and real as the mountains and the mountain people among whom she has lived the last half of her eighty years."

They talked more the next day in between interruptions by visitors who stopped in at her office, which had no door. She answered calls on the old crank telephone mounted on the wall and talked with the campus boiler man who needed to go to Morganton to purchase repair parts. She led the Blythes across the campus, stumbling once on a gravel path and skinning her knees in the fall. Nonetheless, that evening she presided over a reunion of the Crossnore Business School students and led the Blythes into the Cooper Building for the weekly square dance. "She hopped and cavorted in the rhythmical cadence of the mountain square dance until past eleven o'clock," Blythe wrote.

Blythe returned again and again to the campus as he gathered Sloop's stories. She spoke strictly from memory, jumbling a few dates and names and omitting some experiences that still drew pain, such as her broken friendship with McCoy Franklin. A few years earlier, she had scotched plans for a Crossnore employee reunion for fear of opening old wounds. Blythe captured some of the sessions on a recorder. He filled his notebooks with notes. Finally, he began organizing her stories into a narrative that became the book, *Miracle in the Hills: The Lively Personal Story of a Woman Doctor's Forty-Year Crusade in the Mountains of North Carolina*.

The title would give rise to countless other combinations of the words "miracle" and "Crossnore," but it was not the first choice of Blythe or the publisher. It was adopted after a dozen or more alternatives had been discarded. Among those on the list were *A Woman Doctor in the Hills*, *Faith in the Hills*, *A Doctor's Crusade*, *Faith Comes High*,

The town of Crossnore in the 1950s. The campus is up the hill to the left.

and *A Mover of Mountains*. Blythe offered *Sidesaddle Doctor: Mary Martin Sloop, Genius of Crossnore Mountain School*, but his editor said he didn't want Sloop's book confused with another that was titled *Horse and Buggy Doctor*. Besides, he said, this story had far more dimensions than medicine.

Miracle in the Hills was released on Sloop's eightieth birthday, March 9, 1953. A first run of ten thousand copies, sent primarily to regional outlets, quickly sold out. Another printing was ordered. Sales continued to grow, especially after CBS broadcaster Edward R. Murrow mentioned the book on his television show and Charlotte pastor George Heaton did the same on his syndicated radio program. North Carolina's newly elected Republican congressman, Charles R. Jonas of Lincolnton, took an autographed copy to President Dwight D. Eisenhower. It was promoted on sixty-five ABC television stations. Paul Green, a 1949 graduate of Crossnore High School—he was one of the boys who lived in Sloop's "Fresh Air Camp"—was sitting in a movie theater in San Diego with a group of fellow sailors when he saw Cross-nore, Mary Sloop, and his old campus featured in a newsreel.

Blythe was midway through his work on the book when Mary Sloop was hospitalized early in 1952 after she suffered a heart attack. Her illness received little notice outside the immediate community. She subsequently reported in the *Bulletin* that she suffered from "excessive fatigue." She said she planned to be back in the office in time to register two hundred students for the fall semester. In truth, Sloop was in bed for months and wasn't even allowed to deal with the stacks of mail that piled up on her desk.

One disappointing consequence of her long period of recovery was being unable to attend the graduation exercises at the University of North Carolina in Chapel Hill, where she was to have received an honorary degree. She told Chancellor Robert B. House that because of her family's connection with the school in the 1850s, it pained her deeply to decline. Her mother would have been especially pleased. "I can just see how her eyes would beam if she could realize that her daughter had been honored by her beloved University," she wrote.

Nine years earlier, in 1943, she did receive an honorary doctor of laws degree from the Woman's College of the university (later the University of North Carolina at Greensboro). In 1942, Davidson College presented her with its Algernon Sydney Sullivan award "for rendering service to the life of the state and the community."

Sloop's heart attack brought home just how essential she was to the day-to-day operation of the school, especially its finances. Once the flow of letters from her office stopped, the school's income went into decline. Later in the summer, when she was allowed to resume some duties, Sloop sent a letter to parents who expected to enroll pupils in the fall of 1952 that told them of a deficit. As a result, everyone would be expected to pay—or promise to pay—the six-dollar weekly charge for room and board. She encouraged parents of older children to help them get summer jobs and save money to offset their school expenses. She also offered to set up special hours for parents at the Sales Store, where they could buy clothing for their children rather than pay higher prices at a regular retail store.

She sounded almost desperate when she asked every reader of

the *Bulletin* to send in a dollar. If all the subscribers had responded, it would have provided more than enough to offset the drop in donations and given Sloop the $10,000 she needed to finish the dormitory building for the Middle Boys, the one she wanted dedicated in Roadman Hollander's name. The *Bulletin* was going out to thirty-five thousand readers every quarter. It continued to be tightly packed with Sloop's chatty accounts of life on campus, as well as her appeals—which seemed more urgent now—for money to finish ongoing projects. The appeal did bring in an extra $8,000, which went to pay off an outstanding $10,000 loan used to buy building materials.

Mary Sloop made good on her promise to be back in the administration building in time for the fall enrollment, but instead of her usual location in a chair behind her desk, she was in a hospital bed that had been moved into an adjacent room.

12
End of an Era

In the 1920s, Crossnore School provided room and board for students whose daily commute to the classroom was difficult, if not impossible, because of bad roads and iron-cold weather. ·

A decade later, in the 1930s, most of the students living on the campus were there out of necessity. Two-thirds of them were orphans who had nowhere else to go.

By the 1950s, Mary Sloop was trying to cope with yet another kind of challenge. Now, most of the students came from broken homes. Of the 213 children enrolled in the spring of 1953, only 57, less than a fourth, came from what she considered a "normal home" with a mother and father living together. She was dealing with what she called the "Dreaded Ds: divorce, desertion, and death."

"Whoever heard in times gone by," Sloop told her correspondents in 1953, "of a mountain mother or father deserting the children, even babies, to go out and enjoy the lure of bright lights and a well-paying job. We never did—but we do now.

"And then the home breaks up and there's a move to town—even a big commercial center, a crowded apartment—in a degrading location—for who wants to rent to a lot of children—especially with one parent."

During the war, factory jobs had attracted workers off the mountains to towns and cities in the Carolinas. In the postwar years, southern industry continued to hum. Textile mills in the Piedmont and furniture plants in the foothills sought out new sources of labor. Production in the mica mines in the mountains picked up. Steady paychecks were more readily available than they had been at any time most could remember. Fathers and single mothers found jobs in factories within an hour or two from their homes. A sign of the times, perhaps, was a preschool program that Sloop began in 1950. It was discontinued when she became ill and the school was short of money. She tried it again in 1953 and had twelve children attending classes in the basement of the Middle Girls Dormitory.

Sloop was not critical of those seeking work off the mountain. In fact, she saw Crossnore as a place where parents raised in Avery County and working elsewhere could send their children while they improved their financial situation. She once commented: "We read and hear so much about hydrogen bombs, and they seem very real to us because so many of our children have parents who are working at the big South Carolina plant [the federal government's Savannah River facility near Augusta, Georgia]. The parents stay there and work and send their children to us, and we feel like we are being loyal citizens, helping our country to make hydrogen bombs."

"A working mother, a widow, was so glad to find a boarding school for her two boys," Sloop wrote. The mother told her, "I'll know that they are not on the streets while I'm away at work."

Rebecca Vance and three siblings came to Crossnore in 1948 from their home in Tennessee. Their father was a structural steel worker who followed jobs as they became available around the country. Rather than move the family from town to town and the children from school to school, the Vances followed the advice of a family member who knew of Sloop and Crossnore and enrolled their children there. Rebecca was eight years old when she came. She stayed until she graduated from high school.

The postwar years brought new challenges and new opportunities. Crossnore was no longer the isolated community it had once been. The county had paved highways that brought tourists and summer residents to the mountains. The visitors brought money to spend at the Homespun House and the Sales Store. New restaurants and the hotels in the area provided summer jobs for Crossnore girls who had

Students sat in assigned seats for their meals in the dining hall, where houseparents enforced Mary Sloop's rules governing proper decorum at table.

learned how to serve tables in the campus dining hall. Visitors also began to take an interest in helping Crossnore. Sloop got an unexpected visit late in the summer of 1956 from a golfer at Linville whose game had been cancelled on account of rain. "What do you need most?" he asked her. She told him that new tile to improve the sanitary conditions in the dining room loomed large. "We talked. He left. The tile has just been put down, and he paid the bill."

Avery County built a new elementary school on the campus in 1951. A low, one-story brick classroom replaced the early frame school building. (The older schoolhouse that had produced Crossnore's first high school graduates in 1921 was still standing but not in use.) Improvements in public schools in the county prompted some to question Crossnore's unique public-private partnership, with the two-hundred-plus children living in the dormitories and attending the public school without charge. Sloop rallied her allies to defend the arrangement before the state Board of Education, which had been asked to determine the number of out-of-state students in the dormitories who were attending Avery County schools.

The question about tuition arose when special legislation was required to settle the property lines after the old school building was demolished and the land was to be returned to Crossnore School Incorporated. Sloop blamed the intrusion on "some restless citizen" in a letter to B. B. Dougherty, who, with his brother, had founded what was then Appalachian State Teacher's College (later Appalachian State University).

About 10 percent of the campus children came from out of state, she told Dougherty, many of them from homes just across the state line in the mountains of Tennessee. They enrolled at Crossnore because the school was more accessible than their own schools. She said Tennessee authorities accepted North Carolina children under the same conditions. There were other children on the campus whose families owned property in Avery County but were living temporarily out of the county. "They don't want to keep their children in those crowded schools and trailer camps where the influence is so bad, and so they send them here," she wrote. "In nearly every instance the children are from broken homes."

Sloop asked Dougherty to intervene on her behalf. She said it was impossible for Crossnore's boarders to pay an additional charge to attend the public school when many could not afford the weekly room-and-board charge of six dollars. In addition, she warned that if the public school excluded the Crossnore children in its annual census, the state contribution to the local school system would suffer. Most important for Sloop, however, was the education of mountain children. She said she could replace the out-of-state children with children placed there by welfare workers elsewhere in North Carolina, "but somehow or other I would like to have a hand in developing the children whose parents are from the mountains, and most likely the children will come back to the mountains to live as opportunities for jobs open up. We came here to take children from the mountains as nearly as possible, and because they live on the other side of the state line doesn't bother me a bit."

As always, there was a constant struggle to maintain the delicate balance of Crossnore's finances. The school continued to barter with local farmers for vegetables and produce, but Sloop had to find money to buy dining room tables after a health inspector disqualified the homemade tables because they had cracks between the boards that captured bits of food. She also had to discontinue using raw milk—bought at an annual savings of $2,800 from a dairy operated on the school's farm—after state health inspectors condemned the sanitary conditions at the dairy. Pasteurized milk would have to come from a commercial dairy. Due to the school's limited budget, that meant milk could be served only at breakfast and lunch.

Sloop heard from some who believed that in the "modern" age Crossnore was no longer necessary. A "Mrs. X, a had-been friend of

At the close of school each year, the students competed in a variety of contests, including a race made from homemade carts.

Crossnore," wrote her to ask why Crossnore was needed when "every child in North Carolina now lives within reach of a good public school and has free transportation to it." A boarding school was simply an anachronism.

"She may know about roads and public schools," Sloop wrote in a special broadside titled "Why Crossnore School Inc.?" "Many, many children do not have the privileges and rights every child deserves. Many apply for entrance that must be turned away. We try to study case histories and choose those who need us most. Every type of broken home is represented on the campus."

She told her friends about a welfare worker who arrived on campus one day with four children whom she had found living under a rock ledge with their mother. On another day, a neighbor brought children who had been living in the cab of a pickup truck because they weren't safe inside the house with a drunken father. Another boy told her, "I can't go home, my daddy is an alcoholic."

The future of young women remained her special concern. Seeing girls leave school to marry troubled her as much as it had when she first heard about Hepsy. "We count it a red letter year when no high school senior marries during the spring term," she wrote. "That's a catastrophe in our eyes." She encouraged teenage girls to stay in school after graduation and complete the business courses, hoping they would put off marriage until they were at least eighteen or twenty years of age.

Crossnore now confronted problems that didn't always respond to the usual remedies offered by a caring houseparent or a visit to "Miz Sloop." Sloop learned from a teacher that one young girl was having difficulty reading from the blackboard. She arranged for her to be given a thorough vision examination, and the doctor prescribed some medication. When the doctor examined her again, however, he discovered that her vision problems were emotional, not physical. "If the child felt completely wanted, the difficulty would clear itself," Sloop wrote.

Sloop responded to the challenges with all the energy and vigor that she could muster, but it took a toll on her health. In the early months of 1956, she spent another two months in the hospital. She told friends not to worry, and indeed, she rebounded, saying she was "stronger than she had felt for year, and much more spry." Even as she recuperated, she embraced every child with love and compassion and a determination to provide a haven, even when the budget was stretched beyond the limits. The trustees told her not to obligate the campus for any further loans, so she borrowed money in her own name that was necessary to pay the bills. They had told her not to ask for new buildings, but she took seriously her promise to replace those poorly constructed dormitories that now suffered from twenty years of wear and tear.

The dormitories were always full to overflowing. The student population on campus never dropped below 200 during the 1950s, and most years there were more than 210 students living on the campus. The need for more and better housing remained an urgent plea, usually accompanied by a list of items, from shoes to sewing machines, that could fill a full page. The work proceeded slowly, but finally a dormitory for the middle boys—the Roadman Dormitory—and an extension for the big boys were completed. As soon as a new space became available, ostensibly to relieve overcrowding, it was quickly filled.

The Atwell Cottage was finished in 1956. Half the $20,000 needed for the new building had been donated by Mr. and Mrs. Charles S. Atwell of Port Arthur, Texas. Mrs. Atwell was a founding member of a DAR chapter there. Her husband was a top executive at a firm that had built Liberty ships during the war. When he asked Sloop to see plans for the building, she wrote him to say, "Alas, we never spend money on blue prints. That much money would almost finance the foundations. So we use our pencil and ruler and build by that." He looked at her rough drawings, made some suggestions, and work began.

Atwell was different from most of the other campus buildings, and was a sign of new ideas circulating among child care professionals. The Sloop dormitory, dedicated just five years earlier, had followed the old design perfected over the years. It was big and boxy, a Spartan two stories of small rooms with a basement level for a study hall. The new building was low and long, more closely resembling the popular ranch-style houses going up in new suburban neighborhoods in Charlotte, Asheville, and Greensboro. It was designed to be a home for twenty-four boys ages nine, ten, and eleven.

The youngsters moved there from the Reed Dormitory, which had been considered a godsend when it was opened in the late 1930s. It had not been built to last. Over the years, the chestnut bark on the exterior had deteriorated, leaving the interior framing exposed. Further damage had been caused by boys using the side of the building for target practice with small rocks. Sloop caught one rock thrower, who allowed that he did not mean to hit the building, but rather a companion who ducked.

A year after Atwell was opened, work began on a home for the nine-to-eleven-year-old girls. It was paid for by the children of Mrs. William Henry Belk. The new cottage gave Sloop the opportunity to at last recognize the hard work of her good friend and DAR companion. Sloop had wanted to name the administration building in her honor, but Mrs. Belk had declined. The new cottage was more appropriate.

Building a dormitory for the girls had been on Mrs. Belk's mind for years. "We must plan for the children at Crossnore," she once

The Roadman Dormitory was named for a boy who inspired the campus with his enthusiasm and singing voice before his untimely death from appendicitis at the age of twelve.

told a friend, "for they are our responsibility." She was involved in many charities, but Crossnore held a special place among her interests. When the Daughters arrived in the state for the school tour, they stopped first in Asheville for a luncheon sponsored by Mrs. Belk at the Biltmore Forest Country Club. She then led the bus and a caravan of large sedans up the mountain to Crossnore. There were always large boxes of clothing, some of it shopworn merchandise from the Belk stores, stored on the side porch of her spacious home in Charlotte, ready for transport to Crossnore on her next visit.

The cost of the buildings had more than doubled from Sloop's days of severe economy. Materials were more expensive, and workers' wages were higher. The latest buildings also were more complicated in their construction than the earlier ones, so fewer students could be enlisted to help.

Campus jobs remained an important component of the Crossnore day, with a few adjustments. Boys and girls fourteen or older put in fifteen hours a week, but students under the age of fourteen worked an hour a week for each year of age. Older students helped in the dormitories of the younger children, and girls in the sewing room mended clothes. Older boys handled the heavier chores. Sloop begged for a potato peeler to relieve the younger children of one of their chores and give them time for play. A mechanical peeler also meant that less of the meat of a potato would be thrown out with the peel. The young ones were additionally responsible for raking the leaves on campus, keeping the gravel trails neat, and combing the campus for trash on Saturdays. Mrs. Obie Johnson promised a whole cake to the boy who delivered the largest bag of trash.

From time to time former students stopped by the campus for a visit. Some had remained in military service, while others had found their place in civilian life. Sloop knew graduates who had become auto mechanics, ministers, teachers, lawyers, librarians, nurses (lots of them), farmers trained in advanced agriculture under the GI Bill, stenographers, artists, and writers. Some had done well enough to begin making their own contributions for Crossnore scholarships, sending $50 to $150 a year to assist someone like themselves.

Others had continued their education beyond high school with loans from the DAR that Sloop arranged and secured with her signature. It troubled her deeply when these loans went into default. "I hate to think that I have failed to instill enough principle in them to have made those of them who are able, pay their debts," she said in a note accompanying a payment on a delinquent loan.

For Sloop, the children at Crossnore were more likely to inspire than disappoint. She was approached one day by a youngster who had received six dollars from his "scholarship lady" that was to go toward a pair of shoes. He asked Sloop if he could mend his old shoes for two dollars and spend the remaining four on a Bible. The encounter led Sloop to ask her friends to start a Bible fund.

At the award ceremony in New York, someone had estimated that three thousand children had been on the Crossnore campus since the early days. There was really no way to tell how many had been on the campus at one time or another. Twenty-five years of records had burned in the fire that destroyed the administration building, and even if they had survived they would have been incomplete. With many children on the campus for only a year or two and then gone, an accurate accounting of alumni was impossible. Some of those who spent much of their childhood on the campus kept in touch with Sloop, but there were many more who grew into adulthood eager to put their years at Crossnore behind them. They didn't want to be reminded of hard times when they were without a home, suffering from the loss of one parent or both and sent to live with strangers.

The stigma of living in what most people in North Carolina considered an orphanage became attached to the lives of Crossnore children as soon as they arrived on the campus. "We were so close with one another, but we didn't know about one another's backgrounds," recalled Jane Johnson, one of the twin daughters of Mr. and Mrs. Obie Johnson. Although her parents worked on the campus, she lived in the dormitory with the other children. "People didn't talk about what brought them there," she remembered. "Everybody had a past, but you didn't talk about it."

Quite often, children arrived on the campus sullen, angry, and suspicious. Sloop wrote of one girl whom she immediately picked out of a group of newcomers. A neighbor had arranged for her to come to Crossnore, and the girl was not happy about it. Sloop explained: "She fears others will be better dressed, they will know one another and she's a stranger, they know what to do next and will forget to tell her, so she will blunder. She has lost her sense of security, and our first duty and privilege is to build that up. To remind the other girls to do it."

The living quarters prepared for Mary Sloop in the administration building remained a combination office and counseling room. Children with problems often ended up there for quiet talks, during which this kindly, gentle woman would tell them about hundreds of others who had come before them and left to enjoy full and happy lives. She eased their fears like a loving grandmother, encouraging and reminding them of their worth as they played with a box of blocks she kept under her bed.

Sloop believed one remedy for broken homes was building strong families with lessons that began at an early age. She talked to friends about opening a practice house where teenagers could get a taste of what was involved in running a household. It could be a laboratory for the exercises that were part of the standard home economics courses. "Girls marry too young," she said. "They don't know how to meet the demands of everyday life, to prevent or avoid divorce, separation or desertion." These were the "hot beds of juvenile delinquency." Her solution: "Let's prevent. It's better than trying to cure."

Boys needed lessons, too. She confronted one teenager who said he didn't need to learn how to iron. "That's just the point, son. You think a man doesn't need to know about such things, but I'm not raising just men, I'm training husbands, and if you do your own ironing you will know what it means for your wife to have the family washing to do." Keeping themselves and their rooms in good order was the first step toward the young men developing the ability to provide for a wholesome household.

Over the years, Sloop related details about virtually every aspect of campus life in her letters to supporters and in the newsletters that were going out to nearly forty thousand readers in the 1950s. One topic that she never addressed was campus romances, and the consequences when teenagers got too amorous. Sloop's expression of delight in not having girls marry before graduation was perhaps one way of saying that no unexpected pregnancies had occurred. In the 1950s, public schools did not allow pregnant girls to remain in class. If a girl did become pregnant, it was handled very discreetly. "People in the know kept confidences," Jane Johnson said. "I am sure it happened, but I can't remember."

Romances were commonplace at Crossnore, even within the limits of its strict rules of behavior and dress, and despite houseparents who kept a close watch on their girls. A young man could walk his sweetheart home from Sunday evening church programs and maybe linger for a while around the front door of her dormitory until she was called inside. Rebecca Vance met her future husband, Tudor, while she was living on campus. They would race ahead of others walking in a group back to the campus from a movie or off-campus event so they might have a few minutes alone at the door, where Tudor could sneak a kiss before the others arrived.

Courtships between Crossnore students and boys and girls from the town developed during the day at school and carried over to the campus. The town boys often attended the Saturday night square dances. Their presence created tension with the dormitory boys, who were very protective of their Crossnore "sisters."

The girls bore the greatest burden under the rules for proper behavior. Slacks could be worn during bad weather, but only those that were tailored for girls. Skirts were allowed at folk dancing practice. Housemothers in the girls' dormitories were told to confiscate any boys' jeans they found girls wearing. Shorts were prohibited for any girl over the age of ten, and every girl was required to have at least one nice dress for Sunday services and social occasions. Boys over the age of fifteen could smoke cigarettes, but smoking was prohibited for girls, as was leaving campus or entering a car without permission or a chaperone. No one was allowed to chew gum.

The rules reflected the mores of America in the 1950s as much as the Calvinist leanings of Mary Sloop. Crossnore was not a religious institution, although it was organized with a serious religious purpose. Over the years, virtually everyone connected to the place had made their faith a part of campus life, either by teaching or by example. For Sloop, there was always a prayerful dimension to her regular appearances at the dining hall, even when she was talking about table manners or reciting the best lines from the movie she had seen that week in Asheville. Attendance at Sunday services and at least one evening youth program remained a requirement for every student. Yet there was little outward evidence of the Christian underpinnings on a campus that had been built on faith.

Since the early days, the houseparents had mobilized the students for the weekly walk to Sunday services. For those attending the Presbyterian church, the walk over and back had always been a discouragement. Rainy days and knee-deep snow made it all the more difficult to maintain the schedule of religious activities that Sloop considered essential to a complete education. She had experimented with alternative locations for religious services—the gymnasium and the playroom of one of the dormitories had been tried—but neither provided any "spirituality."

In the latter part of 1953, she began writing about the need for a chapel on the campus. "We have so long wanted and needed one—a real Chapel for the weekday and Sunday afternoon and evening inspirational activities for our boys and girls,—activities that develop character, change hearts, and teach our youngsters to go home and do likewise." She pledged a share of the royalties from her best-selling book toward the construction costs, and she pleaded with her friends to help make it reality. The book had by that time gone into multiple printings, and circulation expanded around the world, with translations into Spanish, French, Hindi, and Japanese.

The spot she chose for the chapel was the site of the old consolidated school that had been abandoned by the country school board in 1951. It was the most prominent spot on the campus. Unlike most of the buildings she had erected over forty years, the chapel was designed with patience and care, and it embraced a style that had come to be associated with Crossnore. She wanted it built with stones from the Linville River, just like the Presbyterian Church, her husband's hospital, the Homespun House, the sewing room, and the entrances to the dining hall and the Cooper Building.

By the time she announced her dream of a chapel, she had already set aside a small amount in a separate fund. It grew slowly, but by the fall of 1955 she was able to tell John R. Weaver, who now supervised the school's construction projects, to begin work. The seed money for materials and labor had not come from one generous benefactor but from a variety of donors, many of whom recognized that this was probably Sloop's last project. One gift came from the widower of "an interested friend." She got another from a young man whose donation was a memorial to his mother. She didn't have all she needed in hand—the total cost would be more than $43,000—but just as she had so many times before, Sloop moved ahead, remarking, "These donors had faith, and believed the chapel was needed and could be built, and why should we be 'of little faith?'"

Architects called it a "craftsman-style church building" due to its use of native wood and stone. There were Gothic touches in the lancet-arch window and door openings, as well as the stained wood interior. All in all, it was a simple design: a shallow entrance foyer

The last building that Mary Sloop added to the campus was a chapel built to honor her husband, Eustace. It was faced with stone from the Linville River and dedicated in 1958.

opened into the sanctuary under a high, vaulted ceiling that could seat about eight hundred people on wooden pews. By springtime, the interior walls were up, and atop the roof was an octagonal belfry mounted by a copper cross. Inside of it would go one of the bells that Sloop had collected when she was thumping for a campus bell tower. Sloop tracked down chestnut boards—hard to find since the blight took the tree from American forests—for use as interior paneling. The side windows were of colored glass, which softened the sunlight and added a warm glow to the chestnut interior. The exterior remained rough wood until April, when temperatures warmed sufficiently for rock to be harvested from the river.

The chapel was dedicated on October 16, 1956, in honor of Mary's quiet, steadfast, and attentive husband, Eustace. One of the late Alexander Johnson's sons, the Reverend Monte Johnson, delivered a message entitled, "An Altar unto God." An organ given by national society officers of the Children of the American Revolution accompanied the hymn, "My Faith Looks Up to Thee." A prominent window was a gift of the National Officers Club of the DAR in honor of Mrs. Helen Pouch, Sloop's long-time friend.

Indeed, the chapel was Mary Sloop's final building campaign. The chapel proved as useful as she had hoped. Children gathered there for choir, and the entire campus attended Sunday vespers services at 7:30 p.m. It was used for special events, including presentations by special campus visitors. One evening in the fall of 1958, the guest speaker was Clarence Taylor. He was one of the boys who had lived in the loft of the grist mill, and he had returned in the 1930s to supervise construction on campus buildings.

Mary and Eustace Sloop were both in declining health. Doctor was hospitalized in 1958. A year later, Mary suffered another heart attack, this one more serious than before. Neither would return to the active lives that had sustained them for more than eighty years. Sloop continued to talk about Crossnore's future, dreaming of a day when the campus would have a cultural center where mountain arts and music could thrive.

Eustace died on February 6, 1961. His wife remained gravely ill. Her daughter, Emma, who had assumed her father's duties at the hospital, said she had difficulty recognizing people. She died as winter closed tightly around Crossnore on January 13, 1962, just a little more than fifty-one years after she and her husband had arrived at the tiny mountain crossroads to begin their medical practice.

Mary Sloop and her beloved husband were not people of pretense. They both had lived simply and modestly, accumulating little in the way of wealth. The doctor had always charged his patients a trivial amount for his services. Many had never paid him anything at all, even though his care saved their lives. He did sell his interest in the Linville Power Company in 1949, when a power cooperative began consolidating electric power systems in the mountains. The money may have helped him pay for a large black Lincoln that was demolished when a former Crossnore boy crashed an airplane into it as it stood, parked, beside the Crossnore Presbyterian Church. The pilot, a 1949 graduate named Wimpy Holloway, emerged unin-

Eustace and Mary Sloop in the 1950s.

jured. The doctor was said to have told him, "Wimpy, you are late for church." Photos of the crash were published in national magazines.

The only income his wife drew from her years in building the community was a few thousand dollars in royalty checks that came from her publisher, and she put half of that into the construction of the campus chapel. She bought her clothes at the Sales Store, just like many of her neighbors. When she was ill and taking her meals from her bed in the administration building, she would neatly fold and return the waxed paper that covered the tray. She expected it to be used for her next meal.

She seldom had money in her purse. Martha Guy succeeded her father as a member of the board of trustees in 1955. At the conclusion of the meeting one year, Mary Sloop invited her to join in a luncheon with Mrs. Belk at the Eseeola Lodge at Linville. On the way out the door, Sloop warned her that she never carried cash, and she was sure Mrs. Belk, one of the wealthiest women in the state, had none with her either. Martha Guy paid for lunch.

Both Mary and Eustace Sloop were passionate about their community and devoted to their faith. They never faltered in allegiance to either one. Their funerals were held at Crossnore Presbyterian Church. Tommy Hartley, the new music teacher on campus, was asked to play the organ for Mary's service, which took place on a blustery winter's day. He was told Sloop had asked for a simple service, with no eulogy, and he drew his selections from the Presbyterian hymnal. Children from the campus rose from their places in the pews to talk about the influence Mary Sloop had had upon their lives. Then the older boys carried her casket to the grave site in the church's cemetery on the hill overlooking the valley, where she was buried beside her husband.

13
What Now?

Robert Woodside was a tall, serious man who, even in his late forties, looked as lean and fit as he had when he was a two-miler on the Davidson College track team in the early 1930s. He had spent his adult life in Crossnore, where he was a teacher in the high school and a houseparent for the older boys, who now called him "Pop." Woodside was such a mainstay on the campus by 1959 that the Crossnore board of trustees asked him to take over the campus operations a few months before Mary Sloop's last, and most serious, heart attack.

Crossnore's future without Mary Sloop had been a topic of conversation for ten years or more. In the late 1940s, she brushed such talk aside, saying the Lord would provide. She dismissed as too expensive the recommendation of outsiders that she share the burden of running the campus, which she continued to do almost single-handedly even when she was nearly eighty years old. Then came her first heart attack in 1952 and a subsequent hospitalization three years later. She worked on a reduced schedule from a bed in living quarters arranged for her in the campus administration building. Various assistants picked up some of her duties. It was only on the insistence of her doctor—her daughter, Emma—that she finally accepted Woodside as "assistant business manager," a position he held as her health continued to decline. After her death, Woodside was named executive director.

Sloop's death changed everything. At the same time, it changed nothing. The loss of the founder meant the campus was without its most dynamic presence, its chief fund-raiser, publicist, advocate, and, most importantly, emissary to the DAR. Wealthy benefactors considered Sloop a dear friend and trusted supplicant. She was the campus counselor and confessor—for students and staff—as well as the chief administrator, planner, and the only one who could correct the behavior of wayward youths. There was no one else associated with Crossnore who possessed her range of talents. She could brow-beat a stubborn tradesman into delivering goods on time and in her next breath convince the bank to lend a few thousand dollars more on the strength of her smile.

Woodside, however, was savvy enough to know that he was no Mary Martin Sloop, and he was not about to try to fill her shoes. He told a newspaper reporter that life on the campus would continue as before. Sloop had talked about building an auditorium with seat-ing for fifteen hundred to serve as a center for music and dramatic productions reflecting mountain life and culture. That would have to wait. Woodside said he wasn't going to promote anything new: "We would rather improve what we have for our present number of stu-dents than look to new things."

Launching bold new initiatives was not in Woodside's nature. When he had free time, which was rare, he preferred to stretch out and read a book. Not long after he came to Crossnore, Sloop had told him to get busy with the laying of a foundation for a new build-ing. When he protested he had never built anything, she turned to him and snapped, "Well, get out there and find out." He was a teach-er whose interests ran from social studies to Spanish. Until he left for service in the navy in World War II, he had run the campus print shop. Not only was he an unlikely successor for Sloop, he was bur-dened with duties beyond the campus, as well. At about the same time that he was named executive director, he became the princi-pal of Crossnore High School, a job that left him with but one or two hours a day to deal with campus affairs.

As a result, the campus would operate for much of the Sixties on the momentum, the methods, and the model of the Sloop years, with only minor adjustment from Woodside or the board of trustees.

The years would be difficult as the board struggled to maintain the equilibrium of an institution whose mission appeared to have run its course. Residential care in places like Crossnore was in decline, while less expensive options like foster homes were on the rise. For the first time in Crossnore's forty years of operation, the trustees would have to determine what sort of institution it would be, rather than just follow the lead of Mary Sloop.

The trustees had altered the charter in the 1930s to declare that Crossnore was a child care institution with the hope of gaining financial support from the Duke Endowment, which provided aid to orphanages in the Carolinas. That never materialized, as Crossnore did not qualify. No orphanage accepted the payment of tuition for its residents or closed its doors during the summer months when public schools were not in session. Other institutions accepted responsibility for the children placed in their care. Crossnore children were treated more like guests, free to come and go, than as wards of the management. Only on very rare occasions did Sloop assume guardianship of children. If children misbehaved, they were sent on their way.

Crossnore remained a unique public-private arrangement. It had no sponsor like the children's homes run by the Baptists, the Methodists, and the Presbyterians. It was not a state institution, although some uninformed outsiders believed it was a correctional facility for juveniles. It only indirectly received state aid from parents or guardians who qualified for Aid to Families with Dependent Children and used the money to pay tuition. Stripped to its essentials, Crossnore in the 1960s was what it had been since the 1920s: a place that provided room and board and supervision for students while they attended a nearby public school.

After forty years of Sloop's constant fund-raising and tub-thumping, Crossnore had appreciable resources to offer room and board at free or reduced rates to students whose families couldn't afford to pay. The school's two hundred and fifty acres of land and the nearly two dozen buildings scattered about the campus were worth an estimated $461,000 in 1962. The Sales Store was a profitable enterprise that produced about a third of the money needed to cover the annual operating expenses. And there was income from tu-

Until a proper bell tower was built in the 1950s, campus activities were regulated by an old bell donated by a Pennsylvania farm family that was mounted on top of a campus building.

ition, which was raised to ten dollars a week in 1962, the year Mary Sloop died. Enrollment was reduced to below two hundred in the early 1960s. The lower census allowed Woodside to close the Fleshman Dormitory, which had been used for the youngest girls and was in bad repair.

The DAR remained essential to Crossnore's continued financial health. Bequests from wills of Daughters helped Woodside balance the books each year. Plus, Crossnore was due hundreds of thousands of dollars in the years to come from friends who had included bequests to Crossnore School Incorporated in their wills. Not long before Sloop's death, she learned that Mrs. Isabelle Weeks had left $94,000 in securities and cash to be used for student college loans. That fund would double in value in ten years. The largest legacy was $439,000 that was sitting in a trust established after the death of Mrs. Rhoda Barkley Bayles of Pennsylvania.

The Bayles bequest had caused Sloop no small amount of concern. When the will was made public in 1956, she stirred from her sickbed to explain that the money was not immediately available, and current donors should not close their pocketbooks. She emphasized to friends that the money was in an endowment for use by Mrs. Bayles's daughter as long as she lived. In a note to friends, Sloop wrote, "She is 52 years old, and suddenly has decided to marry for the first time, which may rejuvenate her quite a bit. When it does come to us, the will decrees that it shall be used to build a building on the campus, which will honor Mr. and Mrs. Bayles, the donors. Imagine our little campus with a third of a million dollar building on it—but our descendants will have to decide that!"

As Woodside assumed the management of the campus, he had a reservoir of experienced staff members to draw upon. Many of them had been in their jobs for some time. One of the relatively new staffers was a dean of students, a position created in the 1950s to assist Sloop in supervision of the houseparents. For a while, the dean was a former teacher named Blanche Welch, whose icy stare and stern commands were quickly obeyed. Mrs. Bonnie Coffey Rash managed the school's finances, a job she had perfected under Sloop's tutelage for twenty years. She had worked so closely with Sloop that she continued answering Sloop's mail after her death, virtually channeling her absent mentor to old friends. Rash even wore her hair in the same style that Mary Sloop had favored. Mrs. Obie Johnson remained as the dietician in the dining hall, and her husband handled odd jobs on the campus. Fern Monson had joined the staff in 1960 to handle fund-raising and public relations after the founder was no longer able to travel.

Ossie Phillips was one of the best-known of the Crossnore weavers. In 1998, she received the North Carolina Folk Heritage Award from the North Carolina Arts Council. Her specialty was baby blankets.

The most profound staffing change occurred in the spring of 1960, when Mrs. Newbern Johnson, "Aunt Newbie," retired from the Weave Room. Widowed for some years, she moved to Raleigh after marrying widower George Coggin, the man who had directed the Smith-Hughes money to Crossnore's weaving department. Ossie Phillips, Mrs. Johnson's assistant since 1939, took her place and was the campus representative who made the annual pilgrimage to Washington, D.C., with woven goods for sale at the DAR's Continental Congress.

Crossnore's student population remained much as it had been in the 1950s. Like the young inhabitants of other institutions, two-thirds of the children at Crossnore came from homes where there had been a breakdown in the family. Woodside depended on houseparents to help children through the most difficult times in their lives. Some children arrived as victims of abuse and neglect, cut off from their own kin and wanting only one thing—a stable home life in a familiar setting. Crossnore's answer was rigid rules of behavior that promoted good manners, proper decorum at the dining table, and an unyielding program of work and study. Family contact was kept to a minimum. Parents and family members were allowed to visit one Sunday a month. Housing was crowded. Professionals recommended that no more than twelve children be placed in a housing unit. At Crossnore, the dormitories held twice that number.

Crandle and Roland McClellan were a married couple in their late twenties with two boys of their own when they became houseparents in the aging Reed Dormitory in 1963. Woodside had been looking for houseparents when the campus night watchman told him about Roland's ability to manage the busload of children that he drove to the school each day. On the strength of that recommendation, Woodside hired the McClellans to look after twenty-four boys between the ages of ten and fourteen. Their sons lived in a room across the hall from their small apartment.

"Most of the kids were good kids after you could get them settled down after school started," Crandle McClellan recalled. The challenges were the children who had been placed at Crossnore by social workers, rather than family. "You had to explain that you are here to get a good education. You might not understand it yet, but when you get older you will be so glad that you studied and made good in life. Once you won their trust—that you wouldn't double cross as I call it—then, you have got good kids."

The McClellans were much like the other married couples and single men and women who served as surrogate parents over the years. Their wages were low—each received one hundred dollars a month—but they had a place to live and food to eat in a county where steady jobs remained hard to find. In the beginning, Crandle tried to manage academic courses of her own in the hope of getting her high school diploma, but looking after two dozen youngsters plus her own two children proved to be as great a load as she could bear.

Mary Sloop helped organize the Crossnore chapter of the Daughters of the American Revolution with eleven others in 1931. The DAR Chapter House was reconstructed in 1958–59 from the logs of a cabin built in 1904, and it stands on the campus across from the Sloop Chapel.

One of the old-timers they could count on for advice was Walter G. Jarvis, who was a teacher in the elementary school and the house-parent for the older boys. He had been on campus since 1948. Like the other men on campus, he was called "Pop" by his boys. Jarvis was one of Sloop's favorites. She had defended him in the early 1950s when some said the thirty twelve- and thirteen-year-olds he was responsible for didn't get to the showers often enough. At about the time the McClellans arrived on the campus, Jarvis had married another teacher. In 1965, he became the first North Carolina teacher to receive the Terry Sanford Award, named for the former governor in recognition of his innovative approach to teaching and counseling.

Two years after Sloop's death, Woodside told the trustees that Crossnore needed an executive director who could devote full attention to the management of the campus. The request weighed heavily on Martha Guy, the chair of the trustees. She had taken on the job after the death of Eustace Sloop. Mary Sloop had arranged her election to the board after her father's death in 1955, and she had been running the meetings ever since. She and Emma Fink, who had been elected to succeed her father, formed the Avery County contingent on the board.

Guy brought more than a local perspective to her efforts on behalf of Crossnore. She had grown up with the campus and the Sloops as topics of conversation at her family's dinner table. Doctor had treated her for ailments when she was young. She knew Crossnore's finances in and out and was sympathetic to Mary's missionary zeal. At the same time, she had a banker's eye, and she didn't cloud her judgment with sentimentality or the fog of legend in *Miracle in the Hills*. She knew Crossnore's bulldog of a leader irritated many with her single-mindedness. "A lot of people could not stand Mrs. Sloop," she said many years later. "She'd give them a good lecture if things weren't going well. A lot of people were afraid of her because she would do that."

Guy played a pivotal role and was well suited to the challenge ahead. She kept the campus connected with the local community and was a sounding board for Woodside and the staff. At the same time, she had earned the respect of a small but influential group of Charlotte businessmen who had joined the board in the late 1950s. They would be critical to Crossnore's future and weren't shy about prevailing on their wealthy friends for help.

For most of the board's first fifty years, the trustees were the close friends of the Sloops, and they always bent to her will. They apparently never reprimanded her, even after they voted to restrain her plans for buildings and drafts at the bank and she went ahead without their consent. Rather than seek out board members of substance and influence, Sloop preferred the ex officio representatives from the DAR and other members with long-time connections, such as former teachers R. Q. Bault and T. Russell Nunan, who shared her philosophy and beliefs. These old ties were important. In the late 1950s, one new member was Betty Bayley Gillen, who lived in Connecticut but who had maintained a connection with Sloop for nearly forty years.

The composition of the board began to change in 1957. This time, the new members included William Barnhardt and Frank Dowd of Charlotte. Barnhardt was a Presbyterian, civic leader, and very suc-

The management and some of the trustees of Crossnore School Incorporated in 1964, after the deaths of the Sloops. (Standing, left to right) Robert E. Woodside, S. Lambert Johnson, William H. Barnhardt, W. Frank Dowd, Tully Blair, E. P. Dameron, James J. Harris, Milligan S. Wise, and S. DeVane. (Seated, left to right) Mrs. Bonnie Rash, Mrs. Betty Bayley Gillen, Mrs. W. O. Geer, Mrs. A. B. Cornwell, Martha Guy, and Dr. Emma Sloop Fink.

cessful textile man. Dowd ran Charlotte Pipe and Foundry and was equally prominent in the city's affairs. He was the unexpected visitor from Linville who had stopped by in the mid-1950s when his golf game was rained out and asked Mary Sloop what she needed most. Three years later, Mrs. Belk's son, Tom, became a trustee. Soon, he was followed by other executives with connections to the region's wealth and power. Among them were Charlotte's James J. Harris, a businessman and real estate developer, and Ross Puette, a paperboard manufacturer, along with Newton textile mill owner and philanthropist J. W. Abernethy and John Harden of Greensboro, the North Carolina business establishment's favorite public relations man.

Woodside's appeal for a replacement went unanswered at first. Another year passed before two men from the Duke Endowment arrived at Crossnore to have a look at the place. Though Crossnore didn't qualify for endowment aid, the endowment's executive director, Marshall Pickens, was well-known by men like Barnhardt,

Dowd, and Belk. "That's the good old boy system working," said Robert Mayer II, who was then the endowment's director of child care services. He could think of no other reason why he and Pickens's assistant, B. G. McCall, were called on to visit Crossnore, assess the program, and make a report to the Crossnore board. They spent the day on the campus, talking with Woodside and Guy and generally looking around. Neither had been there before, nor did they know of its history. Mayer carried away a copy of *Miracle in the Hills* to read before he made a return visit. A month later, he spent two more days on the campus in conversation with staff members. His frank and concise report focused the trustees on the challenges ahead.

The campus was on autopilot, Mayer said, and there was no way Woodside could continue attending to his responsibilities at the high school and the affairs of the boarding department without endangering his health. As teacher, principal, and director of a campus with 160 children, he did not have enough time to deal with campus problems, or even to tell staff members they had done a good job. First and foremost, Crossnore needed a leader who could focus on the task at hand, hire qualified staff members, and prepare an operating budget—something Crossnore had never had.

The houseparents were doing as good a job as they could, and Mayer commended their efforts despite their lack of experience in group child care or training in managing youngsters with troubled lives. Woodside had a "sixth sense," Mayer said, for selecting good people to be responsible for the care of the children. In addition, Mayer said, the campus rules needed updating, and parental visitation had to be adjusted to suit the needs of the children, not the convenience of the staff. Discipline was to be administered with an understanding of the child and his or her ability to learn from mistakes.

Mayer also recommended a year-round program to offer children more continuity and security. He said the dislocation the children experienced during the holidays and summer was detrimental to their care, especially for those who did not have a family member to take them in. "They never learn to trust an adult," he wrote, "because they are aware that their stay is only temporary."

Mayer was especially disturbed by the condition of the campus

Students in the Crossnore music program sponsored a dance in the early 1960s that was held in the Allen Gymnasium. Photo courtesy of Tommy Hartley.

buildings. All the problems resulting from the expediency of Sloop's building program—large buildings that were put up fast and cheap—were evident. There were too many children in each building, leaving houseparents unable to pay attention to any individual child's needs. "There should be time for the houseparent to listen sympathetically as a child expresses his feelings; time devoted to help the child meet social expectations appropriate to his age and developmental level in such areas as cleanliness, duties, etc., time for the creation of a pleasant and orderly atmosphere in which the child can live."

Most of the buildings were simply worn out. The construction shortcuts taken years earlier on bathrooms and conveniences for residents meant the buildings had become unsafe and unsanitary. In some buildings, the bunk beds blocked windows that might be needed for escape in the event of a fire. With no drinking fountains available, each child was required to keep his own glass or cup to draw a drink of water from a faucet in the bathroom. Mayer noted: "These few items—

fire, substandard bathrooms, and lack of water—would not have occurred, had an architect's services been employed or if the State Board of Public Welfare had had an opportunity to review the plans."

Furthermore, Mayer wrote, "Crossnore has, for the past few years, been caring for a type of child quite different from that of twenty-five years ago, yet many of the methods and practices have not materially changed since then." Crossnore's residents now were even more likely to come from homes broken by Sloop's "Dreaded Ds" and not be merely in need of help because of poverty.

Overcrowding and stark living conditions were nothing new. The most radical departure from the past in Mayer's recommendations was a suggestion that the campus shift to a year-round program. Except for a handful of children for whom a summer placement could not be found, the campus emptied at the close of school. From time to time, some of Sloop's friends would come and stay as guests for the summer in the apartments emptied by staff members. Woodside had managed to boost the school's income by making the campus facilities available to outside programs. A college coach conducted a basketball camp on campus in the summer of 1962, and the possibility of a summer drama program and a music camp like the Transylvania Music Camp at Brevard was explored. Some suggested the school offer its housing and dining facilities to businesses and organizations looking for a spot for a summer retreat. However, no one at Crossnore had considered maintaining the normal student body when the public school was not in session. To do so would have changed everything.

Mayer's report was followed a year later by another from architect Grayson Annas of Lenoir. His survey of the campus was even more devastating. There was not a single building on the campus that he could rate "as Class 'A', or non-combustible." Further, he reported, "many can not even be classified as safe for occupancy." There were dead-end corridors in the big dormitories like Roadman, which had rooms fifty feet from fire escapes. Hardly a single multistory building on the campus was in compliance with fire codes. Most buildings were in such poor repair that he advised they be replaced immediately.

In addition, the lighting was poor, even in spaces designed for study hall, and houseparents had only their apartments for use in counseling students. The heating system—one furnace for each building—was inefficient, as was the electrical service. Consequently, Crossnore was probably paying three times what it should for electricity. The unpaved walkways that meandered about the campus linking one building to the other resulted in mud and dirt being tracked into the buildings, thus creating a constant headache for housekeepers. The grade of the streets and roads was too steep, and they also needed paving. Annas proposed a complete redesign of the campus. "This campus should be designed, not as an institution, but rather as a beautiful and inviting home for the children who live here, so many of whom so desperately need a home."

The Avery County Board of Education finally forced the board to act in 1967 when it decided to close the high school at Crossnore and move all the students to a new consolidated high school located about eight miles away near Newland. Woodside informed the board that when the new school opened in 1968 he would no longer be able to manage the campus and continue teaching. He would then resign as executive director.

Any doubt about the threat of fire to the campus buildings was removed in February 1966 when a fire broke out in the upper-story apartment of the sewing room, where the janitor at the elementary school lived with his wife. This was one of the two buildings erected in the 1930s to replace the log Weave Room after it had burned. It stood less than a hundred yards away from Crossnore's fire-fighting equipment—war-surplus pumps and hoses that drew on a small pond at the campus entrance for a water supply. After the fire had been put out, the building was still standing, but interior floors and framing were heavily damaged. Annas called it "unsalvageable," even though the stone veneer, made of river rocks collected by that battalion of children on a cold October day thirty years earlier, was unaffected by the fire.

After the fire, the charred top story of the sewing room, which stood right at the campus entrance, was like a metaphor for Crossnore itself. The exterior looked strong, but the structure was weak, and its future was in doubt. With Woodside's departure from the administration building, the Sloop era had finally come to an end. The trustees organized a long-range planning committee, but its work had just begun.

Townspeople watched with anxiety. They had always reacted to every twitch and ache on the campus. Most took a proprietary interest in what happened on the hill above the town. The campus was the town's largest employer in a county where nearly 60 percent of the households lived below the poverty level at the beginning of the 1960s. The water and sewer system for the community was owned by Crossnore School Incorporated. The volunteer fire department got some of its equipment from the campus. Indeed, the campus and the hospital were all that kept Crossnore on the map. As a result, changes—or even talk of change—were regarded with suspicion and outright hostility. Even in her day, Mary Sloop had complained that local folks could react to decisions made on campus even before the trustees adjourned their annual meeting.

Many attitudes in Avery County—and living conditions, as well—really hadn't changed much since the Sloops arrived fifty years earlier. A recently completed study of Appalachia focused on the problems of the southern highlands, where poverty remained endemic and children were growing up in rough cabins with no running water and an outhouse in the back. Only 20 percent of the roads in the county were paved. The average education amounted to a little more than seven years of schooling. There was some stirring among a few farmers in the county who were turning their steep mountain pastures into fields planted with Christmas trees. It was a new crop that was just beginning to show some promise as a possible answer to the subsistence operations that had long characterized Avery agriculture. Even the romanticism of the mountain life that had captured McCoy Franklin's listeners in the 1920s remained vivid among tourists and others who weren't living near the edge of poverty. The director of an antipoverty program created in the mid-1960s to serve Avery and neighboring counties heard a middle-class resident talk nostalgically about the simple mountain life. "I don't know if she's tried it or not," said Ernest Eppley, the program's first director.

In the spring of 1968, Martha Guy announced that Crossnore's new director would be John M. Gatling, a native New Yorker who was then living in Asheville. He had been a corporate executive with the Johns-Manville Corporation, but for the previous decade he had worked at raising money for colleges and universities. Gatling and his wife were on the campus even before the last class at Crossnore High School had graduated. They moved into the burned-out sewing room, which had been repaired and renovated for their use. He planned to use his time that summer to prepare for the fall term.

He put the incoming class on notice that a new administration was in charge. In a letter to prospective students, Gatling promised "a completely new attitude and philosophy" in a terse, blunt letter to prospective students he mailed out in July. "What has been permitted, allowed, and accepted during the last few years is no longer satisfactory. A much higher standard, response and accomplishment is demanded and necessary. Do not be stupid or silly in thinking you can get away with things."

The Sloop era had indeed come to an end.

14

A Rough Transition

Mike Stanley was a scared fifth grader when he arrived on the Crossnore campus late in the summer of 1969. His mother had died the year before, and his father, a truck driver, was unable to look after Mike, his older sister, and a younger brother. An aunt had suggested Crossnore. With his brother as a companion, Mike moved into the Atwell Dormitory for little boys, where they faced a tough first year, punctuated by scrapes with his bunkmates. Some of these were settled on Sunday night, when boys tied on boxing gloves and slugged away at one another. Years later, Mike said it seemed to help.

Crossnore in 1969 was almost as troubled a place as Mike Stanley was a boy. Like his, its future was uncertain, and its present wasn't all that great. There was some activity on the mountainside, where two new buildings were under construction. With the help of the DAR chapters in North Carolina and money from other donors, the trustees had raised what they needed to build two dormitories. These would allow the school's new director, John Gatling, to move children out of structures that were unsound and unsafe.

Gatling had been on the campus for a little more than a year when the Stanley children arrived. His introduction to the community had not gone well, and it would only get worse before he left about eighteen months later. Part of his problem was a shortage of tact and diplomacy, as well as what seemed an inherent inability to refrain from salting his conversation with mild profanity—even when speaking to the students at the Sunday evening vespers. He excused his language by saying that was the way folks talked in upstate New York, where he had spent much of his life. His explanation only made things worse among people suspicious of outsiders.

Even if Gatling had exhibited some grace, he had taken on a job that was sure to enrage the local community. During his nearly three years at Crossnore, Gatling would dismantle a comfortable culture of accommodation between the campus and townspeople that had begun in Mary Sloop's years and had become even more entrenched after her death. Like others who had examined the operation in recent years, Gatling questioned whether the campus, firmly anchored in habits of the past, existed for the benefit of the children or for those who counted on it for their daily bread. Board members urged him to "use the broom," a not-so-veiled reference to their hope that he would relieve the campus of workers who weren't up to their responsibilities.

None of that made much difference to Mike and his siblings. They were in a strange place and surrounded by people they didn't know. At the same time, they had beds, new clothes from the Sales Store, and regular meals served family style around big tables in the dining hall, where a houseparent enforced proper table manners and decorum. Everyone dressed for dinner. A sport coat was standard issue upon arrival. When Mike outgrew his, he exchanged it with someone who had broader shoulders, who, in turn, went looking for something larger.

Dining together meant music. John Gatling loved patriotic hymns, and each evening the children and staff sang all the verses of the national anthem. "America the Beautiful" and "Kumbaya" were other favorites, as was "Michael, Row Your Boat Ashore." The director enjoyed jazz hits from the 1920s, and his appreciation of show tunes was such that he hauled campus children to Asheville to see performances of Broadway musicals. He also recruited the campus piano teacher, Tommy Hartley, to play popular numbers at the dining hall during the evening meal. Hartley once heard a guest from off campus ask his host, "When are you going to get your cabaret license?"

Behind the gaiety of the dining hall was growing turmoil and dissention as the campus began a transition away from Mary Sloop's boarding department, where children were housed, fed, and bathed regularly, to something else. Just what Crossnore would become was not clearly defined, and Gatling and his successors would struggle to find an answer in the years ahead. For the time being, the changes would shake the campus loose from a cozy relationship with the community that had served both well in another era.

Crossnore was stuck in the past. Through the Woodside years, the operational plan was simple: the activities of one year followed the path of what had been done the year before. It was a sleepy place where retired DAR matrons worked in the campus office, usually for little more than their meals and the use of a small apartment on campus. The campus telephone operator was one of these. She left shortly after Gatling's arrival rather than learn how to operate a new phone system. The man who ran the campus supply room had "retired" in 1965, but he remained on duty, working about one day a week for pay of $60 a month. The new director allowed him to stay on and receive his pay as a "pension" after learning that he had worked on campus for twenty years for the same salary, $200 a month. Obie Johnson was reduced to mopping floors in the dining hall. The days of folk and square dancing were over and gone. When these old-timers were replaced with people who lacked a local mailing address, it drew frowns. "Too many in the community believe only local residents should be employed whether employable or not," Gatling reported to the board. "They look upon Crossnore School Inc. as the personal fief of Crossnore Village and Avery County area."

Virtually no aspect of the Crossnore operation went untouched, from the daily habits of the students to the operations of the weaving department. Much of the talk among the folks who gathered around the gurgling water fountain in the center of the village touched on Gatling overturning arrangements of long-term employees whom he believed took their situations for granted. Campus employees who had once set their own schedules, especially around the holidays, now found an administrator who wanted a proper accounting of their time. Major adjustments were made in the bookkeeping department, which was run by Mrs. Rash, one of the senior members of the old regime. In his first year, Gatling introduced the campus's first operations budget so that he could determine just how much it cost to feed and house the roughly 140 students living on the campus. (In 1969, the cost was $4 a day, compared to $7 and $10 at other children's homes in the state.)

The new accounting methods didn't sit well with Rash. She had learned her job under Mary Sloop, and nothing had changed since. Over the years, she had been a good steward, paying the bills on time (at least when money was available) and doggedly pursuing collection of past-due tuition payments. She groused about the new arrangements, and her complaints were heard in town, too. Gatling attributed rumors that he was bankrupting the school to disgruntled employees, who, he said, didn't appreciate the challenge he faced. Not long after he arrived, he discovered that Crossnore School Incorporated employees weren't covered by workers' compensation insurance, a violation of state law. Other adjustments came from recommendations of new auditors who were in charge of installing accounting procedures designed for child care institutions by the Duke Endowment, which had taken a new interest in the campus.

Of special concern to Gatling and others, including Robert Mayer II at the Duke Endowment, was the handling of grocery store coupons and trading stamps that arrived by the pound from Crossnore's friends. The advent of these promotions had produced a bonanza for nonprofit organizations like Crossnore. By the late 1960s, savings from coupons accounted for $60,000 a year in the school budget. There was little oversight of the accounting of the coupons redeemed in supplies from a Newland grocery store. Gatling and others believed the program was fraught with error and potential for misuse and legal liability.

Other long-time practices drew Gatling's attention as he tried to take control of campus finances. The Crossnore weaving room was losing money, as it had for years, but no one could determine the extent of the loss, because an inventory hadn't been conducted in twenty years or more. One was undertaken during the off season early in 1971, but six months later the accounts were out of balance again. Weave Room manager Ossie Phillips, a beloved member of the

Crossnore community, was given strict instructions on what to produce and how to compensate weavers for the goods that were sold. Gatling also imposed new rules requiring hourly workers to receive at least the minimum wage. Word circulated that the weaving department might be closed.

In his regular reports to board members, the director worried aloud about having enough money to pay bills on time. It was the same old story. Crossnore's balance sheet was strong, but there was little ready cash in the bank. Some days, Gatling depended on the receipts from the daily mail to cover outstanding checks. Most of Crossnore School Incorporated's wealth was tied up in land and buildings. As a result, board members began considering unused real estate as an asset that could be converted to cash, and the 155-acre farm looked like a place to start. The farm buildings were of no value. A former dairy barn, unused for many seasons, was in severe disrepair. Portions of the land had been planted in trees a few years before Gatling arrived. Mountain property wasn't nearly as hot as it would be in another decade, but the economy was just beginning to shift. What had once been a single summer season at resorts like Linville was transforming into a year-round attraction with developers promoting skiing in the southern mountains during the winter months. The owners of Tweetsie Railroad, Harry and Grover Robbins, had created another major attraction on top of Beech Mountain near Banner Elk. They called it "the Land of Oz" and sent their public relations man to Los Angeles to buy the red shoes that actress Judy Garland had worn as she skipped down the Yellow Brick Road. People were looking for land to build second homes on the side of Beech Mountain, at Sugar Mountain, and at other new resorts.

All in all, the campus was at a critical turning point in 1969. Gatling reported to the board: "We, therefore, must determine the service and niche we must give and fill. I do not believe anyone wants Crossnore to be solely a housing and feeding facility, as to a large extent it has been in the past, glorious as its past has been." Yet aside from an assessment that, after forty years, Crossnore had outlived its initial purpose as a boarding department for students—especially since a majority of the Crossnore students had to be bused to classes at the new consolidated high school—there was no consensus on what purpose the campus would serve in the years ahead.

In the meantime, Gatling was charged with keeping the doors open and the beds filled while he prepared for Crossnore School Incorporated's first major capital funds campaign. New residential living space was needed immediately in the face of the alarming reports from architects and others who had surveyed the campus buildings. Not long after Gatling arrived, the trustees set out to raise $500,000 that was to be used to build two dormitories, renovate some of the existing buildings, and construct an indoor swimming pool. The North Carolina DAR agreed to raise $125,000 toward the cost of a new residence for teenaged girls. The wealthy businessmen and textile manufacturers on the board dug deeply in their own pockets and tapped their friends for contributions to raise 80 percent of the goal.

An unintended consequence of the building campaign was a more thorough examination of the kind of campus that Crossnore would later become. In the past, residential buildings had been built to house dozens of students. Beginning in 1961 with a visit to the campus by Dr. Alan Keith-Lucas, one of the leading consultants in the field of child care, the trustees had been advised to reduce the number of children living together under one roof. The latest advice to shift to smaller units came in the 1966 report from the Duke Endowment's Robert Mayer, who was now a regular guest at meetings of the trustees. The unmistakable message was that institutions like Crossnore that housed large numbers of children in dormitories were a thing of the past.

By the late 1960s, the prevailing consensus called for a child-centered approach, with smaller groups living together in a home-like setting, not assigned to bunk beds in what might be mistaken for barracks. Moreover, outsiders recommended the campus program should be run for the benefit of the child, rather than the convenience of their caretakers. That meant more family contact and counseling for children troubled by their circumstances. It was not enough to provide a safe, wholesome, patriotic, and Christian environment, as Crossnore advertised. Rather, child care institutions should offer a broader program that took into consideration the entire family.

The tradition of Christmas gifts coming from the Bird Cage began in the 1930s and continues today. Children with their presents in the old dining hall before a tree decorated for the holidays.

Crossnore's problem was that it didn't fit the model, and not just because of the living arrangements. While the trustees called Crossnore School Incorporated a child care institution, in reality it remained the "boarding department." Most of the professionals who came to the campus had never seen anything quite like it. Crossnore was unique, said Clifford Sanford, a colleague of Keith-Lucas who in 1969 made a study of the campus for Group Child Care Consulting Services, which was located within the School of Social Work at the University of North Carolina in Chapel Hill.

Sanford was just one of the professionals who looked in on the campus in the late 1960s. He said a thorough study and plan for the future should be prepared. Mayer warned, however, that such an investment in planning was bootless unless and until Crossnore had the resources to put together the kind of staff and campus support necessary to implement the recommendations that might come from such work. That clearly was not the case in 1970, when Gatling warned the trustees repeatedly that without sustained financial support, Crossnore's future was in jeopardy.

In short, the choices were clear: The trustees could close the campus and end a remarkable era of service to families in the southern Appalachians, or they could embrace a new mission for Crossnore as a bona fide child care institution similar to other children's homes in the state. Apparently, closing was never given any serious consideration. Mayer warned that even a temporary cessation would be fatal. Likewise, it probably was not an option considered by trustees such as Dr. Emma Fink, nor by those who had long been soldiers in arms with the Sloops. R. Q. Bault, a teacher and school principal associated with Crossnore since the 1930s, and Lambert Johnson, who with his father had helped move the Sloop family to Crossnore, were regular in their attendance at board meetings. As a result, it was by default more than by decision that the trustees chose to move in the latter direction by building more residential space—but within the context of Crossnore School Incorporated's unique situation.

The new residential halls complemented the mountain setting. Their exteriors of rock facing and board-and-batten siding reflected the style that Mary Sloop had favored. They were set higher on the hill, within sight of the campus gymnasium. The size of the buildings was similar to dormitories of the past, with living space for up to thirty-two children, not the twelve to fifteen that Mayer had urged the trustees to consider. One of the buildings, to be called DAR, was intended for high-school-age girls. A second, to be called Carolina, would be for preteen boys. The planners did nod to the prevailing bias against dormitory living, however. Each of the residence halls was partitioned, with one group of sixteen living on the first level with houseparents and another group of sixteen with separate houseparents assigned to the second floor. The buildings also became known as "cottages," although promotional material continued to refer to them as dormitories. The DAR building was dedicated in October 1969 during the tour conducted by DAR officials.

Aside from this adjustment, no formal declaration was made about Crossnore's future. Rather than demolish the old buildings, Gatling got a second opinion on the viability of the Roadman, Belk,

When two new dormitories—Carolina and DAR—were dedicated in 1969, they were called "cottages," but they still housed more than thirty children under one roof.

Sloop, and Atwell dormitories. This second expert declared them salvageable and targeted them for renovations. Fire alarms were installed in wooden structures that could have ignited and burned to the ground in a matter of minutes. Gatling envisioned turning Fleshman Dormitory into a gathering space for the students.

When the building campaign fell short, the campus did not get the indoor swimming pool, which would have cost as much as a new dormitory. The pool had ignited Gatling's enthusiasm, and he promoted it tirelessly. It had been on a campus wish list since the early 1960s, when one report recommended a building with a pool on the lower level and a new gymnasium on the floor above. Proponents argued that mountain children were handicapped because they did not know how to swim. Indeed, the only available swimming hole was the pond behind Eustace Sloop's dam on the Linville River. The last swimming pool of any description in the immediate area had been

The Fleshman Dormitory housed Crossnore children for more than thirty years before it was closed in the late 1960s. Executive Director John Gatling proposed using it for a campus social hall.

built in the 1920s by McCoy Franklin and a troop of Boy Scouts. He was given a donation to pay for construction, and the Scouts created a large rock basin that caught the chilly waters of a small stream at the foot of a ravine the children passed on their way from the campus to the Presbyterian church. The pool and an accompanying building used as a gymnasium didn't survive the Depression, although remnants were still visible in 2011.

The only hint of a new direction for Crossnore School Incorporated appeared in a campaign brochure. It made no mention of the campus providing accommodations for children during the school year. Rather, it said the campus would provide year-round care for children from "upset homes" and produce future good citizens "through carefully disciplined Christian training." Consistent with Crossnore's past, students were expected to work during their stay, make their beds, and care for their own belongings, and they would

Over the years, various symbols appeared on the Crossnore logo to signify the Christian tradition of educational achievement and the clasped hands of caring found in a home in the mountains.

receive the "training and upbringing a child would receive in normal, proper, compatible homes of moderate circumstances." It was a program founded on the virtues of hard work, rectitude, and wholesome living that were part of the Crossnore tradition.

Apparently, the new dormitories and the renovations of the old buildings were enough to satisfy state authorities of Crossnore's worthiness. By the 1970s, Crossnore School Incorporated was licensed as a child care facility and became eligible to receive payments directly under programs like Aid to Families with Dependent Children. While social workers had often escorted children in their care to Crossnore in the past, licensure provided a greater guarantee of payment. There was another new element to the campus program. In 1970, Crossnore School Incorporated contracted with a psychologist to spend one day a week on campus to meet with children and consult with houseparents. Gatling also hired a campus life director, the Reverend Max Tussey, who organized programs for the children. The rental of campus facilities for summer athletic camps was discontinued.

Gatling began actively courting social workers to place children at Crossnore. His pitch was urgent, and it flaunted the righteousness of Crossnore's mission. Crossnore had strict rules, and obedience was expected. "We stress responsibility, citizenship, love of country, and old fashion flag-waving patriotism." Students were expected to be well-groomed and obedient, and to work. "Is there anything wrong with these methods and philosophy?" Gatling asked. "We think highly of them." He indicated that Crossnore corrected the lack of discipline developed by many children in foster care.

The rigid conformity of the campus and its unabashed patriotism suggested Crossnore was an island of salvation in a youth society that favored long hair, flamboyant dress, political protest, and self-expression, all of which ran counter to Gatling's own political faith. He wrote one correspondent that he had given up on *Time* magazine because it was too liberal and had become a regular reader of William F. Buckley's *National Review*. He had no patience for students who refused to pledge allegiance to the flag. That included two Panamanian children who objected for religious reasons. Gatling told a state welfare official, "If a child cannot pledge allegiance to the flag of this wonderful country they are not welcome here."

Gatling proposed to make Crossnore available to those who were in need, but he didn't want troublemakers. He said "recalcitrants and incorrigibles should be avoided," and any children with mental problems were too expensive to manage. "In my opinion," he wrote, "we should seek out the well deserving youngster who is either destitute in a number of ways or who requires a decent home. We then should do an outstanding and excellent job with them."

The screening of prospects probably wasn't all that different than it had been in the past, however. It was just more clearly stated. During her era, no child entered Crossnore without Mary Sloop's endorsement. She kept problem children off her campus with an innate sense of child behavior and the character of the children she accepted each year.

Of course, she never experienced the 1960s, when society was shaken by protests, marches, and street demonstrations that brought profound changes to America. She also was never confronted with the acceptance of African Americans. Very few blacks lived in the North Carolina mountains, but the few African American children living in Avery County didn't begin attending schools with whites until 1968. By the late 1960s, the campus dormitories were integrated. Despite Gatling's intention to screen problem children, those living in the dormitories included young people who had been in trouble with the law or who had been more than foster parents could handle. There was grumbling in the village about "Crossnore going downhill," and complaints about the children reached Gatling's ears. He defended the integration of the student body as the right thing to do. It was essential, moreover, if Crossnore was to be eligible for reimbursement under Aid for Families with Dependent Children. His answer to troublemakers was to expel or restrict to campus those who disobeyed the rules. He also made plans to keep children out of

John Gatling (at left) presided over Crossnore School Incorporated during a period of wrenching change. With him is a delegation of DAR officers who came to the campus in 1969 for the dedication of a new dormitory. Board Chair Martha Guy is second from the left.

the town. He believed renovating the Fleshman Dormitory as a gathering spot for students on campus would deprive students of the opportunity to make "trysting arrangements."

Two years after Gatling became director, the campus had an improved infrastructure and new employees, but it also had an unwelcome reputation. Negative feelings in the community ran high. One day, storeowner Corbett Johnson intervened in an exchange between Gatling and some students who apparently were not supposed to be off the campus. Johnson threw a punch, and Gatling went down. Asked why he hit him, Johnson said, "He sassed me."

On another occasion, Gatling reported to the board that "a group invaded the campus" and had to be scared off with warning shots. The McClellans, houseparents in the Reed Dormitory, were asleep one night when Gatling called and told Roland to come quickly and to bring his gun. They found that dynamite had been placed near a campus building. Chains were put across campus roads at night, and an off-duty prison guard with a dog was hired to patrol the grounds.

In time, trustee chairwoman Martha Guy called a summit meeting with the mayor, town aldermen, and others so they could publicly air their complaints. Sheriff's deputies guarded the road into campus. Gatling took a long vacation.

The campus troubles extended beyond the immediate vicinity. Social workers began steering children elsewhere. Some were concerned about what they considered a lax admission policy at Crossnore, the strict rules, and Gatling's autocratic style, which was mentioned as a problem in a study of the campus by one of the members of Alan Keith-Lucas's Group Child Care Consulting Services.

Accounts of Gatling's confrontational behavior also reached the trustees. Mike Stanley and his tablemates had finished their meal one evening not long after he arrived when Gatling rang a bell for silence. He saw Gatling stand up and unfurl a bedsheet with a familiar stain in the center. "Let me tell you who did this," Gatling announced. Forty years later, the moment was still vivid for Stanley. "You thought, I am never going to pee in my bed," he recalled. "It was a boy from Roadman Dorm, one of the big boys. And he pointed him out. Look at this. Everybody knew what it was. Every kid's heart dropped. He pointed to the kid." A South Carolina minister who interviewed for a counseling job reported to Guy that he had witnessed Gatling browbeating students who had misbehaved. "I cannot believe that such an attitude should exist even in a penal institution," he wrote.

One of Gatling's staunchest defenders, trustee William Barnhardt, sent the director a copy of Norman Vincent Peale's book, *How to Stand Up to a Tough Situation*, but the Gatlings had had enough. Early in 1971, the trustees began looking for a new director, and the Gatlings left the campus.

Over the next year, the situation on the campus changed dramatically. Gatling's successor, Richard Brown, could not have been more different. While Gatling had no prior training to suggest any qualifications as director of a home for children, Brown was an ordained Baptist minister with a degree in psychology. As part of his candidacy for a master's degree at Appalachian State University, he had worked with Mel Gilley, the psychologist who counseled children at Crossnore during Gatling's term. The new man looked like a good fit. He was thirty years younger that his predecessor, expansive in his ideas, and appeared to be well suited to the appointment as director.

Brown dressed up the school's public relations, and board member John Harden helped with the creation of a new Crossnore logo. The earlier version had shown a shield bearing a cross in the upper right quadrant, the lamp of learning next to it, and below, from left to right, clasped hands and a relief of the mountains. The slogan, "Noblesse Oblige," appeared on a ribbon below the shield. The new logo showed only the clasped hands, suggesting the larger hand of an adult holding that of a child. Brown ordered buff-colored stationary printed with the new logo in brown ink. It was the same color he chose for pens used by the staff and the ribbons of the office's electric typewriters.

The program changed, but only slightly. By the end of the year, Brown had created what was called a "Skills Center" in the Cooper Building, the dorm for older girls built by the DAR. It was a place for students to receive tutoring and other help with their course work. Rooms in the old Goodfellow Hall, aged but useful, were being rented to the area antipoverty agency, WAMY, which planned to begin Headstart classes for preschoolers in the community.

By the end of his first six months, however, Brown was beset by complaints from teachers who said the campus children arrived for class improperly dressed and unprepared. The county school superintendent called Brown in for an explanation. At the same time, trustees, especially those associated with the DAR, questioned the elimination of Gatling's nightly patriotic rituals, such as the recital of the Pledge of Allegiance. Board members also didn't like Brown's relaxed attitude toward religious services, which drifted from the traditional program to what he called "a form the children could understand." Furthermore, Brown was in hot water over additions to the staff, which included new positions not authorized by the board. Some of the jobs—as well as houseparent appointments—were filled by young people whose long hair and eclectic clothing were noticed by the locals. Rumors of unseemly behavior by the staff found its way to the trustees. "We went from POWs to anything goes," Mike Stanley later recalled. "Mr. Brown hired every young hippie that was out there."

Brown was relieved of his duties before the end of his first year, and the board drafted Anderson Greene, who Brown had brought in as campus life director, to be interim director. A search for a new director began. More than a year would pass before Brown's replacement would arrive.

A decade after the death of Mary Sloop, the campus was a troubled place. Its direction had swung from one extreme to the other. Community support was at a low ebb. Some locals may have objected to Mary Sloop's firm hand, but they had kept their complaints to themselves. She was gone now, and tradition was no shield. As *Miracle in the Hills* slid into "out of print" status with its publisher, McGraw Hill, the challenge for the school's new leadership would be to blend Crossnore's storied past with the conditions that confronted children in 1970s, not those of half a century before.

15
A Revival

Henrietta Colgate Cannon—she preferred her nickname, "Bobbi"—came from wealth, as her middle name suggested. Further, she was married to Charlotte's James G. Cannon, a textile financier and grandson of the founder of Cannon Mills, the manufacturing behemoth large enough to own its own town, Kannapolis. Educated at Princeton and Harvard, James G. Cannon was a quiet, conservative man and a dedicated civic leader who, despite his wealth and position, always worked "like he was behind on the rent." His wife was equally energetic. Some called her bold, pushy, and opinionated, not one to let others stand in her way when she set out to get something done.

When Martha Guy called the Cannon residence in Charlotte to recruit either of the Cannons as a trustee at Crossnore, Bobbi Cannon answered the phone and was the first to say yes. She attended her first board meeting in the fall of 1971, just as executive director Richard Brown was being shown the door. The board elected her to chair the search for a new director.

The Crossnore board of trustees included some of the most influential businessmen in the Carolina Piedmont. The names of Belk, Harris, Dowd, Barnhardt, Abernethy, and others caused prospective donors to take notice and open their checkbooks. Only a crowd like that could have convinced the recently retired executive director of the Duke Endowment, Marshall Pickens, to become a trustee. Endowment executives, Olympian in the world of philanthropy, never deigned to work in the trenches for charitable organizations. Crossnore was an exception. Pickens stepped into emeritus status before the endowment made its first grant to Crossnore School Incorporated in 1971.

These businessmen did what they could for the campus. They opened their own checkbooks, they leaned on friends for more money, and they added prestige to what was otherwise a relatively obscure charity in the North Carolina mountains. Crossnore School Incorporated would have gone out of business without their support. But like the busy banker Martha Guy, these executives had many demands on their time, and they were limited in what they could do on Crossnore's behalf. Their attendance at meetings of the trustees was spotty, at best.

Bobbi Cannon was entirely different. There had been women trustees since the late 1940s, when the board majority tilted heavily in their favor after Sloop recruited DAR officers to serve. Over the years, these ex officio board members had participated largely as Crossnore's roving ambassadors. They helped raise donations for the Sales Store and kept the Crossnore flame alive at the DAR headquarters in Washington, which controlled a steady flow of funds. Cannon was the first woman from outside the world of the DAR or Avery County who devoted her time, as well as her money, in aid of Crossnore.

During her years on the board—she remained a trustee for more than twenty years—she would bring the same energy she devoted to all manner of A-list charities and civic causes in Charlotte, from the Mint Museum to the Florence Crittenden Home. Through her own labor and that of others whom she brought to Crossnore, she would help shape a new direction for Crossnore School Incorporated.

Her first project was to overhaul the Sales Store. Though it had long been a reliable and irreplaceable source of income, the Sales Store had been taken for granted during the tumult of the Gatling and Brown administrations. Even Robert Woodside had given it little time or attention. As a result, store operations had bumped along much as always. Used clothing and other goods arrived on the cam-

The Sales Store was overhauled in the 1970s by Bobbi Cannon of Charlotte, a Crossnore trustee who energized the school's board by encouraging a younger generation to volunteer in service to the school.

pus, where they were sorted, priced, and put out for sale. The selections for children helped campus residents become some of the best-dressed students in school and a source of envy for local youngsters of modest means. Financially, however, the Sales Store was sliding into stagnancy, beset with some of the same problems it had had at its last renovation twenty years earlier.

As testimony to the long-standing reputation of the enterprise among the DAR chapters around the country, the flow of goods remained steady even in the absence of the desperate pleas that Mary Sloop had included in her chatty newsletters. Publication of the *Bulletin* had been discontinued upon Woodside's retirement and didn't resume until 1972. Yet shipments continued to arrive, encouraged mostly by habit and by the presentations that Gatling and others

Henrietta Colgate Cannon, known to all as Bobbi, energized the board of trustees in the 1970s, overhauled the Sales Store, and brought to the board new members like John L. Fraley, with her in this photo taken at the wedding of trustee David L. Clark in 1982.

made at the DAR gatherings they attended. The notion of turning old clothes into gold remained part of Crossnore's compelling story.

The trustees surrendered the store to Cannon. She closed it in June 1973 and organized a midsummer fire sale to empty the shelves and clear Crossnore's attic of shopworn merchandise and surplus goods that had suffered from storage in the lofts and basements of various unused campus buildings. Meanwhile, she spent the summer renovating a building fronting on the town's main street that had been occupied by the campus's Fabric Shop, where surplus fabric solicited from Carolina textile mills was sold at discounted prices. The Fabric Shop was not earning its keep, so it was closed. The space got a fresh coat of paint, and the store fixtures were repaired and improved. The Sales Store reopened in September with a more appealing retail appearance. A few months later, the trustees were told that sales had tripled. The 1950-era Sales Store was demolished to add to the parking space for Sloop hospital.

Fixing the Sales Stores was far less complicated than finding new leadership for the campus. Anderson Greene remained in charge as acting director throughout 1972 until early in 1973, when Cannon's committee recommended to the trustees that they offer the job to Robert Martin, who was then the director of development at nearby Lees-McRae College. Martin had the fund-raising experience the board was looking for, but he also was a college-trained educator who had run schools for the federal government in stations abroad, from Midway Island in the Pacific to Kinshasa in the African nation of Zaire. Martin had grown up in Winston-Salem, North Carolina, and had earned his undergraduate and master's degrees at Appalachian State Teachers College (later Appalachian State University) before heading off to government jobs around the world. The Martin family included five children—three of whom would live on campus and attend Avery County schools—and he had family ties to Avery County. His wife, Lou Ann, was a Burleson. Her kin had greeted the Sloops when they arrived in Plumtree in 1908. Martin started work under a temporary arrangement in February. His appointment was made permanent a few months later.

When Martin arrived on campus, he found an institution struggling with new demands on its financial health. One of his first thoughts was, "I've got to get out and raise some money." He hit the road, often with his family in tow and a fat Rolodex of the names of Crossnore donors tucked beside him in the front seat of the car. He rode along armed with the legend of Mary Sloop's Crossnore and the warm welcome that the story provided him when he rose to talk to the Daughters at their state meetings and chapter sessions across the country. All the while, he knew Crossnore had moved well beyond the days of just feeding and housing deprived mountain children who were yearning for an education. The future of Crossnore would be another story indeed, and a more expensive story to produce.

By the time Martin was installed in office, the trustees had responded to the pressing physical needs of the campus. Their fund-

Robert Martin was director of Crossnore School Incorporated during the transformative years of the 1970s and early 1980s.

raising had produced the new residential living space, paved some of the dirt roads on the campus, and put new equipment in place. Largely overlooked in the urgency to raise new buildings and avoid the calamity of a fire were the changes that had overtaken the student population. The striking difference between the Crossnore students of the 1970s from those of ten years earlier was apparent in a report to the trustees submitted on the eve of Martin's appointment by Group Child Care Consulting Services.

The Crossnore student body had undergone a churning transformation. In the three years from 1969 to 1972, six hundred children had been enrolled, indicating a turnover that virtually flushed the campus of one group of students and replaced it anew with another. The average length of stay on campus was less than six months, and campus officials had no record of why half of those at Crossnore had been sent there in the first place. Out of three hundred and fifty case records studied closely, there was evidence of "sound planning" for only two children.

Three-fourths of Crossnore's student population were teenagers, and a third or more of them had serious behavioral problems and were having trouble at home or with the law when they arrived. According to GCCS's Margaret Faraday, who compiled the data, the prior records of delinquency probably accounted for the disciplinary problems that were cited in a preponderance of cases of those expelled from campus. It was known among the boys that if they misbehaved, their next home would be the state-run Jackson Training School.

Of those students with records to show a reason for their placement at Crossnore, about a third had what was considered a valid reason to be away from their homes. These reasons included evidence of abuse or neglect, a lack of a safe place to live, or a need to finish their high school education away from some problem at home. In short, Faraday told the board, Crossnore officials knew little about the children who came to the campus and left almost before anything could be learned about them. How, then, Faraday asked, could Crossnore prepare a program to serve the children? The report reinforced earlier complaints of county social workers that Crossnore was too lax in its admission policies, taking in children mainly to fill a bed and receive the state payments for their care.

That report and others laid out clearly the challenge for Martin, who would be the one to ease Crossnore School Incorporated into a new role as a component of the state welfare system serving children and families in crisis. It would be a transformational change that would make Crossnore more of a client of the state and would determine the type of service it provided. The campus would retain its independent status, and administrators would hew as closely as state regulations would allow to the traditions of the past, including the emphasis on religious and patriotic themes—two components that were essential for continued good standing with the DAR. A few boarding students placed by family members would be admitted from year to year, but dependence on state placements would soon expand. In a few years, eight out of ten of the children on campus would have arrived in the car accompanied by a state-employed social worker.

When Martin became executive director, about half of the student population still lived in buildings of questionable integrity. In short order, he turned Roadman Dormitory into staff housing and made it available to a gathering of bagpipers who rented space on the Crossnore campus in the summertime. Goodfellow Hall, used by the campus Scout troop and other groups, was torn down. Fleshman Dormitory, already decommissioned for student use, was earmarked for demolition. Until it was removed, it was used as a warehouse. The same was true of Reed Dormitory and, eventually, the campus infirmary. The latter building was feared by students. Children too sick to attend school were given a bed for the day in one of the infirmary wards. If there was no on-duty nurse, the wardroom doors were locked from the outside. It was as close to a jail cell as existed on the campus. Before he left as director in 1981, Martin claimed the distinction of tearing down more buildings than were built.

One of the reminders of the past was Sloop Dormitory, where a number of the older boys lived. Mike Stanley was beginning high school when he moved there. It was still little more than a barracks. The lower level was used for study hall and an occasional dance party with campus girls. On some weeknights, the boys turned it into a killing field for rats. They'd place food smuggled out of the dining hall in the middle of the floor, turn out the lights, and wait. When the lights were back on, they'd flail away at the large rodents with brooms. "Everybody got in a corner," he said, "and then flip the lights on and it was kill as you can. They were big old rats. We thought it was great."

New job descriptions appeared on the organization chart. Martin hired the first full-time social worker, whose job was to coordinate the arrival of children, get them assigned to a cottage (they were no longer called dormitories), and, when appropriate, work with family members. H. Dean Bare, a Berea graduate and former Avery County schoolteacher, was first hired to run a summer recreation program. After attending a Group Child Care Consulting Services seminar in Chapel Hill, he began work on a master's degree in social work at the University of North Carolina in Chapel Hill. He later became Crossnore's first director of child care services.

Other staff members, from houseparents to office workers, even-

In the 1970s, H. Dean Bare became the first trained child care professional on the Crossnore staff. He later succeeded Robert Martin as director of Crossnore School Incorporated before leaving for The Tamassee School, a DAR school in South Carolina.

tually became certified in child care through Group Child Care Consulting Services seminars. The new positions, plus the training of the staff, signaled a major change in Crossnore's approach to helping children who arrived on its doorstep. For the first time, Crossnore acknowledged that the problems that brought a child to the campus could not be addressed in a void. The entire family would need to be involved whenever possible. Crossnore School Incorporated remained largely an institution for custodial care—not a treatment center—but the staff was obliged to do more than merely provide room and board.

The housing space lost through the closing of the old residence halls, as well as from the belated recognition that large groups of children living together was no longer acceptable, forced a reduction in the campus population. Crossnore simply didn't have enough safe buildings to maintain the large count that previous administrators had attempted to push to two hundred or higher. By the time that Martin arrived, the number of students had already been cut in half to about a hundred. By the end of the 1970s, the number of students would shrink even further to about sixty. The smaller number meant less income from tuition, which made Martin's job of fund-raising all the more urgent. At the same time, it opened opportunities that hadn't existed before. Martin traded in enough S&H Green Stamps to get a campus van that was used to carry students to games of the Little League team or follow the campus basketball and football teams to away games with the students at Grandfather Home in Banner Elk or down the mountain to other similar institutions. Such outings would have been impossible when larger numbers of students lived on the campus.

Martin discontinued the use of the grocery coupons that had been exchanged for staples at the Newland store. Despite the hefty contribution these coupons made to the program budget, the system had become too unwieldy and fraught with problems. The campus gladly received trading stamps (and Campbell's soup labels), and they arrived in sufficient volume to be exchanged for appliances, furniture, and even the van Martin got from a Cleveland County auto dealer. Trading stamps arrived by the pound, and office workers, students—any campus help available—swiped the stamps with a sponge and mounted them in books. Some years, the volume was measured in hundreds of pounds.

Martin cultivated better relations with the community and held a campus open house. New trustees in the 1970s included more local residents, including Andre Tenille, a pharmacist; nurseryman William Aldridge; Alexander Lyerly, a Newland attorney; and Don Thompson, the director of the Avery County Department of Social Services. Bobbi Cannon recruited Hugh Fields, the manager of Grandfather Golf and Country Club, one of the largest resort developments in the area, as a trustee, and he became chair of the board.

Further, Martin made an effort to establish more of a family atmosphere on the campus. His wife and children took their meals in the dining hall, and his children rode the school bus to Avery County High School with the rest of the Crossnore children. Off-campus activities remained limited, and he made travel away from the campus a genuine adventure. "They stopped in Marion, at some hamburger place," his daughter Melynda Martin Pepple later recalled. "He went in and bought them all food. Some of those kids cried. They had never had anything like that. That gesture was so big to them."

During the summer, children, houseparents, and staff packed up and headed to a beachside retreat center in Garden City, South Carolina. The facilities at the nondenominational Garden City Chapel and Retreat Center were available at no charge. Houseparents packed enough food for the week, and the campus transported everyone to a spot just back from the edge of the Atlantic Ocean, about a dozen miles south of Myrtle Beach. For many of the children and adults, Garden City offered their first experience at the ocean. In the fall, the center's director, the Reverend Hal Norton, brought his staff to the Crossnore campus.

John and Ramona Sturgill were in their twenties when they became houseparents to the preteen girls living in the Carolina Dormitory. Ramona had just finished her first year as a teacher at Crossnore elementary school. She was second-generation Crossnore. Her mother, Elizabeth Roth, had been a dormitory child in the late 1930s, along with her brother Jesse. Mary Sloop had found her summer jobs, usually as a nanny. She had met Ramona's father at a school dance. After a year of teaching dormitory children in her classes, Ramona told her husband, John, that they were needed on the campus. Neither had experience raising children, but during the seventeen years they spent at Crossnore they gained a family of girls far larger than they could have had on their own.

"Those were wonderful years. We didn't have a lot; the kids didn't have a lot," Ramona said. They arrived in August 1971, at the tail end of the Gatling administration. During their first year, they were responsible for twenty-eight girls on both floors. They worked double duty for one paycheck—John was the only Sturgill of the campus payroll. Crossnore got Ramona for the same money. "I'd tell them when they'd come," said John. "We are not your momma, we are not your daddy. No matter what goes on we cannot be that. But if you come to Crossnore, we will be the next best thing."

Ramona continued. "We took them where they were. You've got to meet physical needs first. Then you start to work on emotional needs. Some didn't want to be hugged. A lot of them didn't want a man round them at all. Their daddy, preacher, step dad, their coach—somebody who was supposed to have loved them—had done them bad sexually." John eventually won their trust, and after another houseparent took over the second floor the Sturgills could get the eight or nine girls in their care into a van they purchased so the "family" could travel together. "They hated to get in a van that said Crossnore School Incorporated on the side of it. Ramona and I went and bought a van, nothing on it. When I pulled into a ballpark or a movie theater, I just wanted to look like a normal family."

Casual bystanders sometimes didn't understand, especially when the Sturgill family included African Americans. John was in the parking lot of a discount store in Boone talking with someone he had not seen in years when an African American teenager ran up to them, called him "Daddy," and asked for a dollar. He reached in his pocket and gave her the money. "You could see the blood leave his face," he recalled. "All I said was, 'You ought to see her mother.' He didn't say a word and I didn't either." One of the Sturgills' girls, an African American, was named Miss Congeniality of Avery County High School in 1972.

The Sturgills didn't try to shut out the world beyond the campus. At Christmastime, she and her girls carried presents to Avery County children who lived in tumbledown houses amid poverty and deprivation well back from the paved roads. "Half of the girls would be boohooing," she said. "I wanted them to know they could give back to somebody even though they weren't at home and didn't have mother and daddy, there were a lot of kids in worse shape."

Church attendance remained mandatory, as were weekly vespers services in the chapel. Houseparents and staff set a tone for upright behavior. Wilma Biggerstaff on the business staff held students accountable for their manners, correcting slouching behavior wherever she saw it on campus. Sandra Waycaster kept boys from pestering her teenage girls. One day, a group of boys paid a call on Dean Bare in the administration building. "They said we would like to talk to girls after dinner and walk them back to cottage," Bare recalled. "I said, 'Well what seems to be the problem?' They say, 'Well, Mrs. Waycaster says, Boys, this is not the time, this is not the place.' I said, 'She probably knows what she is talking about.'" He thought the conversation was over. "Well," they continued, "could you tell us, when is the time and where is the place?"

Sports was Mike Stanley's ticket off the campus and into a life that more closely resembled those of his classmates at Avery County High School. He compensated for his shortcomings in the classroom—he was at best a B student—with his abilities on the playing field. He was chosen as Player of the Week by the *Winston-Salem Journal* in September 1976 when he started his senior year, during which he excelled in football, basketball, and baseball. The Avery High jersey helped him shake the stigma of Crossnore. Associating with teammates who weren't living on campus prepared him for leaving Crossnore when the time came. After high school, he earned his way through Mars Hill College, received a business degree at Appalachian State University, and began a career in campus finance there. In 2006, almost forty years after he had arrived as a frightened ten-year-old, Mike Stanley returned to the campus as the commencement speaker at the Crossnore Academy graduation.

When Stanley had arrived on the campus in 1969, the newest buildings were residence halls built for up to thirty-two children each. A year after he left, the campus opened Gilchrist Cottage, which would become home for nine preteen boys and girls, who would live together with houseparents in a setting that more closely resembled a suburban home than anything any of them had ever seen. Gilchrist had a large living room with a fireplace and a second-story deck shaded by the overhanging branches of an old oak. There was a kitchen, a laundry room, and private baths. It sat on the site of Reed Dormitory, the Depression-era building that had been constructed for the youngest boys. The new hall was named in honor of a North Carolina Daughter—Mrs. Ruth Gilchrist Bowen—but the total cost of construction, $187,000, made it the most expensive building yet. It would not have been possible without funding from a broad range of sources, including foundations and corporations.

The school invited Dr. Alan Keith-Lucas to the dedication. He said putting up such a building thirty years earlier, in an era when children living on charity were expected to be grateful for depriva-

The Gilchrist cottage opened in 1978 and became the new model for campus housing. It replaced the large dormitories of the Sloop era.

tions, would have been considered "an unpardonable extravagance." At forty dollars a square foot, the cost was more than half again as much as one of the two-story buildings that had been erected just a decade earlier. Nonetheless, Keith-Lucas said Gilchrist should be the model for what child care was about for the future. "Not only its donors, but its designers, testify to a desire to love one's neighbor as oneself; to want for other people's children what one wants for one's own and perhaps a little bit more."

The current challenges for child care providers—the lowest-paid and least regarded among society's workers, Keith-Lucas said—were helping families work out their problems, either together or apart in a residential care setting, and reconnecting children with their parents, their schools, and their home communities. These children weren't mentally ill or criminals, but they could become either.

These were the children knocking at Crossnore's door. "To serve them well," he said, "is Crossnore's opportunity to serve in the spirit of its founder."

"The future is not going to be easy for places like Crossnore School," he continued. The campus had to weather many challenges from those who couldn't escape the past and those at the other end of the spectrum who wanted "to sweep away places like Crossnore and put all children in private homes or small group homes in the community, neither of which is a practical solution." He reminded the trustees that the charter provided the opportunity to adapt to changing conditions. "Dr. Sloop foresaw that needs would change and wanted the school that she founded to have enough flexibility to move with the times."

The Gilchrist cottage was the result of a new energy among the trustees. This was especially true of vice chair Bobbi Cannon, who at board meetings sat next to the chairman, Hugh Fields, ready to pinch his thigh when the discussion began to drag and she became impatient to move on. "The school needed to pare down the numbers," Fields later recalled. "It was trying to serve everybody, but it couldn't serve everybody. It needed to focus on child care and family situations. Bobbi Cannon was leader in that movement."

The Gilchrist Cottage was just the beginning. The dining hall was on the critical list. It had been built in the 1940s with the usual care to sound construction taken at that time. For a time, cottage dining and meals from a catering service had to suffice until a new dining hall opened in May 1980. The building was a reduced version of its predecessors, with seating for 125 instead of more than 200. It stood on the site of the old infirmary. Three years later, a gymnasium was under construction at a cost of $500,000. The chair of the campaign for the new gymnasium was John Fraley of Cherryville, a new trustee recruited by Bobbi Cannon.

Fraley was subsequently joined by other young recruits, such as Rush Dickson III of Charlotte and Robert Stowe III of Belmont. They were called "Bobbi's Boys." The three were scions of wealth and social position, and they did what they were told when Cannon called and enrolled them as a new generation of trustees for Crossnore. The

For many years, philanthropist E. H. Little provided each child at Crossnore with a crisp dollar bill at Christmastime—until he accounted for inflation and raised his gift to five dollars.

Stowes were old textile money in Belmont, a mill town midway between Charlotte and Gastonia. Fraley's father had founded Carolina Freight, a major long-distance trucking company, after growing up in a children's home in Georgia. Fraley's mountain connection was a home at Grandfather Golf and Country Club. Fraley was a first-rate golfer who gave up time on the course to lend a hand to Fields and Crossnore affairs. Dickson's grandfather had handled stock transactions and business deals since the 1940s for men like Spencer Love, the founder of Burlington Industries. The family had owned one of Love's houses at Linville since World War II. His father and uncle ran Ruddick Corporation, a regional holding company that included Harris-Teeter supermarkets.

The board included other newcomers representing a younger generation. One of them was Alexander Lyerly, a young Banner Elk attorney who handled legal work for Martha Guy's bank and the Crossnore hospital. Guy recruited him for a one-year term. He was still on the board three decades later. Another was Newland attorney William Cocke Jr., a nephew of Hugh Morton, the owner at Grandfather Mountain. Like Fields, Cocke was another Cannon recruit. When Crossnore School's status with the DAR was questioned in the early 1980s, Fields, Lyerly, and Cocke became the front line of defense. Working with the national schools chairman at the time, Mrs. Robert Jackson of Maryland, they successfully turned back an attempt to disconnect Crossnore from DAR support in favor of another institution.

Mrs. Jackson managed Crossnore's defense and invited Fields, Lyerly, and Cocke to attend the Continental Congress. "[National schools chair] chair Barbara Taylor saw that we got an opportunity to talk to all the people who were able to see Crossnore as a school that really needed their assistance," Lyerly recalled. The objections were met, and Lyerly and Cocke celebrated at the formal DAR dinner by appearing in kilt.

The list of DAR-approved schools was subsequently reduced to only six institutions, with Crossnore remaining in good favor along with Berry College in Georgia, the Hillside School in Massachusetts, Hindman Settlement School in Kentucky, Kate Duncan Smith DAR School in Alabama, and the Tamassee School in the mountain foothills of South Carolina.

In 1984, Mrs. Sarah King, the DAR's president general, notified the Crossnore board that the national DAR school tour would come first to Crossnore. Said Fields, "Mrs. King praised Crossnore for being an 'inspiration' and 'pattern' for the other DAR-approved schools. It is ironic that the school survey several years ago was prompted because of our school and yet Crossnore proved to be the number one of all the schools at the conclusion of the survey."

16
The Children's Plan

In the winter of 1975, Phyllis Crain and her husband, Keith, were newly married and living in a faded two-story rental house whose furnishings were as spare as their own prospects. Phyllis was seventeen years old, pregnant, and one course shy of qualifying for her high school diploma. With Keith working nights and attending classes at Furman University during the day, Phyllis was often alone in an empty place that could be a bit eerie. She slept with a rifle nearby. On one cold February day, with the wash hardening on the line as she hung it out to dry, she broke into tears. It was not a sorrowful cry, but one that was deep, soul wrenching, even angry. Out of it came a firm resolve to get as full an education as possible and make sure that the child she was carrying did not grow up in poverty.

She completed the missing English course in night school and had the credit transferred to her high school in Polk County, North Carolina, in time to graduate with her class. Because of her "indelicate condition," she was required to walk at the end of the procession of seniors. The Crains' daughter, Holly, was born two months later in July, seven weeks before Phyllis entered North Greenville College with the help of student aid. She excelled and won a scholarship for her final two years of undergraduate education at Wofford College, where she completed a double major in just eighteen months. She became a classroom teacher while she worked on a master's degree in special needs education at Converse College. By the time Holly entered kindergarten, Phyllis was, at twenty-one, the youngest member ever elected to the board of education in Polk County. She took quiet satisfaction that those in the teaching establishment who had inflicted humiliation on her on graduation night now reported to her.

By the time Phyllis Crain became superintendent of the Avery County schools in 1995, she was Dr. Phyllis Crain, Ed.D. (University of South Carolina, 1990). She was responsible for nine schools, a staff of hundreds, and a student population of more than two thousand. Her challenge was clear: only one-fourth of Avery County high school graduates pursued any further education, reading literacy rates were low, and students finished their education without the opportunity to learn a second language. It was a more limited curriculum than what Mary Sloop had helped establish seventy years earlier. In part, these challenges were what had brought her to the mountains. She chose Avery County over another system that already had a strong academic record because she thought she could make a difference in the education of children.

Her ambition was not especially welcomed by the locals, however. When she appeared before the board of county commissioners to tell them that state law required them to adopt a school budget, the chairman wondered aloud if a woman was up to the job. Years later, that bracing bit of eye-opening candor ranked up there with the call she got one morning from a principal who asked what he was to do about two students who had worn their father's Ku Klux Klan robes to campus as part of school spirit week. Some of those overseeing the school system considered a blackboard and chalk to be high-tech.

She found the county full of stunning contrasts. It was not hard to find families living in deep poverty and wretched conditions, while just across the ridge stood lavish resort homes whose owners visited but once or twice a year. One day, Crain attended a county politician's family reunion where moonshine was served along with the barbecue. That evening, she sipped cocktails with the swells in a fine home at Linville.

Nonetheless, she continued to push the boulder up the hill. Inspired teachers began to turn the postgraduate education rate around.

Dr. Phyllis Crain became the executive director of The Crossnore School and drew her inspiration for transforming the campus from the dreams of the children.

Within a few years, nearly half of the county graduates were seeking education beyond high school. The county system was recognized as having one of the best reading literacy programs in the state. The number of children reading below grade level dropped by 40 percent. Early childhood classes were introduced at the county's six elementary schools. French returned to the high school curriculum. Crain had also helped Avery and other small, low-wealth school systems secure supplemental grants from the state legislature to replace aging and inadequate school buildings. On Crain's replacement list was the elementary school adjacent to the Crossnore campus.

For Crain, the public-private partnership at Crossnore was just one more of Avery County's curiosities, sort of like the four separate patterns of winter weather that the county's rugged topography could produce simultaneously. She had the unique Crossnore arrangement explained to her by its gregarious director, Joe Mitchell, whom Crain met not long after she arrived. Once she had the money for a new elementary school building, Crain began negotiating with the Crossnore trustees for thirteen acres on the back side of the campus, where she planned to build the new school.

Joe Mitchell had been on the Crossnore campus for nearly a decade by the time Crain got to Avery County. His earlier career had included responsibilities at a children's home in Mississippi. He was the development director at King College in Bristol, Tennessee, when he heard about the Crossnore job late in 1985. He applied and was hired to succeed H. Dean Bare, who was already installed as director at Tamassee School, a DAR school in South Carolina, by the time Mitchell arrived at Crossnore in the spring of 1986. Bare had followed Robert Martin as director at Crossnore.

Mitchell was a tall, heavyset fellow with an easy manner and a ready smile. He was an accomplished amateur musician, and over the years his piano playing made him a favorite with the Daughters. He had a quirky sense of humor, along with an impressive collection of rubber ducks that lined the shelves of a bookcase in his office.

Mitchell's major contribution to the Crossnore program was spending the Bayles benefaction. The legacy announced in the 1950s finally came available to Crossnore and had grown by $200,000 to more than $700,000. That was enough to build a handsome administration building on the site of the old dining hall and a large, airy residence for Crossnore's executive director. The house had an interior of chestnut paneling, open beams, and a stone fireplace, and it sat at the top of Christmas Tree Hill, the old sledding haunt that was now covered with a forest of white pines. Visitors to the back deck were rewarded with a million-dollar view of Grandfather Mountain a dozen or so miles away to the northeast. The new offices reflected the special needs of the staff and were a decided improvement over the warren of tiny rooms and staff apartments in the old building where Mary Sloop had lived and worked in her declining years. For the first time, conversations with children, their caretakers, and the social workers who accompanied them to the campus could be undertak-

One of Crossnore's best-known students was Harlan Boyles, North Carolina's state treasurer from 1976 to 2000. With him in this picture is Virginia Foxx, a graduate of Crossnore High School who learned to weave on the campus. She served in the state legislature before being elected to Congress in 2004. Joe Mitchell, Crossnore director from 1986 to 1999, is on the far right. At far left, in the back, is Margaret Lauterer, a great-niece of the Sloops.

The Bayles Administration Building was built in the late 1980s with money from the legacy of a generous Daughter. It incorporated the styling of the Cooper Building with its balcony and stone entry.

en in private. The new space spruced up Crossnore's first impression considerably.

Mitchell trimmed away some of the Crossnore legacy. He dismissed Tommy Hartley, the last Crossnore music teacher in a line of succession that dated to the 1920s. Hartley's share of the payroll was turned over to remedial education for students. At the same time, he presided over a revival of the Weave Room, which returned to the fold of the Southern Highland Craft Guild in 1989. Mary Sloop had helped found the organization in 1928, but she let the membership lapse in 1938 after finding a better use for the ten dollars in annual dues. The Weave Room had rejoined in 1950 but became inactive again a year later.

Ossie Phillips and her weavers found a champion in Joe Mitchell. The Weave Room was expanded, and a new manager, Eleanor Hjemmet, was put in place. As Phillips's career came to a close, she attended her fiftieth Continental Congress as a Crossnore weaver. A few months earlier, she had learned that Mrs. Barbara Bush was using one of her bedspreads at the presidential retreat at Camp David.

Mitchell clung tightly to the homespun nostalgia of the Weave Room and was able to wring thousands of dollars in sales out of the Daughters at their annual meeting. He even resurrected and put on sale a Depression-era doll dressed in colonial garb called "Susie Crossnore." Sewing teacher Helen Stedronsky had created the doll in the 1930s to help novices learn how to handle needle and thread. Students followed a simple pattern and used fabric scraps to create the doll Ossie Phillips named "Susie."

Mitchell delighted in buffing Crossnore's image with uplifting stories of boys and girls who got misty-eyed while singing "God Bless America" and who were taught the "value of sitting on the porch in the summertime, listening to the peep frogs sing." Stories like these kept the Daughters in thrall and faithful in their shipments of used goods to the Sales Store. Each year, DAR chapters also showered Crossnore with up to three hundred pounds of labels from Campbell's soup cans. Crossnore redeemed them for appliances and equipment for the cottages, or for use elsewhere on the campus.

The continued success of the Sales Store clearly demonstrated

The Blair Fraley Sales Store opened in 1998 and was built in memory of the young daughter of trustee John Fraley. It operates just as it did when the Johnsons sized up sales items and customers in a small frame store that stood just across the way.

that if the sales floor were larger, its annual contribution of $100,000 to Crossnore's bottom line might be greater. The building that had been renovated twenty years earlier suffered from the same complaint as the one it replaced. There just wasn't enough space to properly display the full range of merchandise, from clothing to furniture, appliances, and anything else that arrived aboard the Crossnore truck dispatched for pickups. A new building—with ten thousand square feet of space instead of eighteen hundred—was designed, and construction began in May 1997. The trustees announced it would be called the Blair Fraley Sales Store in memory of the daughter of John and Guyann Fraley and of John's work as chair of the trustees. Blair, the Frayley's eight-year-old daughter, had been killed in 1996 while riding her bicycle in her Cherryville, North Carolina, neighborhood.

The new store opened in the summer of 1998. Beneath its foundation were the old footings for Treasure Island, the all-purpose building that Mary Sloop had erected once the county had built the two-room school. Later, Treasure Island was brought down and the soggy bottom dredged for a small pond that provided a reservoir for firefighters and gave Eustace Sloop a place to ice skate in the winter. The Blair Fraley Sales Store was bright and open inside, with a loft, smooth timbers, stone accents, and a broad front porch complete with rocking chairs. It was a handsome addition to the village and one of the largest new buildings constructed since the Baptist church had moved off the hill and down to a spot across from the hospital in 1956.

The new store was some salve to Crossnore's wounds. As it went up, the community was preparing for the loss of the hospital and the business that it had brought to town. Garrett Memorial was due to close soon in favor of a new eighteen-million-dollar facility that combined it with Banner Elk's Cannon Memorial. The new Charles A. Cannon Jr. Hospital opened near Linville in 2000, along with the Sloop Medical Office Plaza.

The campus weaving program was one remnant of the past that remained much as Mary Sloop had left it forty years earlier. The patterns on the looms were the same, and the feet of local weavers still worked the treadles. Enlarging Homespun House to accommodate more looms had not altered the picturesque stone building. It had only made it more functional. The board continued to operate it at a loss. Its defenders argued in favor of its public relations value. No one, it seemed, wanted to call a vote to end a program that had been Crossnore's own for nearly eighty years.

A few student weavers continued to work there, but self-help wasn't the watchword it had once been at Crossnore. Students no longer worked to earn a portion of their tuition. Instead, those with campus jobs received modest wages for their assistance in the dining hall, the Sales Store, the office, and elsewhere. Hours of weekly labor that had once been the hallmark of the Sloop era had fallen to state restrictions on child labor and the changes in Crossnore's student population.

Campus jobs also had become more problematic because some children weren't on the campus long enough to learn the regimen of hard work and Christian living. Crossnore had become a way station for the state's social welfare system and was no longer a way of life. A student who remained in a cottage for more than a year was considered an exception. Some children were in care for only a few weeks, or just long enough for social workers to make arrangements for placement in foster care or to find a family member to take them in. After Mitchell and his wife moved to their new home, the former director's house—the old sewing room at the campus entrance—became a second emergency care facility on the campus, where children could stay up to ninety days and receive special attention from social workers while an alternate home, perhaps foster care, was arranged.

Other campus programs had been adapted to meet the new conditions and new realities. Roadman Dormitory became "Roadman House," home to a handful of teenagers in their senior year of high school. It was an effort to teach independent living, which these young people would face soon once they reached the age of eighteen and lost the support of the welfare system. The teenagers made trips to the grocery store for food to fill menus they planned together. An old clunker of a car was available for their use.

The turnover in the cottages was such that some children never made it to the public schools. It was easier to put them in the remedial classes taught in the Cooper Building, built by the DAR in the 1930s, than to go through enrollment in public school only to be removed a few weeks later when they were withdrawn from Crossnore. The Skills Center had been organized in the early 1970s to provide students with help on their homework and other assignments. By the 1990s, it was equipped much like a standard classroom and employed full-time teachers who held daily classes for students who arrived on campus too far behind their peers to function effectively in public schools.

Most of the Crossnore children attended Avery County schools, as they had in the past, although the arrangement with the public schools was suffering from official disfavor. In 1992, the board of education refused to accept students from the Crossnore campus and the Grandfather Home for Children. The suspension notice appeared without warning on Joe Mitchell's desk in the morning mail. Each child would have to apply for admission, he was informed. None was accepted. When he inquired into the reasons why, he was told the board wasn't being compensated for teaching nonresident children. It was an argument almost as old as Crossnore School Incorporated itself. Mary Sloop had fought this battle in the 1920s and later in the mid-1950s. Behind this excuse was something more. Deeply troubled and emotionally disturbed children from the Grandfather Home had threatened to harm teachers and principals, disrupted classes, and one had set a fire at the school, according to subsequent court testimony. There were no similar complaints aired about Crossnore children.

The two institutions sued the school board to overturn the decision. They won an injunction in superior court in August 1993, just before the opening of school, but only for those students who had already applied. Any others who were living at Crossnore or Grandfather Home would not be allowed in the public schools. It was nearly a year before the case was finally settled and children from the two homes were returned to the public schools as before.

"They just about shut us down," Mitchell said some years later. Crossnore's student population dropped from an already low census of about fifty to twenty or twenty-five, the number who had lived in one dormitory just twenty years earlier. The episode demonstrated just how dependent Crossnore was on the welfare system for its residents. Social workers ceased to send children to Crossnore from elsewhere in North Carolina when the children could not be guaranteed a proper education.

Crain was unaware of the lawsuit that had embroiled the county—over three hundred people turned out for the first court hearing—when she took over the superintendency in 1995. She learned about it soon enough after Mitchell and Jim Swinkola of Grandfather Home came to call. Both were interested in mending fences. They invited her to board meetings and other events. Crain began thinking about a long-term solution; the charter schools that had been approved by the North Carolina General Assembly in 1996 looked like the answer. She worked with both institutions. Grandfather Home's charter was among the first thirty-seven schools approved in March 1997.

She and Mitchell worked closely together on an application for

Crossnore at the same time she was negotiating with the Crossnore trustees for the land on which to build the new elementary school. As they met and talked, Mitchell began pressing Crain to consider leaving her public school job and joining him on the staff at Crossnore as his assistant. He had talked of retiring in a few years, and board chair Rush Dickson III was nudging him to find a successor. Mitchell believed Crain was a very strong candidate. Crossnore would need someone like her—an administrator with a background in education—as it developed its charter school and became an educational program with a social services component, rather than the other way around.

Crain didn't share Mitchell's enthusiasm. Indeed, she was weary of the political arm wrestling required in the running of public schools. She was frustrated by "visionless decision making" and mind-numbing debates over the hiring of an athletic coach while substantive educational matters were given lip service. The ministry of Crossnore's work was appealing, especially after pressure-filled years in the spiritual desert of secular education. Yet she didn't see her next career move as likely to take place against the backdrop of the North Carolina mountains. Her husband had kept his job down the mountain with the Rutherford County school system. The flatlands still looked good to her. She told Mitchell no. She only had to recall the horrid, frozen days of the prior winter to be reminded of why she wanted a change.

Her options ran beyond running a public school system. She considered enrolling at Duke Divinity School. Phyllis and Keith shared a deep faith in the Lord. She'd made her first visit to the mountains to attend a camp on the grounds of the retreat owned by the Church of the Brethren just a few miles from Crossnore. Returning to teaching, this time at the college level, also looked promising. She was a good teacher and had the credentials and experience to make her résumé attractive. She continued to answer Mitchell's invitations to attend school functions, however, even taking a part in the dedication of the Blair Fraley Sales Store in the summer of 1998, where she sang at the ceremonies in the Sloop Chapel.

Joe Mitchell's offer to make a career change in favor of Crossnore continued to play on her, however. "First of all, I prayed for serving children in a place where there was purity of purpose. That is as specific as I can share for you," she said some years later. "But when the door opened here, for three months I said no. So, then, it was sleepless nights with an 'Aha.' Crossnore is everything you have prayed for. Go and be second in command and go and really enjoy being a momma these next four years for our son's high school career. Be at the soccer games, and still give an organization all of your God-given gifts in writing and communication."

Crain began work on January 1, 1999. The irony of her new situation was not lost on her. She had been hired to raise money for Crossnore; for all her many skills, that was one thing she had no experience with. She was determined, however, to see that when the Crossnore Academy students began classes later in the year, they would have proper classrooms. The current learning environment was woefully lacking. Classes were held in rooms on the lower level of the Cooper building and two other old dormitories. The only thing that suggested education was finally an integral part of Crossnore School Incorporated was a new sign that hung over the rock entrance to the Cooper Building and read "Crossnore Academy."

Crossnore's new executive in charge of fund-raising had never asked a donor for a dollar in her life. She had written proposals for state and federal grants in aid, and she had some limited experience with foundations, but nothing quite compared to what confronted her now. Nonetheless, she soon was sitting across the table from trustee chair Rush Dickson III with a handful of grant applications.

Crossnore required a school, she told Dickson, with classrooms and the best teachers, whose instruction could renew the promise of Mary Sloop that education provided the best path out of poverty. "This is the heart of who we are," Crain argued that day in Charlotte. Everything else was just icing on the cake.

The two didn't know each other as well as they would in years to come, when admiration and confidence would take hold. That February, thirty days into her new job, Crain was just another new employee, one of many that board veteran Dickson had seen in his quarter-century as a trustee. The tributes to Mary Sloop, the glory of the Crossnore mission, the duty to the children—he could recite it all himself. Now here was a woman he barely knew talking about raising $2 million and building a school. The trustees still had not paid for the Blair Fraley Sales Store. Crain finally stopped talking, her excitement stilled by his response. "If you can raise the money," he said dryly, without any hint of an endorsement, "you can build it."

It was not the answer she had been looking for. In fact, Dickson sounded like the dismissive males who had greeted her when she was introduced to the county commissioners. She brushed her rising frustration aside and simply told him, "Well, great, I've got some papers for you to sign."

Raising the money would be a challenge. Crossnore had never taken on any project quite this bold. A few months later, Phyllis and her husband were in Miami, where she was absorbing everything she could at a seminar produced by the Association of Fund Raising Professionals. Just before heading home, she got a telephone call from Dickson. Joe Mitchell was retiring earlier than planned, the chairman told her. "Stop through Charlotte on your way back to Crossnore and pick up the keys. You've just been hired as the new executive director." Crain knew God had a sense of humor. She was looking for it as she hung up the phone. The four years of on-the-job training that she had anticipated came to an end in four months.

In early June, the extended Crossnore family—children, staff members, trustees, the Crains, and their family and friends—filed into Sloop Chapel and filled the pews for a ceremony of installation for Crossnore's new executive director. Just beside the walkway, on the right side of the lawn in front of the chapel, the ground was still rough around the thin trunk of a newly planted weeping cherry tree. It had been planted in Crain's honor to signal a new beginning for Crossnore. Tied with ribbon to the tender, drooping branches were heart-shaped pieces of colored construction paper. Each one carried a wish from a Crossnore child, the answer to a request to express whatever was in each heart.

When the ceremony concluded, Crain went to the tree, gathered the pieces of paper, and carried them home with her. Later in the evening, she settled into a chair and began reading them one by one. The message was profound.

Phyllis and Keith Crain with a Crossnore student stand beside the weeping cherry tree planted in her honor on the occasion of her installation as director in 1999. Children decorated it with paper hearts carrying their wishes for Crossnore.

"I said, 'Oh my God. I get this.' The bottom line of the children's hopes and wishes were things that are so characteristic of a normal healthy childhood. Dr. Crain, I want to live in a real neighborhood. Dr. Crain, I want to have a backyard. Dr. Crain, I have always wanted a puppy. Dr. Crain, can you make William's mom come and see him. Dr. Crain, can we have a swing set? And one, an Olympic-size pool. I heard from the hearts of these children, written on construction paper hearts, and with God as my witness, it became my strategic plan."

17

Miracles, Always Miracles

As Phyllis Crain rebounded from the surprise of her unexpected promotion, she told board chair Rush Dickson III that she wanted to talk with the Crossnore trustees so that together they could map out the "where to from here" of the eighty-year-old institution. There was a pause, a moment of empty silence, but Dickson didn't follow with an offer to schedule a weekend of brainstorming. Instead, he said, "The role of leadership is to lead. Lead."

Crain thought to herself: "I think I can like this job. Almost anybody else would have said, 'I am running from here. They don't know what they are doing.' I was like, Whew. If I could invent anything I wanted to, to truly meet the needs of children in this state who had all the odds against them, what would it look like? What would it feel like? Sign me up."

Over the next decade, Phyllis Crain would lead the trustees into establishing The Crossnore School (a new name) as one of the nation's leading residential education programs for children in crisis, especially siblings who might otherwise have been sent to separate foster homes. In short order, she organized what would eventually become a $16-million Make a Miracle campaign. The first phase, for $5 million, brought in more than $7 million. The money built and equipped a modern education building and three cottages, replaced aging water and sewer lines, and aided in the transformation of the

Crossnore campus into a neighborhood of homes where children had dogs to play with and bicycles they could call their own. At the same time, Crossnore's modest endowment of $1 million, which had been nibbled on annually as previous administrators borrowed from it to pay operating expenses, grew to more than $20 million with a commitment to reach $100 million as soon as possible.

Along the way, Crain created opportunities for serving children and sustaining Crossnore by borrowing ideas and inspiration from Mary Sloop. Her predecessors had loyally paid lip service to Sloop's genius, but Crain saw *Miracle in the Hills* as more than a fascinating story. It became a handbook on how to continue Crossnore's mission a half-century after Sloop was gone. For example, Crain revived Sloop's formula for paying weavers in order to save the weaving department from financial ruin. In 2012, Crossnore's weavers were still at work preserving a mountain art form in a new way. "There is an old saying that if we are not in touch with the history, we are doomed to repeat past mistakes," Crain said. "The other side is that if you are not fully in tune with the past, you might lose some of the golden nuggets from the past."

As Crain moved about the campus in the summer of 1999, however, she had yet to find clarity of purpose. It was evident that Crossnore was at perhaps the lowest point in the long arc of its eighty years. The institution lacked a definitive mission and was struggling to survive in the backwash of the shifting preferences of child care professionals, many of whom said institutions like Crossnore would soon be gone, and the sooner the better.

There was little to suggest that Crossnore's days weren't numbered. The daily census of about forty children was a reflection of the bias of state and national policy makers who discouraged social service agencies from placing children—especially those under twelve years of age—in residential care. In addition, the campus looked tired and disorganized. To reach Crain's office in the administration building, visitors had to first pass by an abandoned elementary school and the patchwork of additions that had expanded the service of Garrett Memorial Hospital over the years. The hospital's outer wall literally sat at the edge of Crossnore's main street. There was talk that an Avery County Christmas tree grower was interested in acquiring the vacant building for use as housing for his migrant workers.

When Crain and Asheville architect James Padgett did a campus walkabout in the early summer of 1999, they found buildings that needed immediate demolition. Roadman remained a firetrap. Sloop—a sad, gray, two-story block of a building that stood right in the middle of the campus—was useful only for storage. Gilchrist Cottage, which Dr. Alan Keith-Lucas had held up as a model twenty years earlier, was the only residence hall that provided anything like a home setting for children. One teenager told Crain that the concrete-block interior walls of Carolina and DAR reminded her of a juvenile detention facility.

Moreover, the institution's financial underpinnings were weak. Previous administrators had all said they were opposed to balancing the books with unexpected bequests. Yet that was what happened more often than not when income for the year didn't cover expenses. In addition, chronic problems that drained the school of cash had been pushed aside rather than resolved. Crain was stunned when she got her first look at the books and discovered the weaving department's deficit was running about $40,000 a year.

Looming large was the new responsibility to create Crossnore Academy. The charter school had received state approval in the spring of 1999, but there was no classroom building or teaching staff qualified to support a full academic program. The school could change Crossnore's future and give it purpose, but first it had to be built, staffed, and paid for.

Mounted against these challenges was a petite, charming, and engaging woman of forty-two who was unknown to the Crossnore staff and trustees. She was an educator with an admirable record, but she lacked experience in the care of children facing the most difficult days of their lives. She had been hired as Crossnore's chief fundraiser, the one job she was least qualified to undertake. The irony was not lost on her. What Crain's résumé did not include was a measure of the boundless energy and creativity, stone-hard determination, deep religious faith, and compassion for children that would mark her years at the helm of Crossnore. Beginning that summer, with those heart-shaped messages piled in her lap as a guide, Crossnore became Phyllis Crain's ministry to children.

Crain brought the determination and righteous conviction of Mary Sloop's original mission back to Crossnore. By the end of 1999, she had convinced the trustees to embrace Sloop's commitment to educating children by developing Crossnore Academy as a first-rate boarding school to serve what she called "society's orphans." These were the abandoned, neglected, and abused children whose parents were in prison, on drugs, or simply just gone. It didn't require a degree in social work to understand the formula. Crossnore's children needed the same things that Crain wanted for her own son and daughter—the best that she could provide. Paraphrasing philosopher Mortimer Adler, Crain explained, "If really fine prep schools make sense for privileged kids in society, why not least privileged kids in society?" Keith-Lucas had suggested the same formula for Crossnore nearly a quarter-century earlier at the dedication of Gilchrist Cottage.

Crossnore would build on its ability to take in brothers and sisters and keep them united rather than dispersed in foster homes while beginning the rebuilding of their lives. As she put it, Crossnore could give children back their childhood. "That and lifting up our charter school and being able to take children where they are and really move them," she said. "We could factor in the children's education as a part of what ought to be in any plan for a child that can't live at home." Quality care in a strong educational environment would lift Crossnore above other institutions and secure its future.

It was a bold declaration, perhaps even reckless in the face of the current thinking of those setting child-welfare policy. "Congregate care," the bucket into which institutions like Crossnore were tossed, was on its way out. Foster care was the preferred option, because it kept children closer to their home communities and within reach of social workers. Budget-minded administrators in the county and state departments of welfare also were mindful that foster care was considerably cheaper, a consideration that often outweighed others.

Crossnore's trustees soon discovered that Crain's plan was not just high-sounding hyperbole. She was serious, and she confronted the board with an added sense of gravity for their own responsibilities. She applied for and received accreditation from the Council on Accreditation of Services for Families and Children, a national agency that certified Crossnore was following best practices in its care and providing quality services. Among other things, the council's endorsement required the full participation of board members. Trustees with spotty attendance patterns were elected to emeritus status; their replacements were chosen for what they could bring to the aid of the cause. Crain called it "loving people through change." She explained, "When you take an organization to this level, people either had to come with you or be left behind."

Meetings of the trustees became more than a prelude to an afternoon of golf. In the years before her arrival, the annual report from the long-range planning committee was usually about four paragraphs long. Crain had been on the job only a few weeks when she distributed a six-page document titled "Strategic Plan (First Draft)." In it, she walked the board through the stages necessary to reach a desired result. Trustee John Blackburn, who had been Crain's civic workmate in Avery County projects and her friend before he rejoined the board after an absence of about ten years, told his fellow trustees: "Put your seatbelt on. It is not going to be just rowing the boat. We are taking off."

For Crain, there was no time to lose, especially with the academy. She was determined to get Crossnore's students out of the makeshift classrooms as soon as possible. She had commitments from foundations for a third of the cost of the Wayne Densch Education Building in hand when the trustees announced the "Make a Miracle" campaign late in 2000. Rather than the $3 million figure that had been bandied about earlier, the new goal was $5 million. In addition to paying for the school facilities and contributing to the endowment, the money would build three new cottages, upgrade aging heating systems in old buildings, improve staff housing, build tennis courts, and overhaul the campus infrastructure.

Work began on the educational building in early 2001, and in June 2002 the first class of graduates were handed their diplomas. By the end of the year, campaign chairwoman Carol Dabbs announced the fund-raising campaign had surpassed it goal by $200,000. When

The home of the Crossnore Charter School is the Wayne Densch Education Building. It was built with money raised as part of the Make a Miracle Campaign, launched in 2000, which also paid for new cottages and campus improvements.

the campaign was finally closed out a year later, the total amount raised was more than $7 million.

"That lady can raise money," Dabbs said some years later. Dabbs was a relative newcomer to the board when she agreed to chair the campaign. She had grown up in Charlotte and first heard of Crossnore when her DAR mother pulled dresses from her closets to send to the Sales Store. "I know a lot of people who had the funds to give," Dabbs said. "But Phyllis Crain, well, once they met her, that was it. They gave. I was just the facilitator."

Foundation directors who had never heard from Crossnore before were impressed with Crain's ideas, as well as her unbounded energy, thorough planning, and attention to detail. Grants for six-figure amounts came from Asheville's Janirve Foundation, the Duke Endowment, Florida's Wayne Densch Charities, and Georgia's Thoresen Foundation, as well as North Carolina's Kate B. Reynolds Charitable Trust and the Cannon Foundation.

Individuals may have been initially drawn to the effort by Crossnore's remarkable history, but it was Crain who convinced donors to turn loose their money. They felt the warmth of her personality and the depth of her commitment, both to the children at Crossnore and to her faith. Sloop had cultivated a small group of benefactors in Charlotte, but Crain reached deep into the pockets of a broader audience, most of them wealthy seasonal residents of Avery County's resorts whose permanent addresses were all across the Southeast. The largest single individual gift in the campaign's first phase came from a Florida couple, Glenn and Carol Arthur. They came to see Crain to learn more about Crossnore after talking with one of her students, who had been their server at a local restaurant.

Her message penetrated hearts and melted resistance. It was clear, simple, and poignant. "What children in North Carolina's foster care system are grieving for and longing for is a healthy childhood," she said. "They are grieving for a childhood that has been literally and figuratively raped. I started using the terminology with donors that one of our passions here is to give children back their childhood. That became part of the language. Everything we can do would be around that." It was a message donors found hard to deny.

Crossnore's wealthy friends brought more than money for new buildings. On the same day that Arthur Cottage for boys was dedicated in the summer of 2002, the campus gathered to bless a sculpture by Richard Hallier of Boone. His bronze likeness of three children, two brothers and a sister, caught them in a moment of joy as they ran down the slope of a grassy lawn across from the Belk Dining Hall. It was a gift of philanthropist Irwin Belk of Charlotte, given in honor of his mother. Not long after, another sculpture of children, one holding a ladder for another, was given by Margaret Guy Penland, a daughter of Mary Sloop's banker, E. C. Guy. It was installed at the entrance to the school. Others would follow.

Muddy ditches criss-crossing the campus soon brought the prom-

The later cottages at The Crossnore School were designed to provide a living environment as close to a normal home as possible.

ise of clean water and sewer lines that wouldn't break. Fiber optic cables linked the campus buildings. And Crain began to fulfill some of the dreams of the children. By the end of 2002, Crossnore had seventy children and ten dogs in residential care. For Crain, the therapeutic value of the warm nuzzle of a dog against a troubled child outweighed the demerits Crossnore earned from the health inspector, whose regulations discouraged household pets. A generous donor offered to build the swimming pool that was also on the list. Crain convinced him to put it at a new YMCA to serve the entire county. Crossnore cottages received family memberships.

Crossnore School Incorporated got a new name, more fitting to its renewed mission. It became The Crossnore School. "I don't like the 'inc.' thing," Crain said one gray November day in 2010. "It sounds like a corporation making widgets. Or a reform school. You don't see 'Inc.' after Woodberry Forest School. Berea College is not Berea College Inc." She had rambled into this aside as she traced the challenges from one era to the next. "Dr. Sloop always called it a school. Without a doubt, she had constructed a boarding school for poor children. It was sort of like Berea College on an elementary, middle school, and high school level. In Dr. Sloop's time, she could pile thirty boys into the two-story structure and have one cottage momma. I have to have two staff members for every cottage of five to ten kids. [Dr. Sloop's daughter] Emma would pat me on the hand and say, 'My momma could never run a school with today's regulations.'" Crain laughed.

She was nestled into an overstuffed chair in her office in the Bayles Administration Building. Even with a desk, the blank stare of a computer screen in a far corner, piles of working papers, and award plaques on the walls, the space had the feel of a living room, not an executive's office. French doors opened onto a terrace. Campus visitors, staff members, and others rambled in and out all day; Crain's door was usually open. A Daughter from Texas had arrived that morning with a horse trailer full of donations for the Sales Store. Crain invited her to an all-campus luncheon in the gymnasium, where she made a ceremonial presentation of class rings—handsome in gold, with a dark stone—for the academy's seniors. All twelve had plans to further their education on campuses of community colleges and universities.

The day had been long, but Crain remained lively and animated as she talked about Crossnore and the children. "Precious" was one of her favorite words, whether she was talking about a generous donor or a troubled child. There was no hint of fatigue in a woman who three months earlier had resumed an aggressive treatment for cancer that had returned, as threatening as ever, after six years of relative dormancy. Only her close-cropped gray hair gave testimony to the recent weeks of radiation and chemical treatments.

The cancer had first been discovered just as summer was turning to fall in 2001. The Make a Miracle campaign was under way, and students were settling into classes in the new educational building that had just opened for the fall term. Crain was fixing a cup of tea to help her nurse mild back pain when she sneezed and collapsed to the floor in unbearable agony. Hours later, at the hospital, she learned she had broken vertebrae weakened by breast cancer that had metastasized to her spine, ribs, clavicle, and hip. Trustees with the right connections soon had her on a private airplane to M. D. Anderson Cancer Center in Houston, where oncologists only confirmed the gravity of her condition. Their prognosis: she would live for a year, maybe eighteen months.

This could not be. Her ministry at Crossnore—that's what her job had become—had only just begun. To be told there was no hope, no healing, could not be correct. "I've read the book [the Bible]," she later told an interviewer. "I know how things are to end. I'm a Christian, but I'm not at peace. I knew I wasn't finished."

Once again, she was that defiant young mother-to-be hanging out wash on a cold winter day. Even in the face of the harsh reality presented by medical professionals, she told anyone who asked that the prognosis simply would not do. A year was not sufficient to finish everything on her to-do list. Crossnore Academy was in its formative year, a new cottage was under construction, and promises had been made to Crossnore's children. She hadn't told her board that she was working on a twenty-year plan. A year! Pshaw. She had to have more time.

The doctors insisted—she had a year. The trustees wrung their hands. Some talked about finding a replacement. She was sitting with other cancer patients, gowned and waiting for treatment, when one of her seatmates told her to pack it in. It was time to retire and apply for disability. Fighting cancer was hard work, he insisted. She would need all her energy for that. He wouldn't be quiet until he had her address and had promised to walk her through the applications. "That day, they were doing an MRI on my spine," Crain remembers. "The machine makes a sledgehammer sound in your ears. All I could think about was this is not who I am. I was not raised to live off the government. I was raised to work, and by golly as long as I am vertical, I am serving the Lord. I just felt like that is what I have to do."

She submitted to regular treatments with an energy that prompted her call to the cancer center in Boone to be ready when she arrived for her "drive-by chemo." She was not going to waste any more time than necessary on this disease. For months, the body cast she inhabited limited her movement, but with the help of her husband and father, she forced herself to stand erect. She went to the office when she could, checked on construction when she could. When necessary, her assistant, Kathy Dellinger, brought the office to her. She called donors and talked with her staff. Many days, she sat with Keith on the deck of their home, looking toward Grandfather Mountain, a dark outline on the horizon. They talked, they cried, they planned and prayed.

She wrote the annual year-end appeal to Crossnore donors and explained her condition. She told them of the candles (electric ones) that students had placed in the windows of the cottages, the school, the Weave Room, and at the Sales Store: "They assured me that when I am too weak to pray, some member of the Crossnore family is praying for me. I want to thank you for your spirit, for your generosity, for your concern, prayers and love. To love me best, love my children." There was no hint of retreat. She would "emerge a stronger person."

By spring of 2002, Crain was not only walking, but she had pedaled a recumbent bicycle forty miles along the New River Trail in Virginia. In June, she stood for pictures with her arms around the academy's graduating class. Her dark brown hair was long again, falling to her shoulders. Reports from her doctors encouraged her and confounded them. One finally admitted she was just an "outlier" from the usual statistics. The bone cancer was contained. There were no signs it had spread to major organs. Then, in the summer of 2003, she heard the news that she had been praying for. Her latest body scan showed no evidence of cancer. In a report on her good news to the trustees, she sent along a copy of a student's drawing of an angel holding a trumpet raised to on high. The student, she said, had "wanted to portray what the angels in heaven were doing when they heard the news of my healing."

"Prayer has wrought miracles in these hills. I know it," Mary Sloop had written a half-century earlier. "Through long years I have seen it. Joyously and out of a full heart I declare it. If any would doubt the power of prayer, only this I say to him, and humbly, try it."

Now Crossnore had another miracle to enjoy. And for Crain, there was no question it was a miracle. After the dedication of the Phyllis Crain cottage early in 2004—an event most believed she would never live to see—Crain said, "The medical world describes this miracle as my cancer being 'in remission.' I describe it as God's amazing grace."

Crain's story drew magazine writers and television producers to the campus. UNC-TV's William Friday made her one of his *North Carolina People*, and some viewers unlimbered their checkbooks and adopted the school. Crain's story became Crossnore's story, in much the same way that Sloop's tireless efforts had captured the imagination of an earlier generation of donors and sponsors. Trustees and friends became energized by her example. The first phase of the Make a Miracle campaign was followed by a second, and then a third. Crain and Crossnore raised another $10 million for further enhancements to the campus, including more cottages, renovations of the dining hall, the creation of a sports complex, and, finally, the building of a performance hall like the one Mary Sloop had dreamed of in her dying days. In time, a barn and paddock became the focal point of a program in equine therapy, where rescued horses helped rescue children.

The school recovered the hospital property, and when the demolition company arrived to tear it down, Crain convinced the foreman to dismantle it rather than simply bulldoze it off the hill. As the additions came down, the original stone walls that Will Franklin had laid in 1928 were discovered intact, and the old building stood like a Phoenix rising out of the rubble. Restoration began to preserve an architectural gem from an early era of mountain life. Architects even found replacement roof tiles—made of concrete and unique in their day—stored away in the basement. Dedicated as the Edwin Guy building, it was renovated to provide four guest rooms for campus visitors, a boardroom, and space for a medical clinic staffed by a family nurse practitioner who could serve the campus children, as well as patients in the community.

Meanwhile, Crain salvaged the Crossnore weaving program in a collaborative effort with trustee Freda Nicholson of Charlotte. Draw-

The equestrian therapy program at The Crossnore School was one of the innovations developed by Dr. Phyllis Crain and generous donors who provided a barn for rescue horses.

ing on Nicholson's experience in helping create Discovery Place as a kid-friendly exploration of science and imagination, Crain turned Homespun House into a working museum where local weavers could continue to demonstrate their art and make money from the sale of their goods. The museum allowed Crossnore to continue an important part of its heritage and provide local weavers with a steady market for their work from visitors, as well as the annual sales at the DAR's Continental Congress in Washington, D.C. "We moved away from having full-time weavers on staff to actually what Dr. Sloop did in her days. She was an astute businesswoman. She did piece rate. That is what we do."

Later, other local artists—potters, painters, and carvers—were asked to provide items on consignment for display and possible sale in the gallery. In the summer, a Charleston, South Carolina, dealer in fine arts hung high-end paintings there, sharing commissions on sales.

Tourist traffic to Homespun House increased after artist Ben Long completed a fresco mounted on the back wall of the Sloop Cha-

When years of additions that had enlarged Garrett
Memorial Hospital were removed, the original structure
was found in good condition. The building was
reconstructed to provide a guest house and clinic for the
campus.

The Homespun House became the home of the Crossnore weavers after the log Weave Room burned in 1935. Built of river stone, it later became a working museum and gallery of mountain arts.

pel that depicted Jesus with the children. The second phase of the Make a Miracle campaign had included refurbishing the chapel, which had been largely untouched for fifty years. Crossnore's leader wanted more than newly polished floors, fresh carpet, rebuilt bathrooms, and a new heating system, especially after she settled a sobbing child into her lap during an evening chapel service. Crain said: "She looked up at me and said, 'I have lost everything. Momma is dead. Her friend who is taking care of us died. Even my cat died. I have no one.' And I just broke in a really deep place. Sitting in chapel, facing forward, I would have loved to be able to turn to the back wall and say, 'You know you always have Jesus, who loved children and who always said, "Bring them to me."' He is our heavenly father. At a very child level, it would be an introduction to God as hope and strength when you truly have no one."

Artist Ben Long IV created a fresco that fills the back wall of the Sloop Chapel. It brings to life the words of Matthew 10:14: "Suffer the little children to come unto me."

Long's fresco, "Suffer the Little Children," is sixteen feet wide and nine feet tall. It was finished in the summer of 2006. Long used sketches of Crossnore children as his models. Phyllis and Keith Crain were among those who sat up through the night to watch the artist and his assistants work until dawn to finish the image of Jesus. "There is a lot of theology in that piece," she said later. "The adults are ... Well, they don't have time for these children. He is just radiating that this is my business. You-all don't get it. That was such an exciting time."

The campus was becoming pretty, a description that would never have been uttered before. Utilitarian, yes. Pretty? Perhaps only in the sense that frugality and simplicity can be an art form. A new entrance with a curving drive was built when the elementary school came down. The demolition opened space for handsome new cottages with open decks that offered views to the hills beyond. A donor provided a miniature railroad. Playgrounds were only steps from the cottage doors. An outdoor amphitheater was added, and a playwright's rendition of *Miracle in the Hills* as an outdoor drama became part of the summer program. On opening night in 2007, a power failure darkened the valley. Crain went to the stage and asked for patience, and a miracle. Then, as if on cue, lights flickered back to life in the homes, and the stage flooded with light.

Crain's imagination produced the village's first eatery in decades when the Miracle Grounds Coffee Shop opened in a small stone building just across from the town hall. Formerly the Muscle Farm, a bodybuilding studio, Miracle Grounds became a vocational classroom for older students where customers could find specialty coffees, pastries, and sandwiches, along with a small collection of used books. The student jobs were part of a revived self-help program, with even the youngest children responsible for chores in the cottages.

Ingenuity produced opportunity. A kennel built to care for cot-

Mary Sloop's story as told in Miracle in the Hills *was revived in an outdoor drama performed during the summer in an amphitheater built on the campus. Haley Hanes, the Crain's six-year-old granddaughter, portrayed a young Emma Sloop in the 2011 performance.*

tage pets when the "family" was away for a week at the beach was opened to pet owners in the community and began paying its way. It was staffed by student workers supervised by a vet. One ingenious teenager with a decided mechanical talent opened a repair shop in the basement of the gymnasium to keep the campus fleet of bicycles in good repair. Campus services—a medical clinic, the academy, counseling—were offered to the people of Avery County.

From time to time, grumblings reached Crain from those in the community who were uneasy with the changes taking place all around them. She was "that woman," roundly denounced at the post office after a community baseball field on school property was reclaimed to become part of the Crossnore Academy campus. Crain also ruled the campus off-limits for the Fourth of July fireworks display out of concern that the fireworks would damage life and property. That really riled folks who were accustomed to using Crossnore property as if it were their own. After three generations, there were still those who didn't understand the philosophy of the Sales Store. "People give you this stuff," Crain heard a customer loudly declare one day. "You ought to be giving it away." What with the introduction of class rings, handsome school uniforms, and summer vacations for the children, there was talk that Crossnore was snobby and too good for its neighbors. "It's not what it used to be," old-timers said, but they spoke with disdain, not pride. "Can you imagine criticizing for just making the place lovely?" Crain asked with exasperation one afternoon. "Why would you want it to be ugly? Why would you not want there to be a piece of art in a building or have a lovely school campus?" She soldiered on in the tradition of Mary Sloop, who hadn't been universally applauded either. Crain was told it had been more than bad weather that kept some community leaders away from the founder's funeral.

As Crossnore filled out into the vision Crain had expressed a decade earlier, the comparison of the two women became inevitable, with some suggesting that it was providence, not Crain's desire for a career change, that had brought her to the campus in 1999. The similarities were striking. She and Sloop were both prayerful, hard-working, creative, and compassionate women whose every effort was on the behalf of children. Faced with her own debilitating illness, Sloop

The trustees purchased an old building in town and converted it into a coffee shop, bringing a small café back to the life of the community. Students prepare meals and drinks for customers as part of the campus work-study program.

had never surrendered. Neither had Crain. Mary Sloop built a town; Phyllis Crain restored one. And they both had an amazing capacity to separate people from their money on behalf of an institution that restored hope and confidence in young people.

One day, Crain was visiting with Emma Sloop. "I was telling her something about a little bus we needed for the charter school and we didn't have funding in place yet. But I am ordering it. She reached over and said, 'My mother would love you. That was the same way my mother operated.' You pray a lot and trust the Lord that he will make it happen."

Trustee Alexander Lyerly knew both women. "I almost think of Phyllis Crain as being a reincarnation of Dr. Sloop, because she is constantly looking for ways to get a better place for children and to give them more opportunity," he said. When the Duke Endowment funded the early costs of a mother-child program, one that Crain patterned on something she had seen in Texas, she reminded those who inquired that Mary Sloop had done the same thing in the 1930s when a widowed Naomi Greene, with children in tow, became a house-mother and Georgia Lunsford came with her children to work in the campus laundry.

Affirmation for the new Crossnore came from around the country. The World Children's Center recognized Crain with its humanitarian award in 2007. North Carolina's Z. Smith Reynolds Foundation presented her with the Nancy Susan Reynolds Award for advocacy in 2008, the same year her alma mater, Wofford College, presented her with its Algeron Sydney Sullivan Foundation's Mary Mildred Sullivan Award. In 2010, Crain was named National Administrator of the Year by the Coalition for Residential Education.

Crossnore's future looked bright and hopeful. But like Crain's own prognosis, it remained an outlier. With roughly two-thirds of its students placed by social workers, Crossnore was at the mercy of officials who were being nudged by government regulations to move children out of Crossnore almost as soon as they were admitted. The trend lines were discouraging. A third of Crossnore's children were on the campus for ninety days or less. Just how much repair could be accomplished in that brief window? Crain vented to friends in evening e-mails. "It should be criminal in the state of North Carolina to take a little brother and sister who have been so happy their entire five months with us, now healthy, living in an incredibly loving home like Atwell Cottage and then jerked up and moved like pawns on a chessboard." Some cottage parents had a few hours or less to help the children pack their things. A high school senior was pulled from her cottage just days before her graduation.

"We just lost a family of five—sending all of them back to a father who is out of jail on bail for operating a meth lab," she wrote one evening, explaining that a state auditor reviewing county records on out-of-home care had ordered the children returned to the home county because they were under the age of twelve. "We know of no treatment intervention that has been done in three months that would transform meth lab operators into healthy and caring parents. We have grave concerns for their safety and well-being."

Reuniting a family—the mantra of child welfare agencies—sounded so good on paper. More often than not, on the Crossnore campus, it remained an insult to the children the system was designed to serve. Crain finally succeeded in 2009 in getting legislation approved that recognized the value of a comprehensive care and educational program like Crossnore's even for the youngest on the social services rolls. That did not remove the constant threat to the care of brothers and sisters, who could be removed without notice, regardless of Crossnore's new cottages, its fine school, trained staff, and faith-filled program.

The solution was apparent, and it came directly from Mary Sloop herself. Crain wrote her board in the early fall of 2010, "I know that you are often asked, 'What is Crossnore's greatest need?' Our greatest need is scholarships for children living in poverty, who are not in DSS [Department of Social Services] custody who want and need to attend The Crossnore School. We have turned away another three students in the past few days because we have every scholarship dollar in our budget committed to the eighteen children we already have in care."

For forty years, Sloop had asked for scholarships to pay for the cost of a child's care and education. She asked for fifty dollars a year, a handsome amount in the 1930s. Individuals and DAR chapters responded. Some years, scholarships added more to her bank account than anything else she could do. Crain and the trustees had made growing the endowment a priority since the first phase of Make a Miracle. Now, the need became more urgent than ever. One hundred million dollars was set as the goal.

In the meantime, Crain began asking wealthy friends, Crossnore's largest donors, to consider funding scholarships. The price was high: $22,500 to keep a child for a year. She reinforced her call for help by pledging $1,000 a month for ten months from her own pay. Twenty-seven donors responded, pledging more than $400,000 in scholarship funds. "If you do not believe in miracles," she wrote the board, telling them of the response, "you will now!"

There was a new urgency in Crain's appeal that went out just before Christmas in 2010. Earlier in the year, her doctors had told her that her cancer had returned, this time in her liver. She underwent sixteen

Dr. Crain talked about The Crossnore School at the 2012 North Carolina DAR state conference and visited with Kathryn Herman, incoming regent of the Joseph McDowell Chapter, one of the largest chapters in the state.

hours of surgery for repairs to her spine and then began an experimental regimen of treatment. Nine months later, as she appealed for Crossnore's children, the tumors remained in her liver, and they had enlarged. She and her family labored through highs and lows.

Mary Sloop was once asked about her philosophy of life. Goodness gracious, she said. She had never taken the time to figure it out. There was too much to do. As she put it, she worked as hard as she could, and when she had done all she could, she left the rest in the hands of the Lord. She didn't worry about the future of Crossnore, Sloop said. "I'm only a little envious of the one who's going to have such a fine time helping so many marvelous things happen here."

A half-century later, the same true light guided Crain. She worked as hard as she could and left the rest in the hands of the Lord. "One of my employees and I were talking, and we were saying there is no place quite like Crossnore where you can totally use every single gift you have been given. I can sing here in chapel. I can speak to the student body and to the staff, like I did this morning, or to the New York DAR this weekend. I have a gift at financial management and acumen for investments and savings. I've got strategic planning and envisioning down the road and making things happen. You get to use every single gift you have. Often in the world of work, you are lucky if you work in one area that you are gifted. You can use them all here, every single one."

Too busy living, Crain turned her cancer into a gift in service to Crossnore as her story stirred Crossnore's wealthy friends to convert investments moldering in a bank to use for God's children. "It makes her story more compelling," said one who worked with her through her trials. Her story created an emotional hold on those willing to join in her crusade for children. "This is her life's passion and her life's work," her coworker explained. "While we all are living day to day, she *truly* is living day to day."

At the close of its first century, Crossnore remained in the hands of the Lord and a succession plan that Crain had crafted long ago. Whenever trustees got nervous, she would pull it out and read it to

National Society President General Merry Ann T. Wright (left); Lynn Forney Young (center), Recording Secretary General and past Texas State Regent; and Kay Alston (right), Texas State Schools Chair, in front of the Texas Tack Room in the horse barn. The Tack Room was a gift of the Texas DAR during Mrs. Young's tenure as state regent.

them again. Then somebody would say, "You-all have tried to bury her before. Leave her alone."

A hundred years after Mary Sloop began her work, Crossnore's mission remained founded in pushing back the poverty and ignorance that stunted the future of mountain children. In organizing their modest compact in the bylaws of Crossnore School Incorporated, the founders had proposed to promote Christian education and maintain a school of quality for academic performance and vocational excellence, with the implicit understanding that through education, the dark corners would finally see light. In 2011, that simple mission was refined and restated to reflect those original ambitions. "The mission of the Crossnore School," the twenty-first-century trustees agreed, "is to provide a Christian sanctuary of hope and healing where students in need rise above their circumstances and excel both in school and in life."

But there was more. Nearly a hundred years of service to the children and families of the North Carolina mountains also had produced a vision as undeniable as that mission stated so long ago: "The vision of The Crossnore School is to positively transform the lives of children from families in crisis by breaking generational cycles and creating a hope and future through education, work and service."

In her twilight years, long before Crain was even born, Mary Sloop's confidence in Crossnore's future, and her own, was unshakable, founded in faith and the bounty of her Lord. Her vision was clear as she approached what she called "the uncharted maze of days along the highest slope of the last mountain." Crossnore would endure, she believed. "I know things will be all right—for Crossnore and for me. For Crossnore I cherish—and see—a long and even more accomplishing life, a continually increasing importance to the youth of our beloved mountains."

Notes

1. An Epiphany of Shame

Crain said she experienced an "epiphany of shame": author interview with Phyllis Crain, November 24, 2010.

"God, gumption, and grit" built Crossnore: untitled account of teacher on staff from November 30, 1938, to April 24, 1942, Crossnore archives.

"We are a trauma-informed community": Phyllis Crain interview, November 24, 2010.

2. The Sloops

"I cannot yet decide": Winifred Kirkland, "A Hundred-Horse-Power Woman," *Country Gentleman*, March 14, 1925.

She had come to Crossnore in 1911: ibid.

Even the man who had given his name: Mary Martin Sloop, *Miracle in the Hills* (McGraw-Hill, 1953), p. 3.

However, by 1917: "Right Now, at Crossnore: What We Are Doing and How We Are Doing It," undated broadside, Crossnore School archives.

Sloop came from a family of scholars: *Miracle in the Hills*, p. 8.

She began her formal medical studies: *Quips and Cranks*, 1903, Davidson College archives.

In 1905, Mary's brother William helped draw the plans: Donald B. Saunders, *For His Cause a Little House* (Appalachian Consortium Press, 1988), p. 46.

Mary was a teenager: *Miracle in the Hills*, p. 15.

A year after their move: *For His Cause a Little House*, pp. 52–53.

This old building served: *Miracle in the Hills*, p. 49.

The Reverend Monte Johnson was a boy: Mary Dudley Gilmer, *Panorama of Caring* (Linville, NC: Avery Health Care System, 1999), p. 14.

One-room schoolhouses predominated: "A History of Avery County Schools," Appalachian State University Special Collections, 1989, unpaged.

By the time they arrived: Philis Alvic, *The Weaving Room of Crossnore School, Inc.* (Newland, NC: Avery County Historical Society and Museum, 1998), p. 8.

This time, Sloop wrote to her cousins: *Miracle in the Hills*, p. 72.

Sloop kept writing her letters: Mary Sloop to Mrs. Burt, January 28, 1914, Crossnore School archives.

After Hepsy's first year: published broadsides, Crossnore School archives.

Instead, she substituted a printed broadside: "Teacherage," ca. 1915; "Right Now, at Crossnore," ca. 1917, Crossnore School archives.

In a 1915 report to Berea's president: *The Weaving Room of Crossnore Schools Inc.*, p. 8.

3. We Hope to Rise

He once wrote: J. Wayne Flynt, "'Feeding the Hungry and Ministering to the Broken Hearted': The Presbyterian Church in the U.S. and the Social Gospel, 1900–1920," in *Religion in the South*, ed. Charles Reagan Wilson (Oxford: University Press of Mississippi, 1985), p. 118.

A desire to "save" the young women: ibid, p. 100.

In the mid-1890s, the Episcopalians: Howard E. Covington Jr., *All Saints Episcopal Mission: A Linville Church and Its People* (Linville, NC: All Saints Episcopal Mission, Linville, 2010), p. 3.

Armed with the authority of a new truancy law: *Miracle in the Hills*, p. 96.

The commencement exercises: commencement program, Crossnore School archives.

When Sloop began his work: *Miracle in the Hills*, p. 78.

Some parents had built small cabins: "Right Now, at Crossnore."

If Mary Sloop had a model: *Bulletin of Berea College*, April 1911.

The election was called: *Miracle in the Hills*, pp. 1–8.

Nell and her brother Monte: Nell Buchanan interview with Philis Alvic, November 30, 1995, recording made available to author by Philis Alvic.

4. Spreading the Word

In 1910, at the age of twenty-one: Mildred Harrington, "He Took One Look at the Outside World and Went Back to His Mountains," unidentified clipping, undated, Crossnore School archives.

Will Franklin, McCoy's father: *Miracle in the Hills*, p. 159, and author interview with McCoy Franklin Jr., April 27, 2011.

When he arrived back home, he became the public voice of Crossnore: C. McCoy Franklin testimony, *McCoy Franklin v. Crossnore School Inc. and Mary Martin Sloop*, North Carolina Supreme Court, SC1937F-237, North Carolina State Archives, Raleigh, North Carolina.

She eagerly endorsed the new role: Mary Martin Sloop to McCoy Franklin, June 21, 1921, plaintiff's exhibit 1, *McCoy Franklin v. Crossnore Schools Inc.*

The first of these commuter students: *Miracle in the Hills*, p. 141.

In the Helton community of Ashe County: Committee on Public Information, North Carolina Education Association, *Education in NC, 1900 and Now* (Raleigh, NC: Bynum Printing, 1930), appendix A.

It was built with money donated: *Miracle in the Hills*, p. 144, and Charles M. Battett, ed.,

"The Presbyterian Orphans' Home at Barium Springs, NC, An Album of Memories," August 1994.

Sloop was eternally frugal: Mary Martin Sloop, "How Crossnore Spends Her Money," undated, Crossnore School archives.

In late February, during a public hearing: Cecil Kenneth Brown, *The State Highway System of North Carolina* (Chapel Hill: University of North Carolina Press, 1931), p. 116.

No member of the faculty touched more lives: Maude Minish Sutton, "Crossnore Real Community Work," *Raleigh News and Observer*, June 19, 1927.

Franklin's ability to charm an audience: Franklin interview.

Franklin formed the Save the Children Club: memoir in possession of McCoy Franklin Jr., excerpt provided to author.

In 1922, the Camp Fire Girls of Baltimore: *Everygirl's Magazine* 10 (January 1923) and *Boys' Life*, October 1923.

Throughout the movie, Busey remembers: Jean Busey Yntema interview by Colleen Ogg, September 1984, Y69, University of Illinois at Springfield, Norris L. Brookens Library.

At the time of Busey's presentation: *Twenty-Sixth Annual State Conference, Illinois Daughters of the American Revolution*, p. 108.

Mary Sloop became a "member at large": membership records of the National Society of the Daughters of the American Revolution.

She returned to Washington: *Proceedings of Thirty-Third Continental Congress of the National Society of the Daughters of the American Revolution*, p. 446.

The store had regular hours: H. W. Kendall, "Old Clothing and Fairy Princess Transform Life in Mountains," *Charlotte Observer*, August 22, 1926.

Sloop moved her office into the teacherage: Mary Martin Sloop testimony, *McCoy Franklin v. Crossnore School Inc. and Mary Martin Sloop*.

The sleepy crossroads that a decade earlier: "Crossnore," *Avery Journal*, September 8, 1927.

While the overall attendance rate: *Miracle in the Hills*, p. 169.

5. The Weaving Department

The handicraft of Thomas Dellinger's boys in the carpentry shop: Philis Alvic interview with Dr. Emma Sloop, August 29, 1998.

The school's new looms were made: Forest T. Selby, *Manual Training Magazine* 23, no. 2 (August 1921).

Down the mountain in Asheville: Allan H. Eaton, *Handicrafts of the Southern Highlands* (Russell Sage Foundation, 1937), p. 66.

Edith Vanderbilt, the widow of George Vanderbilt: Howard E. Covington Jr., *Lady on the Hill: How Biltmore Estate Became an American Icon* (John Wiley and Sons, 2006), p. 53.

The new roads paid for by Governor Morrison's: *Lady on the Hill*, p. 65.

In the summer of 1925: minutes of organizational meeting, Crossnore School archives.

A sister, Leota, was one of the girls: Denise Abbey memoir, Crossnore School archives.

"Let me tell you what she did in those days": *Miracle in the Hills*, p. 174.

The Crossnore weaving program would never: various letters in correspondence files,

Division of Trades and Industries, Department of Public Instruction, State Archives, Raleigh, North Carolina, and Philis Alvic, *Weavers of the Southern Highlands* (University Press of Kentucky, 2003), p. 120.

Crossnore became the largest ongoing weaving program: Ann Johnson Stanley, Crossnore School archives.

By the fall of 1924, there were thirty-eight students: *The Weaving Room of Crossnore School Inc.*, p. 17.

In 1926, it generated $3,000 in revenue: *Raleigh News and Observer*, July 19, 1927.

Sloop called the weavers working at home: Weave Room brochure, ca. 1927, Crossnore School archives.

Sloop especially liked the log construction: *Miracles in the Hills*, p. 174.

They huddled in the Penland Weavers Cabin: Lucy Morgan, *Gift from the Hills* (Penland, NC: Penland School of Crafts, 2005), p. 80.

One of the first to arrive was Allen H. Eaton: Allen Eaton, "The Mountain Handicrafts: Their Importance to the Country and to the People in the Mountain Homes," *Mountain Life and Work*, July 1930.

As Crossnore weavers assembled pieces: Mary Martin Sloop to George Coggin, June 7, 1932, Division of Trades and Industries, Department of Public Instruction, State Archives, Raleigh, North Carolina.

6. Eustace

It featured gabled end sections: *Panorama of Caring*, p. 23.

"We figured we were pretty good doctors": Sloop, *Miracle in the Hills*, p. 27.

The power station that housed his first generator: Charles Sloop interview by Danica Goodman, Crossnore videos.

Sloop's practical genius confounded experts: Sloop, *Miracle in the Hills*, p. 83.

Electricity was just the beginning: *Panorama of Caring*, p. 20.

In the early years, the family lived off a small dowry: *For His Cause a Little House*, p. 52.

"Dad just hated to ask his patients for money": *Panorama of Caring*, p. 26

Some believed he suffered a form of narcolepsy: author interview with Rachel Deal, November 9, 2010.

Together, the Sloops helped organize the Crossnore Presbyterian Church: "The Historic Crossnore Presbyterian Church," Crossnore Presbyterian Church, Crossnore, North Carolina.

One who attended his classes said: Doctor Grace Sperry Burns to family, August 1942, Crossnore School archives.

Newland banker E. C. Guy: author interview with Martha Guy, November 12, 2010.

"He's the quiet kind": *Miracle in the Hills*, p. 230.

Emma said years later: Emma Sloop Fink interview by Philis Alvic, August 28 1998, made available to author.

Space was at a premium: *Panorama of Caring*, p. 23.

Denise Abbey worked at Crossnore: Denise Abbey memories of Crossnore, Crossnore School archives.

7. The Faculty

By the 1930s, Crossnore required: Mary Martin Sloop to Mrs. Ralph Van Landingham, November 24, 1934, Crossnore School archives.

"She seems to be the One and Only Authority": Grace Sperry Burns to family, February 18, 1942, Crossnore School archives.

The greater Crossnore family: author interviews with Sally Slaton, June 17, 2011, and Robert Sample, March 4, 2011, and Denise Abbey memoirs, 1980, Crossnore School archives.

Denise Abbey was from Long Island, New York: Denise Abbey memoir.

"Breaking a sweat every day": McCoy Franklin Jr. interview.

The Sloops didn't draw any income: Mary Martin Sloop to Mrs. Ralph Van Landingham.

By 1930, the Linville Valley Power Company: Mary Martin Sloop to State Corporation Commission, August 2, 1920, North Carolina state archives.

Some of the adults who applied for jobs: Georgia Lunsford interview with Anne Winn Stevens, December 29, 1938, Library of Congress, American Memory Collection.

He was struggling with his schoolwork: Denise Abbey memoir.

Joe Powlas's mother became the dietician: author interview with Joe Powlas.

Board members received death threats: unsigned note to Alex Johnson, Crossnore School archives.

Franklin had only recently returned to the campus: McCoy Franklin Jr. interview.

She moved out of her office in the teacherage: testimony of Mary M. Sloop, *McCoy Franklin v. Crossnore School Inc.*, North Carolina Supreme Court, SC1937F-237, North Carolina State Archives.

As he resumed his duties: minutes, board of trustees, Crossnore School Incorporated, June 21, 1932, Crossnore School archives.

It was settled for a single payment: Crossnore School archives and McCoy Franklin Jr. interview.

Forty years later, one of the campus staff pulled: author interview with H. Dean Bare, December 14, 2010.

In Sloop's day, the *Bulletin* was as good: examples drawn from several accounts in *Bulletins*.

A widow who arrived in 1942: Grace Sperry Burns letters.

The houseparent in the Middle Boys: author interview with Joe Powlas, December 8, 2010.

"Ma" Greene, as the boys called her: Fred Hawkens, *My Story*, (Lakeland, FL: Genie Publishing, 2006), p. 28.

One night, a new arrival: Joe Powlas, *Somewhere along the Way* (Kearney, NB: Morris Publishing, 2007), p. 140.

"She has saved many a boy and girl": Grace Sperry Burns letters.

"I don't believe a harsh way": Mary Martin Sloop interview with Legette Blythe, undated, Crossnore School archives and Legette Blythe Papers, Southern Historical Collection, Wilson Library, University of North Carolina, Chapel Hill, NC.

Joe Powlas remembered the DAR: Joe Powlas interview.

8. The Boarding Department

The mission of Crossnore School: minutes, board of trustees, January 10, 1934, Crossnore School Incorporated.

Of the 192 students admitted in 1934: Mary Martin Sloop to Mrs. Ralph Van Landingham, November 24, 1934, Crossnore School archives.

Speaking to the state meeting of the DAR in North Carolina: *Proceedings of the Thirty-First State Conference, North Carolina Daughters of the American Revolution*.

The dormitory was dedicated: *Proceedings of the Forty-Third Continental Congress* (Third Day), p. 405.

Forty to fifty of the older boys lived: Denise Abbey memoir.

For many years, the first task: Fred Hawkens, *My Story*, and *Crossnore School Bulletin* 8, no. 4 (July–September 1941).

Sloop had more than comfort and basic needs: *Crossnore School Bulletin* 8, no. 4 (July–September 1941).

Soon, the population began to grow again after donations: *Crossnore School Bulletin* 4, no. 3 (April–June 1937).

Sloop estimated the cost of a meal: Mary Martin Sloop to Mrs. Van Landingham.

"We substituted potatoes": Mary Martin Sloop interviews with Legette Blythe.

One year in the early 1940s: *Crossnore School Bulletin* 9, no. 1 (September–December 1941).

Like she did with so many other opportunities: *Crossnore School Bulletin* 11, no. 5 (October–December 1946).

It took Sloop nearly three years of fund-raising: *Crossnore School Bulletin* 9, no. 1 (September–December 1941).

The story of Crossnore's wobbly finances: ibid.

Sloop's buildings were as simple as they could be: Grace Sperry Burns letters, February 1942.

Mary Sloop didn't hide the extent of Crossnore's pressing needs: *Crossnore School Bulletin* 11, no. 3 (July–September 1944).

If anyone doubted in the durability: *Miracle in the Hills*, p. 170.

9. The Children

Roadman Hollander was one of the boys: The Roadman Hollander story has been told and retold. An account of his life was first published in the *Crossnore School Bulletin* 7, no. 4 (July–September 1940) and in a separate broadside that included a photograph. Sloop saw to it that it received wide circulation. This account combines information from both.

"What a motley line it was": *Crossnore School Bulletin* 4, no. 4 (July–Sept 1937).

Forty-three percent of all families in the county: Jack Temple-Kirby, *The American South: Rural Worlds Lost, 1920–1960* (Louisiana State University Press, 1987), p. 94.

The plight of little boys troubled Sloop the most: *Crossnore School Bulletin* 28, no. 4 (October–December 1954).

Crossnore applicants came from all around: selected accounts from *Crossnore School Bulletins* published in the 1930s.

Fred Hawkens and his brother, James: Fred Hawkens, *My Story*, (Lakeland, FL: Genie Publishing, 2006), p. 27.

Others were dropped at the door: *Somewhere along the Way*, p. 37.

One Saturday in August: *Crossnore School Bulletin* 14, no. 4 (October–December 1947).

One boy who returned after: *Crossnore School Bulletin* 18, no. 3 (October–December 1948).

"She was surrounded by an aura of love, an aura of acceptance": author interview with Jack Haim, May 23, 2011.

"She made us feel important": *My Story*, p. 31.

One day, Sloop found a girl sitting: *Crossnore School Bulletin* 10, no. 1 (October–December 1942).

One housemother wryly observed: Grace Sperry Burns letters.

Sloop also could scold: Grace Sperry Burns letters.

It was a devastating loss: *The Weaving Room of Crossnore School Inc.*, p. 23.

Mrs. Johnson called the new weaving room Homespun House: *Proceedings of the Forty-sixth Continental Congress*.

In an invocation written for the occasion: Denise Abbey, invocation written for inauguration of Homespun House, Crossnore School archives.

Houseparents and assorted staff members: "Christmas at Crossnore," ca. 1954, Crossnore School archives.

"The dining hall was beautifully decorated": Mamie Shirley Church, "Christmas at Crossnore," December 1939, Crossnore School archives.

Young Jack Haim arrived at Crossnore: Jack Haim interview.

She called them "our English refugee cousins": *Crossnore School Bulletin* 7, no. 4 (July–September 1940).

By the early weeks of 1940: *Crossnore School Bulletin* 9, no. 1 (October–December, 1940).

When America entered World War II: *Crossnore School Bulletin* 8, no. 2 (January–March 1941).

10. Over There

Taylor graduated from the high school: Mary Martin Sloop to Mrs. F. W. Freytag, Kirkville, New York, November 11, 1947, Crossnore School archives.

"Here in our mountains": *Crossnore School Bulletin* 7, no. 3 (July–September 1942).

That may have been why Avery County was third: ibid.

Sloop reported that campus jobs had prepared the volunteers: examples pulled from issues of the *Crossnore School Bulletin* published during the war years.

A woman doctor was unusual: *Panorama of Caring*, p. 24.

She scolded him on winter days: Grace Sperry Burns letters.

A large power company: E. H. Sloop to N. C. Utilities Commission, April 15, 1940, North Carolina State Archives.

Advancing age didn't keep the Sloops: *Crossnore School Bulletin* 8, no. 2 (October–December 1940).

The high school building had been promised: undated, hand-written notes of Mary Martin Sloop, Crossnore School archives.

The Crossnore Business School: *Crossnore School Bulletin* 4, no. 4 (July–September 1935).

The condition of one dormitory was deplorable: letter from working mother to Mary Sloop, November 1941, Crossnore School archives.

Viola Duncan attended the fifty-first DAR Continental Congress: *Proceedings of the Fifty-First Continental Congress*, p. 353.

During the war years: Bill Williams, "How a Fearless Woman Led a Community out of Darkness," *Gaston Gazette*, undated clipping.

In 1944, one former student: *Crossnore School Bulletin* 11, no. 3 (July–September 1944).

"So girls are having to do things": *Crossnore School Bulletin* 10, no. 3 (April–June 1943).

"Many children in the county walk": *Crossnore School Bulletin* 8, no. 4 (July–September 1941).

Yet she was not going to abandon children: *Crossnore School Bulletin* 29, no. 2 (April–June 1955).

Sloop even conducted blackout drills: Bill Williams, "From a Mustard Seed," *Gastonia Gazette*, October 5, 1980.

"The only solution to that problem": *Crossnore School Bulletin* 10, no. 2 (January–March 1943).

Young men and women who had spent: *Crossnore School Bulletin* 10, no. 1 (October–December 1942).

The constant turnover in staff: *Crossnore School Bulletin* 11, no. 1 (January–March 1944).

"A blue jacket on the campus means": *Crossnore School Bulletin* 10, no. 4 (October–December 1943).

It was dedicated in honor: *Crossnore School Bulletin* 11, no. 2 (April–June 1944).

The situation became particularly acute one year: *Crossnore School Bulletin* 13, no. 1 (January–March 1945), and Mary Martin Sloop interview with Legette Blythe, undated, Crossnore school archives.

"Before we start": Mary Martin Sloop interview with Legette Blythe, undated, Legette Blythe papers, Southern Historical Collection, Wilson Library, University of North Carolina at Chapel Hill.

The loss was just as devastating as the fire: *Crossnore School Bulletin* 13, no. 3 (July–September 1946).

Somehow, Sloop told a senior finishing: *Crossnore School Bulletin* 13, no. 2 (April–June 1946).

The regular dormitories were packed: *Proceedings of the Fifty-Sixth Continental Congress of the National Society of the Daughters of the American Revolution*, p. 158, and author interview with Jane Johnson, January 2, 2011.

The first cases appeared in 1947: *Panorama of Caring*, p. 29; Howard E. Covington Jr., *Once Upon a City: Greensboro, N.C.'s Second Century* (Greensboro: Greensboro Historical Museum, 2008), p. 49; Mary Martin Sloop to Dr. George M. Cooper, Raleigh, NC, February 18, 1948, Crossnore School archives.

"If God called me to this work": Mary Martin Sloop to Dr. George M. Cooper.

11. Transition

In the early fall of 1951: "National Visitors Attend Crossnore Dedication," *NC DAR News* 5, no. 5 (October 1951).

The award was presented in New York City: *Miracle in the Hills*, p. 222.

She was in a race with time: *Proceedings of the Fifty-Sixth Continental Congress of the National Society of the Daughters of the American Revolution*, p. 159.

The administration building: *Crossnore School Bulletin* 20, no. 3 (July–September 1949).

All in all, in the years after the war: Crossnore School Board of Trustee minutes, May 25, 1949, Crossnore School archives.

Income dropped from $13,000 a year to $6,000: Crossnore School Board of Trustee minutes, August 13, 1951, Crossnore School archives.

Uncle Gilmer remained on: *Crossnore School Bulletin* 20, no. 2 (April–June 1949).

For a boarder to be chosen to perform: *Somewhere along the Way*, p. 68.

E. H. Sloop would open the meeting: Martha Guy interview with author, November 12, 2010.

"What?" Sloop wrote: *Crossnore School Bulletin* 15, no. 3 (October–December 1948).

As much as Mary Sloop praised the DAR: Mary Martin Sloop, "More Recommendations and Crossnore's Attitude toward These," March 31, 1951, Crossnore School archives.

She was a well-spoken southern lady: Mary Martin Sloop interviews with Legette Blythe.

One very thorough journalist: Bill Sharpe to Judith Crist, *New York Herald Tribune*, August 20, 1949, Crossnore School archives.

"It was with amazement and indignation": Grace S. Whitcomb to Mary Martin Sloop, December 21, 1948, Crossnore School archives.

With the photographers' flashbulbs: *Miracle in the Hills*, p. 220.

At the luncheon in her honor: Margaret Dempsey, "Dr. Sloop Captivates New York," *Greensboro Daily News*, May 12, 1951.

Edward Aswell, a top editor at McGraw-Hill Book Company: Legette Blythe memorandum, Legette Blythe Papers, Southern Historical Collection, Wilson Library, University of North Carolina, Chapel Hill, NC.

Three years earlier: Mary Martin Sloop to Mrs. J. Howard Gillen, May 5, 1948, Crossnore School archives.

Miracle in the Hills was released on Sloop's: Legette Blythe papers and Paul Green interview with author, July 20, 2011.

Blythe was midway through his work: Mary Martin Sloop to Mrs. Helen Pouch, September 3, 1952, Crossnore School archives.

One disappointing consequence: Mary Martin Sloop to R. B. House, July 5, 1952, Crossnore School archives.

Sloop's heart attack brought home: Mary Martin Sloop, "A Very, Very Serious Talk with Parents and Guardians Who Send Students to the Dormitories of Crossnore School Inc.," 1952–53, Crossnore School Archives.

The appeal did bring in an extra $8,000: *Crossnore School Bulletin* 26, no. 4 (October–December 1952).

12. End of an Era

The "Dreaded Ds: divorce, desertion, and death": *Crossnore School Bulletin* 29, no. 2 (April–June 1955).

"Whoever heard in times gone by": *Crossnore School Bulletin* 27, no. 2 (April–June 1953).

A sign of the times, perhaps: *Crossnore School Bulletin* 27, no. 1 (January–March 1953) and 28, no. 4 (October–December 1953).

"We read and hear so much": *Crossnore School Bulletin* 27, no. 1 (January–March 1953).

"A working mother, a widow": Mary M. Sloop, "Why Crossnore School Inc.?" Crossnore School archives.

Rebecca Vance and three siblings: author interview with Rebecca and Tudor Vance, August 16, 2011.

Sloop got an unexpected visit: *Crossnore School Bulletin* 30, no. 4 (October–December 1956).

The question about tuition arose: Mary Martin Sloop to B. B. Dougherty, May 16, 1955, Crossnore School archives.

As always, there was a constant struggle: *Crossnore School Bulletin* 29, no. 4 (October–December 1955); minutes, Crossnore Board of Trustees, August 8, 1953; Mrs. Elaine Graham to David Baird, September 11, 1956, Crossnore School archives.

Sloop heard from some who believed: "Why Crossnore School Inc.?"

The future of young women: *Crossnore School Bulletin* 29, no. 2 (April–June 1955).

Crossnore now confronted problems: *Crossnore School Bulletin* 33, no. 1 (January–March 1959).

The trustees told her not to obligate: *Crossnore School Bulletin* 25, no. 1 (January–March 1952).

In the early months of 1956: *Crossnore School Bulletin* 30, no. 2 (April–June 1956).

The Atwell Cottage was finished in 1956: *Crossnore School Bulletin* 30, no. 1 (January–March 1956) and Crossnore School archives.

Sloop caught one rock thrower: *Crossnore School Bulletin* 31, no. 1 (January–March 1957).

Building a dormitory for the girls: tributes to Mrs. Mary Irwin Belk by Gertrude Carraway and Mrs. Roy Cable, found in Mary Irwin Belk files, Belk Stores archives.

"I hate to think that I have failed": Mary Martin Sloop to Mrs. D. S. Currie, DAR Student Loan Fund, undated, Crossnore School archives.

For Sloop, the children at Crossnore were more likely: *Crossnore School Bulletin* 29, no. 2 (April–June 1955).

"We were so close with one another": Jane Johnson interview.

Quite often, children arrived on the campus: *Crossnore School Bulletin* 25, no. 1 (January–March 1952).

Sloop believed one remedy for broken homes: *Crossnore School Bulletin* 29, no. 4 (October–December 1955).

Rebecca Vance met her future husband: Rebecca and Tudor Vance interview.

She had experimented with alternative locations: Mary Martin Sloop to Mrs. Russell W. Magma, May 4, 1956, Crossnore School archives.

In the latter part of 1953: *Crossnore School Bulletin* 38, no. 1 (January–March 1954).

By the time she announced her dream: *Crossnore School Bulletin* 36, no. 1 (January–March 1956).

Architects called it a "craftsman-style church building": National Register of Historic Places, Crossnore School District, Avery County, nominated by Davyd Foard Hood, May 2006.

Sloop continued to talk about Crossnore's future: *Crossnore School Bulletin* 36, no. 2 (April–June 1962).

The pilot, a 1949 graduate named Wimpy Holloway: Rebecca and Tudor Vance interview.

When she was ill and taking her meals: Jane Johnson interview.

Martha Guy succeeded her father: Martha Guy interview.

Their funerals were held: Tommy Hartley interview.

13. What Now?

"We would rather improve": Bill Connelly, "Era at Crossnore School Ends—What Now?" *Morganton News Herald*, March 19, 1962.

Sloop had talked about building an auditorium: *Crossnore School Bulletin* 36, no. 2 (April–June 1962).

It was not a state institution: Bill M. Jones, "Sprawling Crossnore, N.C., School Gets Most of Support from Prayer," *Johnson City Press-Chronicle*, December 17, 1961.

The school's 250 acres of land: "A Brief Relating to the Expansion Opportunity at Crossnore School Inc.," undated, Crossnore School archives.

And there was income from tuition: minutes, Crossnore School Inc. Board of Trustees, July 20, 1962, Crossnore School archives.

The Bayles bequest had caused Sloop no small amount: Mary Martin Sloop, "Everybody Put His Money Back in His Pocket," undated, Crossnore School archives.

For a while, the dean was a former teacher: Jane Johnson interview.

Like the young inhabitants of other institutions: Alan Keith-Lucas and Clifford Sanford, *Group Child Care as a Family Service* (University of North Carolina Press, 1977), p. 8.

Crandle and Roland McClellan had two boys: author interview with Crandle McClellan, December 13, 2010.

In 1965, he was the first North Carolina teacher: Jay Jenkins, "Meet 'Pop' Jarvis—Innovative Educator," *Charlotte Observer*, undated clipping.

Guy brought more than a local perspective: Martha Guy interview.

The campus was on autopilot: Robert A. Mayer II, "Report to the Board of Trustees of Crossnore School Inc.," Crossnore School archives.

Woodside had managed to boost the school's income: A Brief Relating to the Expansion Opportunities at Crossnore School Inc., undated, Crossnore School archives.

Mayer's report was followed a year later: "Survey Findings and Recommendations for Crossnore School," Crossnore School archives.

Even in her day, Mary Sloop had complained: minutes, Crossnore School Inc. Board of Trustees, August 13, 1951.

A recently completed study of Appalachia: Rupert Vance, ed., *The Southern Appalachian Region: A Study* (University of Kentucky Press, 1962).

"I don't know if she's tried it or not": Robert Korstad and James Leloudis, *To Right These Wrongs* (University of North Carolina Press, 2009), p. 242.

He promised "a completely new attitude and philosophy": John M. Gatling, "To All Students," July 1, 1968, Crossnore School archives.

14. A Rough Transition

Mike Stanley was a scared fifth grader: author interview with Mike Stanley, January 28, 2011.

Part of his problem was a shortage of tact: author interview with Crandle McClellan.

Dining together meant music: author interview with Tommy Hartley, March 8, 2011.

"Too many in the community believe": annual report to board of trustees, 1969–70, Crossnore School archives.

Weave Room manager Ossie Phillips: John Gatling to Mrs. Phillips, Weaving Department, May 6, 1970, Crossnore School archives.

The cost was four dollars a day: John Gatling to board of trustees, June 30, 1969, Crossnore School archives.

The new accounting methods didn't sit well: John Gatling, annual report to the board of trustees, 1969–70, Crossnore School archives.

The campus was at a critical turning point: John Gatling to board of trustees, June 30, 1969, Crossnore School archives.

Not long after Gatling arrived: Development Program, Crossnore School Inc., Crossnore School archives.

An unintended consequence of the building campaign: minutes, board of trustees, January 3, 1961, Crossnore School archives.

Professionals who looked in on the campus: Clifford Sanford, "Report to Crossnore School Inc.," Group Childcare Consulting Services, October 27–31, 1969, visit, Crossnore School archives.

The only hint of a new direction: "Development Program, Crossnore, North Carolina," Crossnore School archives.

The last swimming pool of any description: author interview with Rachel Deal, June 23, 2011.

Gatling began actively courting social workers: John Gatling to social service agency directors, undated, Crossnore School archives.

He wrote one correspondent: John Gatling to Mrs. Milton E. Hartley, December 3, 1970, Crossnore School archives.

Gatling told a state welfare official: John Gatling to Mrs. Margaret Parris, August 25, 1970, Crossnore School archives.

Very few blacks lived in the North Carolina mountains: Avery County Retired School Personnel, *A History of Avery County Schools* (Newland, North Carolina, 1989).

There was grumbling in the village: author interview with Rebecca and Tudor Vance, August 10, 2011.

One day, storeowner Corbett Johnson: Danica Diamond interview with Corbett Johnson.

The McClellans, houseparents in the Reed Dormitory: Crandle McClellan interview.

The campus troubles extended beyond: Margaret Paris to John Gatling, August 21, 1970, Crossnore School archives; Mike Stanley interview; J. Louis Fowke to Martha Guy, July 15, 1969, Crossnore School archives.

Brown dressed up the school's public relations: Jane Johnson interview.

By the end of his first six months: Harry McGee to Ralph Gwaltney, November 19, 1971; minutes, board of trustees, September 12, 1971, Crossnore School archives.

"We went from POWs": Mike Stanley interview.

15. A Revival

Educated at Princeton and Harvard: John Vaughan, "James G. Cannon, 76, Dies," *Charlotte Observer*, January 14, 1992.

Some called her bold, pushy, and opinionated: author interview with Rush Dickson III, January 25, 2011.

When Martha Guy called the Cannon residence: author interview with Martha Guy, August 16, 2011.

The selections for children helped campus residents: author interview with Kathy Dellinger, December 21, 2010.

A few months later, the trustees were told: minutes, board of trustees, November 4, 1972, Crossnore School archives.

One of his first thoughts was: author interview with Melynda Pepple, December 21, 2010.

The Crossnore student body had undergone: November 4, 1972, board minutes.

It may also have had something to do with: Mike Stanley interview.

The report reinforced earlier complaints: Mrs. Margaret H. Paris to John Gatling, August 21, 1970, Crossnore School archives.

Children too sick to attend school: Mike Stanley interview.

One of the reminders of the past: ibid.

Martin discontinued the use of the grocery coupons: *Crossnore School Bulletin*, March 1974, Crossnore School archives.

New job descriptions appeared: author interview with H. Dean Bare, December 14, 2010.

John and Ramona Sturgill were in their twenties: author interview with John and Ramona Sturgill, June 23, 2011.

Church attendance remained mandatory: Dean Bare interview.

He said putting up such a building: Address given by Dr. Alan Keith-Lucas, dedication of Gilchrist Cottage, Crossnore School Inc., May 6, 1978, Crossnore School archives.

Fraley was subsequently joined: author interview with John Fraley.

The board included other newcomers: author interview with Alexander Lyerly, August 24, 2011.

In 1984, Mrs. Sarah King: minutes, board of trustees, Crossnore School Inc., Crossnore School archives.

16. The Children's Plan

In the winter of 1975, Phyllis Crain: Phyllis Crain, "next few weeks," e-mail to Crossnore School Executive Committee, Crossnore School records.

By the time Phyllis Crain became: author interviews with Phyllis Crain, November 3, 2010, and September 21, 2011.

Joe Mitchell had been on the Crossnore campus: author interview with Joe Mitchell, January 10, 2011.

The new offices reflected the special needs: Kathy Dellinger interview.

The Weave Room returned to the fold: archives, Southern Highlands Craft Guild; *The Weaving Room of Crossnore School Inc.*, p. 28.

Mitchell clung tightly to the homespun nostalgia: Joe Mitchell, report of the Approved Schools Committee, Continental Congress, April 22, 1992.

He even resurrected and put on sale: *Crossnore School Bulletin*, January–March 1988.

Some children weren't on http://www.crossnoreschool.org/ the campus long enough: *Crossnore School Bulletin*, April–June 1988.

Crossnore had become a social service agency: author interview with Joe Mitchell, September 5, 2011.

Deeply troubled and emotionally disturbed children: "Judge Rules on School Issue," *Avery Journal*, August 12, 1993.

The two institutions sued the school board: "North Carolina Schools Ordered to Take Troubled Kids," *Charlotte Observer*, August 12, 1993.

She and Mitchell worked closely together: Joe Mitchell interview; author interview with Rush Dickson III, January 25, 2011.

Crain didn't share Mitchell's enthusiasm: author interview with Phyllis Crain, November 24, 2011.

In early June, the extended Crossnore family: Phyllis Crain interview, February 9, 2011.

17. Miracles, Always Miracles

Crain thought to herself: Phyllis Crain interview, September 21, 2011.

"That lady can raise money": author interview with Carol Dabbs, September 25, 2011.

Her message penetrated hearts: Phyllis Crain interview, February 9, 2011.

This could not be: Jo Ann Mitchell Brasington, "Phyllis Crain '79: Living the Life Unexpected," *Wofford Today* 40, no. 3 (Spring 2008), p. 31.

"That day, they were doing an MRI": Phyllis Crain interview, September 21, 2011.

"They assured me that when": Phyllis Crain to Crossnore donors, November 8, 2011, Crossnore School archives.

"Prayer has wrought miracles in these hills": *Miracle in the Hills*, p. 230.

Trustee Alexander Lyerly knew both women: author interview with Alexander Lyerly, August 24, 2011.

Index

Italics refer to illustrations.